Music Festivals in the UK

The outdoor music festival market has developed and commercialised significantly since the mid-1990s and is now a mainstream part of the British summertime leisure experience. The overall number of outdoor music festivals staged in the UK doubled between 2005 and 2011 to reach a peak of over 500 events. UK Music (2016) estimates that the sector attracts over 3.7 million attendances each year, and that music tourism as a whole sustains nearly 40,000 full time jobs. *Music Festivals in the UK* is the first extended investigation into this commercialised rock and pop festival sector and examines events of all sizes: from mega-events such as Glastonbury Festival, V Festival and the Reading and Leeds Festivals to 'boutique' events with maximum attendances as small as 250. In the past, research into festivals has typically focused either on their carnivalesque heritage or on developing managerial tools for the field of Events Management. Anderton moves beyond such perspectives to propose new ways of understanding and theorising the cultural, social and geographic importance of outdoor music festivals. He argues that changes in the sector since the mid-1990s – such as professionalisation, corporatisation, mediatisation, regulatory control, and sponsorship/branding – should not necessarily be regarded as a process of transgressive 'alternative culture' being co-opted by commercial concerns; instead, such changes represent a reconfiguration of the sector in line with changes in society, and a broadening of the forms and meanings that may be associated with outdoor music events.

Chris Anderton is an Associate Professor at Solent University, UK, where he teaches music management, business, history and culture. He is co-author of the book *Understanding the Music Industries* (Sage, 2013) and has published book chapters and articles on music bootlegging, music blogs, progressive rock, and music festivals. He established the in-house music organisation Solent Music (solentmusic.com) in 2011 and is co-Executive Producer of the annual Solent SMILE Festival (smilefest.co.uk). His research interests include the cultural economy of music festivals and live events, the future of the music industries, and the 'hidden histories' of popular, underground and niche music genres.

Ashgate Popular and Folk Music Series

Series Editors:
Stan Hawkins, Professor of Popular Musicology, University of Oslo and Lori Burns, Professor, University of Ottawa, Canada

Popular musicology embraces the field of musicological study that engages with popular forms of music, especially music associated with commerce, entertainment and leisure activities. The Ashgate Popular and Folk Music Series aims to present the best research in this field. Authors are concerned with criticism and analysis of the music itself, as well as locating musical practices, values and meanings in cultural context. The focus of the series is on popular music of the twentieth and twenty-first centuries, with a remit to encompass the entirety of the world's popular music.

Critical and analytical tools employed in the study of popular music are being continually developed and refined in the twenty-first century. Perspectives on the transcultural and intercultural uses of popular music have enriched understanding of social context, reception and subject position. Popular genres as distinct as reggae, township, bhangra, and flamenco are features of a shrinking, transnational world. The series recognizes and addresses the emergence of mixed genres and new global fusions, and utilizes a wide range of theoretical models drawn from anthropology, sociology, psychoanalysis, media studies, semiotics, postcolonial studies, feminism, gender studies and queer studies.

Other titles in the series:

Popular Music, Cultural Politics and Music Education in China
Wai-Chung Ho

Perspectives on German Popular Music
Edited by Michael Ahlers, Christoph Jacke

Music and Irish Identity: Celtic Tiger Blues
Gerry Smyth

Heavy Metal, Gender and Sexuality: Interdisciplinary Approaches
Edited by Florian Heesch, Niall Scott

The Songs of Joni Mitchell: Gender, Performance and Agency
Anne Karppinen

The Singer-Songwriter in Europe: Paradigms, Politics and Place
Edited by Isabelle Marc, Stuart Green

When Music Migrates: Crossing British and European Racial Faultlines, 1945–2010
Jon Stratton

The Twenty-First-Century Legacy of the Beatles: Liverpool and Popular Music Heritage Tourism
Michael Brocken

Music Festivals in the UK
Beyond the Carnivalesque

Chris Anderton

LONDON AND NEW YORK

First published 2019
by Routledge
2 Park Square, Milton Park, Abingdon, Oxon OX14 4RN

and by Routledge
52 Vanderbilt Avenue, New York, NY 10017, USA

First issued in paperback 2020

Routledge is an imprint of the Taylor & Francis Group, an informa business

© 2018 Chris Anderton

The right of Chris Anderton to be identified as author of this work has been asserted by him in accordance with sections 77 and 78 of the Copyright, Designs and Patents Act 1988.

All rights reserved. No part of this book may be reprinted or reproduced or utilised in any form or by any electronic, mechanical, or other means, now known or hereafter invented, including photocopying and recording, or in any information storage or retrieval system, without permission in writing from the publishers.

Trademark notice: Product or corporate names may be trademarks or registered trademarks, and are used only for identification and explanation without intent to infringe.

British Library Cataloguing-in-Publication Data
A catalogue record for this book is available from the British Library

Library of Congress Cataloging-in-Publication Data
A catalog record has been requested for this book

ISBN 13: 978-0-367-58857-1 (pbk)
ISBN 13: 978-1-4724-3620-7 (hbk)

Typeset in Times New Roman
by Servis Filmsetting Ltd, Stockport, Cheshire

For Meriel, Amy and Sean

Contents

List of figures	ix
Acknowledgements	x
Abbreviations and acronyms	xi
Introduction	1
1 Contextualising outdoor music festivals in the UK	7
Music festivals: a countercultural narrative	7
Music festivals and the countercultural carnivalesque	19
Other histories of the music festival in the UK	23
Conclusion	35
2 The proliferation, professionalisation and mainstreaming of outdoor music festivals	37
Proliferation, diversification and volatility	37
Market structure and issues	49
Mainstreaming	61
Conclusion	72
3 Branded landscapes: sponsorship, marketing and mediation	74
The 'brand matrix'	74
Commercial sponsorship	80
Music festival sponsorship strategies	93
Festival audiences and critiques of branding and sponsorship	96
Conclusion	100
4 Always the same, yet always different: music festivals as cyclic places	102
Liminality and the outdoor music festival	103
Cyclic place	111

	Music festivals, Britishness and the rural	128
	Conclusion	133
5	**The social life of music festivals: audiences and atmosphere**	134
	Motivations	135
	Sociality	148
	Atmosphere	153
	Conclusion	162
	Conclusion	164
	Bibliography	170
	Index	

List of figures

2.1 Total number of outdoor music festivals in the UK, 2005–2014   39
2.2 Number of outdoor music festivals in the UK, by month, 2005 and 2014   40
2.3 Number of outdoor music festivals in the UK, 2005–2014, by duration of event   41
2.4 Number of outdoor music festivals in the UK, 2005–2014, that were newly launched in each year, and the number of events that were cancelled or no longer held in each year   47
2.5 Select list of festival and event management related trade associations, pressure groups and conferences   55
3.1 The 'brand matrix' of music festivals   75
3.2 Headlining performances on the Pyramid Stage at Glastonbury Festival for the Contemporary Performing Arts, 1995–2015   79
4.1 Diagrammatic representation of 'cyclic place'   125

Acknowledgements

I should like to thank Keith Halfacree and George McKay for the initial inspiration to undertake doctoral research on a topic that was, in the early 2000s, a relatively new field of study. George's work on Glastonbury Festival suggested a variety of research routes, as did Keith's work on the New Age Travellers and the place of music in the countryside. Keith encouraged me to apply for postgraduate funding from Swansea University, and provided much appreciated advice on the development of my thesis. Prior to the PhD, I undertook the MBA Music Industries at University of Liverpool, which led me to take seriously the managerial and business aspects of festivals in addition to their socio-cultural and political associations. Thanks are due to all of my fellow postgraduates at both Swansea University and University of Liverpool for the friendship and support they provided during those years, as well as to the many festivalgoers who were generous with their time during the initial research process. This book was written while leading and teaching undergraduate courses at Solent University. I should like to thank my colleagues at that institution, as well as the many students who chose to study my Festival Cultures option unit, and the graduates who have worked with me on Solent Music and its various off-shoot projects, including Nicole Pennycook, who undertook some additional data collection on my behalf in 2015. Thanks are also due to Stan Hawkins and Lori Burns, series editors of the Ashgate Popular and Folk Music Series, for their feedback and support, and to the editorial team at Routledge, including Heidi Bishop and Annie Vaughan. Finally, and most importantly, I should like to give special thanks to Meriel for her emotional support and proof-reading advice throughout the research and writing process, and to Sean and Amy who weren't there when it all started but make it all worthwhile today.

Abbreviations and acronyms

ACMD	Advisory Council for the Misuse of Drugs
AEG	Anschutz Entertainment Group
AEME	Association for Event Management Education
AEO	Association of Event Organisers
AFO	Association of Festival Organisers
AIF	Association of Independent Festivals
AMG	Academy Music Group
ANPR	Automatic Number Plate Recognition
BAFA	British Arts Festivals Association
BBC	British Broadcasting Corporation
BIFF	British and International Federation of Festivals for Music, Dance and Speech
BMA	British Medical Association
CAMRA	Campaign for Real Ale
CCTV	Closed Circuit Television
CJA/CJPO	Criminal Justice and Public Order Act 1994
CSR	Corporate social responsibility
DCMS	Department for Culture, Media and Sport
DEAG	Deutsche Entertainment AG
DJ	Disc Jockey
EFDSS	English Folk Dance and Song Society
EPA	Event Planners Association
HMSO	Her Majesty's Stationery Office
ICC	International Chamber of Commerce
IEG	International Events Group
IEM	Institute for Event Management
IFEA	International Festivals and Events Association
IFF	International Festival Forum
ILMC	International Live Music Conference
LNE	Live Nation Entertainment
NAA	National Arenas Association
NAO	National Audit Office
NASS	National Adventure Sports Show

NJF	National Jazz Federation
NME	*New Musical Express*
PLUR	Peace, Love, Unity, Respect
PRS	Performing Rights Society
RFID	Radio-Frequency Identification
SEFA	Scottish Events and Festivals Association
SIA	Security Industry Authority
SPS	Special Police Services
TEN	Temporary Event Notice
TESA	The Event Services Association
TMSA	Traditional Music and Song Association of Scotland
UK	United Kingdom
UME	Unlicensed Music Events
UNESCO	United Nations Educational, Scientific and Cultural Organization
US	United States of America
VIP	Very Important Person
Wi-Fi	Wireless computer networking providing access to the Internet
WSTA	Wine and Spirit Trade Association

Introduction

In the twenty-first century, outdoor pop and rock music festivals on greenfield sites have become an integral part of the British summer, with over 3.7 million festival attendances recorded in 2015 (UK Music, 2016). For festivalgoers, they offer a break from the everyday world of work and a chance to socialise with friends, families and like-minded others in an atmosphere of fun, freedom and excess. The media presents them as 'catalysts of life-affirming exhibitionism, festivity and transcendence' (Rojek, 2013: 103), while the recorded music industry views them as invaluable opportunities for up-and-coming artists to reach new audiences, and for established artists to gain significant press and broadcast coverage while collecting substantial live performance fees. The sector has expanded considerably since the early 2000s, with the total number of events doubling between 2005 and 2011, and an estimated 500 outdoor festivals now held each year. The post-millennial market has also seen growth in media coverage, corporate ownership, commercial sponsorship and entrepreneurial 'added value' activities such as pre-erected accommodation and special VIP areas for those festivalgoers willing to pay more than the standard ticket price. In addition, there has been continued development in event formats, including boutique festivals (small, mixed arts events), hybrid festivals (which give equal billing to non-music attractions such as adventure sports, classic cars or food) and a wide range of niche events catering to specific genres, lifestyles and demographics.

The current festival market is a far cry from my first encounters with festivals in the 1980s – a time when there were relatively few large commercial festivals, but many smaller 'free festivals' that were managed on a non-commercial and participatory basis. These free festivals were strongly associated with post-hippie countercultural, alternative and radical lifestyle groups such as the so-called New Age Travellers: people who sought to escape the conventional capitalist world of their upbringing to live an itinerant life in converted buses and trucks. During the 1970s and 1980s, the Travellers created numerous events around the country, but their politicisation in the 1980s led to a moral panic in the mainstream British press about their lifestyle and events, based on fears of rural invasion, drug use, criminal activity and waste. By contrast, those involved in attending and running the festivals saw them as a temporary and hedonistic escape from everyday life, as an attempt to enact utopian dreams, or simply as part of an ongoing alternative lifestyle where the festival provided social interaction, collective identity, and opportunities for trade (Martin, 1998; 2002). Free festivals existed on the periphery of the mainstream leisure economy and society and featured a range of artists who were unlikely to be heard on the commercial music charts or played on the radio, such as Hawkwind, Here & Now, Ozric Tentacles and the Magic Mushroom Band, as well as a host of amateur and semi-professional acts performing a variety of folk, ska, punk and reggae music. A similar range of acts could be found at the Glastonbury Festival, while the small number of other large and commercial events (such as Reading Festival and Monsters of Rock) focused predominantly on the hard rock and heavy metal genres. I was too young to attend these festivals at the time, but as I read about them in the weekly music papers or saw news reports about battles between Travellers and the police, I built up a picture of music festivals as dangerous places populated by hippies and bikers, places of poor sanitation, violence and drug use. Yet, by the early 2000s, when I first began my field research into the contemporary festival market, I found that it was dominated not by small-scale non-commercial events, but by national and international concert and event promoters who sought to provide safe, customer-friendly environments, and to appeal to a broad range of music fans rather than those with 'alternative' views (Anderton, 2007). At the time, McKay argued that these contemporary commercial festivals represented 'dull, homogenised mass events', and contrasted them unfavourably with the countercultural, alternative and radical 'tribal gatherings' of the past (2000: ix) – a commonly-held view in academic and activist accounts of music festivals. Yet, it is the commercial sector that has gone from strength to strength during the past twenty years, while 'tribal gatherings' have dwindled in importance and number.

This book adds to a developing field of 'music festival studies', as distinct from the broader fields of event management, event studies and tourism studies – fields which are often instrumentalist and managerial in their focus, emphasising such topics as market demand factors, economic and environmental impact assessments, and the stimulation of local and regional economic growth. Music festival studies is interdisciplinary in nature and encompasses a wide range of theories and perspectives. Webster & McKay (2016) provide an excellent overview and annotated bibliography of this emerging field, which includes Robinson's *Music Festivals and the Politics of Participation* (2015a), the first full-length text to examine the British boutique festival sector. There are also recent edited collections from Bennett et al. (2014) and McKay (2015) that offer analyses of various social and cultural issues related to music festivals, while St John has written extensively about the emergence, development and meaning of electronic dance music festivals (2009; 2017). In addition, there is growing academic, industry and policy interest in the ecology of the live music sector in general. For instance, Frith et al. discuss the development of the British concert and arena circuits (2013;

forthcoming) while the lobbying organisation UK Music, which represents the interests of the UK music industry as a whole, has published annual reports about the contribution of live music to the UK economy since 2011.

This book will provide the first extended investigation into the commercial rock and pop festival sector in a British context and move beyond romanticised accounts of outdoor festivals as a cultural form co-opted by commercial interests. It will examine a range of topics including the proliferation and volatility of the sector, the use of brand sponsorships and mediation, and the roles of places and audiences in the creation of the festival experience. It will consider the impacts of corporatisation, regulation and professionalisation on the sector, as well as the broadening audience demographic seen since the late 1990s. A broad-based 'cultural economy' approach is adopted, extending the analysis of festivals beyond their social, cultural and political roles to incorporate perspectives related to their marketing and management. The book will 'resist the dualism between culture and economy' (Pratt, 2008: 44) seen in past studies of music festivals, to show how commercial events are not only constructed within a web of economic constraints and possibilities but are also influenced by non-economic understandings of festival culture, history and place. In particular, the book will examine the continued relevance and influence of the counterculture on contemporary festival practices, while also exploring the forces of commercialisation, professionalisation and mediatisation which have transformed the sector over the past twenty years. It will question whether modern events offer a commercial simulacrum of a past which has been simplified and mythologised as a set of symbols, ideas and ideals, and whether this affects the meanings that are ascribed to them today. Can music festivals still be experienced as special and unique when so many of them have the same basic structure and form, and when so many of the same bands, stallholders, and activities can be found at multiple events across the summer months?

To address the influences and questions noted above, the book is organised into five chapters. The first chapter explores the history of music festivals in the UK and examine how countercultural discourses arose from the mediation of key events in the late 1960s and early 1970s, including iconic films of the Monterey Pop Festival, the Woodstock Festival and Glastonbury Fayre. It then charts the development of British festival culture from the 1970s to the 1990s, with particular emphasis on the free festivals and free parties that dominated the festival landscape during this time, and which extended the countercultural ideas of the 1960s hippies. The attitudes, beliefs and behaviours associated with those festivals have been likened to the medieval carnival: a time of licensed irreverence and inversion when the everyday world of work and rank was temporarily overturned and mocked (Bakhtin, 1984). A countercultural version of the medieval carnival can be identified in the work of authors such as Kevin Hetherington (1998a) and Andy Worthington (2004), who analysed British free festivals and attributed a radical social and environmental stance to them. This 'countercultural carnivalesque'

4   *Introduction*

(Anderton, 2008) is also found in popular accounts of festivals which quote festival attendees, organisers and musicians, such as those concerning Glastonbury Festival (Aubrey & Shearlaw, 2004) and Reading Festival (Carroll, 2007). These accounts demonstrate carnivalesque inversions related to drug-taking, alcohol, nudity and hygiene, as well as foregrounding communitarian values, political ideals and spiritual awakenings (see also Larsen & O'Reilly, 2007). However, the countercultural carnivalesque is not innate to the music festival as a cultural form, but that festivals reflect the social, cultural and political milieux in which they are held. As Chapter 1 demonstrates, commercial and non-commercial festivals devoted to music have been staged in Britain since the seventeenth and eighteenth centuries, and these precursor events reflected the social mores and concerns of their organisers – either by satisfying a commercial niche or being used as part of a broader attempt at social education or control of the working classes.

The second chapter focuses on the post-millennial outdoor music festival market and charts the growth of the sector from 2005 to 2014, using a data set collated from a variety of festival listing sources. It covers festivals of all sizes, from well-known large-scale events such as Glastonbury, V Festival and T in the Park, to the many hundreds of much smaller events held each year on country estates, farmers' fields and parklands. The market is shown to be highly volatile, with events typically lasting between one and three years, and only a quarter of those staged in 2014 having a lifespan of more than ten years. The chapter discusses how changing demographic profiles, legislation, mediatisation and corporatisation have promoted the commercialisation, professionalisation and mainstreaming of several areas of festival provision, and how the rise in boutique and hybrid festivals is a response to changing tastes and interests. It then draws on the pioneering work of Clarke, who described four cardinal points of festival culture in the 1970s: sex, drugs, squalor and disorder (1982: 27–34). The chapter examines the stereotypes associated with these cardinal points and apply them to the contemporary festival market to show how these aspects of the countercultural carnivalesque remain important cultural markers, and how they have become increasingly controlled and sanitised through the design and marketing of events. The chapter concludes by considering why unlicensed free parties continue to be staged despite concerted legislative and police actions to prevent or disrupt them.

The third chapter explores an important commercial aspect of staging contemporary music festivals: the need to attract sponsorship funding to offset the considerable risks involved in building events on site prior to the receipt of ticket income to pay contractors and artists. In order to examine the branding and sponsorship activities found at music festivals a 'brand matrix' is proposed, which connects the brand of a festival (a set of musical, social, cultural, geographical and behavioural meanings and expectations that develop over time) with the brands associated with its performers, sponsors and location. The chapter outlines and discusses different forms of sponsorship support, ranging from reciprocal agreements with local contractors and media through to formal cash sponsorships and a variety of 'added value' branding opportunities. The latter have grown increasingly sophisticated, with marketers using the data-mining possibilities of social media in an attempt to incorporate their brands into festivalgoers' longer-term lifestyles and identities. The rising importance of online and broadcast media are also discussed and the chapter shows how these are further implicated in the mainstreaming of contemporary events, and the widening of the audience demographic. In the second half of the chapter, three strategies for sponsor engagement that may be seen at festivals are outlined and the chapter considers both neo-Marxist critiques of festival sponsorship and post-modern notions of a supposed millennial generation that playfully accepts hyperreal brand activities for their entertainment value and is therefore unconcerned by questions of authenticity. Some festival organisers and attendees are, however, resistant to what they regard as the co-optation of true festival culture (derived, in part, from the ideologies of the countercultural carnivalesque); consequently, those events which explicitly avoid commercial brand sponsorships and instead promote social and environmental ideals are also examined.

Chapter 4 turns to the locations in which music festivals are staged, and to the broader meanings and understandings of place that affect both how organisers manage their events and how festivalgoers make use of them. Prior conceptions of festival space as marginal and countercultural (for example, Hetherington, 1998b; St John, 2001) are no longer appropriate for understanding the contemporary positioning of events as mainstream leisure experiences. Instead, festival sites may be able, despite their temporary existence in physical form, to build a strong sense of place and belonging over a period of years, and that this may be linked both to pre-existing understandings of host locations and to broader ideologies of the British rural landscape. Drawing on the findings of two case study events and the spatial ideas of Lefebvre (1991), Foucault (1986) and Massey (2005), the notion of 'cyclic place' is introduced as an alternative means of understanding how festivals relate to their host locations, and then examine such cyclic places within broader conceptions of Britishness and rurality.

Finally, Chapter 5 addresses the social life of festivals by exploring the contribution of festivalgoers to the experience, atmosphere and image of events. Four broad motivations for attendance may be observed, and that the influence of the countercultural carnivalesque continues to be pertinent. Those motivations are: freedom from everyday life and behavioural restrictions; the search for authentic and meaningful experience; socialisation and a sense of belonging; and transcendence of the self. The chapter also offers a critique of neo-tribal ideas on sociality, before introducing the concept of 'meta-sociality', which refers to an event's over-arching identity and image: a shared frame of reference for attendees which is performatively produced on a festival site and supported by ongoing and informal mediations during the rest of the year. The chapter concludes by arguing that the cyclical recreation of meta-sociality helps to construct an event's unique atmosphere and sense of 'specialness', and that these are influenced by the actions of event producers and festivalgoers.

These five chapters offer new knowledge and ideas about the contemporary rock and pop festival sector. They demonstrate the ongoing, if weakening, influence of the hippie countercultures of the past, and of academic understandings of festivals as modern forms of carnival. Festivals and carnivals may be characterised by a combination of reversal, intensification, trespass or abstinence (Falassi, 1987: 3), yet they also serve 'the commercial, ideological, or political purposes of self-interested authorities or entrepreneurs' (Stoeltje 1989: 161). There is, therefore, a need to look beyond carnivalesque understandings of music festivals, and to examine the intersection of culture and commerce. This intersection lies at the heart of this book, and the following chapter, Chapter 1, places it in historical context.

1 Contextualising outdoor music festivals in the UK

This chapter provides a historical overview of the development of outdoor popular music festivals in the UK. The chapter does not seek to replace the detailed histories available elsewhere (e.g. McKay, 2000; Worthington, 2004), but instead examines aspects of those histories in order to show how a 'countercultural carnivalesque' reading has become dominant within the academic fields of popular music and cultural geography (Anderton, 2008). It is argued that two sets of discourses have become conflated: the first emerges from the late 1960s transatlantic hippie and rock counterculture, and develops in a British context through the 1970s and 1980s, before becoming associated with the acid house rave scene of the early 1990s (Anderton, 2011); the second derives from Bakhtin's concept of the carnivalesque (Bakhtin, 1984), which he introduced in relation to the festive behaviours of medieval Europe, but which has since been modified to fit the rock counterculture and its festivals (Hetherington, 1998a). These discourses are discussed in the first two sections of this chapter, which demonstrate how they have fused into an important narrative history with ideological, aesthetic and political aspects. As will be seen in subsequent chapters, this countercultural carnivalesque reading of music festivals continues to have ongoing relevance to and influence upon the production, mediation and experience of events in the twenty-first century. Yet there are other histories and contexts which have influenced the development of outdoor music festivals, including the first and second British folk music revivals and the development and growth of charitable, municipal and commercial events. These will be explored in the final section of the chapter to show how festivals can be understood in other terms, and to demonstrate the limitations of the countercultural carnivalesque.

Music festivals: a countercultural narrative

In the popular cultural imaginary, outdoor music festivals are strongly associated with the transatlantic hippie counterculture of the late 1960s and the emergence of rock music as a genre ideologically separate from pop music (Frith, 1978). For instance, Gebhardt suggests that a belief arose that 'rock somehow embodied the essence of the counterculture' (2015: 55) and that a strong relationship between rock, counterculture and festivals became firmly established on a global level through the mediation of the US Monterey International Pop Festival of 1967. This festival was held on the same site as the pre-existing Monterey Jazz Festival (established in 1958) and was organised as a not-for-profit event by John Phillips of The Mamas and the Papas, Lou Adler (the band's manager) and Alan Pariser (who produced the event). Its board of governors included Paul McCartney, Mick Jagger, Andrew Loog Oldham and Beatles' publicist Derek Taylor, thus forging connections with the UK music industry (Kubernik & Kubernik, 2011). It was filmed by D.A. Pennebaker, who is acknowledged as one of the pioneers of Direct Cinema, a style of journalistic documentary film-making designed to make the viewer feel as if they are experiencing events as they happen (Renov, 2004). The film, released in cinemas in December 1968, focused mainly on the musical performances of the event, which included major international stars such as The Who, Eric Burdon & The Animals, Jimi Hendrix, Janis Joplin, Simon & Garfunkel, Hugh Masekela and Ravi Shankar, in addition to local San Francisco bands such as Jefferson Airplane and Country Joe and the Fish, soul music from Otis Redding, and pop music from The Mamas and the Papas (*Monterey Pop*, 1967). At 79 minutes long, the film misses out many of the performers and performances from the three-day-long event in favour of limited highlights interspersed with images of the festival site and audience, and a small amount of backstage footage featuring organisers, performers and the local police commissioner. The overall feeling of the film is one of innocence and playfulness, with the hippies presented in a generally positive light despite the use of drugs, and despite audience members sleeping in the open air in local parklands. The film highlights the spectacle of a fashionable hippie scene with its celebration of the 'flower power' era of peace, love and harmony, while the final performance of the film is a long raga by Ravi Shankar which emphasises the hippie search for spiritual meaning through the mysticism of Eastern religions. The festival received considerable press coverage as a high point of the 1967 'Summer of Love' in San Francisco, and this coverage, as well as the film itself, helped to promote the hippie movement and ideals, while also commercialising them.

The Summer of Love became a global phenomenon, and Britain saw a number of large-scale open-air rock concerts and festivals in the late 1960s, including free events in London's Hyde Park and Hampstead Heath, and the establishment of the first Isle of Wight Festival in 1968. Many of the events were explicitly linked to the US counterculture through their music, symbolism, imagery and politics: for example, the 14 Hour Technicolor Dream at Alexandra Palace in London, and the Festival of the Flower Children at Woburn Abbey, both held in 1967. The US counterculture also influenced and inspired British 'underground' clubs such as UFO and Middle Earth, which used the psychedelic imagery, lighting effects and liquid slideshows seen in the acid rock concerts of San Francisco (Boyd, 2006; Rycroft, 1998). The cultural, spiritual and aesthetic interests of the UK counterculture were summarised by an article in *The Observer* magazine published in 1967, which described 'an elite ever moving outwards towards new fields of astrology, music, reincarnation, mysticism, fantasies, to an anarchist fairyland' (cited in Sandford & Reid, 1974: 10). These interests could be embraced and enacted at the outdoor festivals of the late 1960s and early 1970s, which also provided a public forum for anti-authoritarianism, experimentation with sexual relationships, and the public consumption of drugs such as marijuana with, as Clarke notes, 'the minimum interference from straight society, without at the same time involving a total and permanent rejection of that society' (1982: 26).

Frith argues further that, for the emergent rock and hippie counterculture of the late 1960s, the principal role of outdoor music festivals was to provide the material experience of community and the public expression of youth solidarity in opposition to the traditional values of commercial pop music culture (1984: 66). This role of festivals as a public and visual celebration of countercultural community is echoed by Hetherington's analysis of the Stonehenge Free Festival (1974–1984), in which he discusses the symbolic centrality of that event to the social reproduction of the post-hippie counterculture of the New Age Travellers in the 1970s and 1980s (2001). It can also be seen in three other festival films which reached a global cinema audience in the early 1970s and helped create the popular media conception of a hippie music festival: *Woodstock – Three Days of Peace and Music* (1970), *Gimme Shelter* (1970) and *Glastonbury Fayre* (1972).

In *Woodstock – Three Days of Peace and Music*, the US counterculture is presented as triumphing over adversity, with people-power overcoming the commercial intentions of the event, and creating a free festival suffused with a 'back to the garden' narrative of a simpler, more natural life. Held in July 1969, the festival attracted hundreds of thousands more people than had been expected or prepared for, leading to ticket booths and fence-building being abandoned and the event being declared free. Bad weather turned parts of the site into mud baths, and gridlocked roads meant that supplies had to be airlifted to the site (*Woodstock*, 1970). The film shows young people taking drugs, bathing naked, making music, dancing, wallowing in the mud and making love. There are also interviews with audience members and others that reinforce the cultural innocence and naivety that was seen in *Monterey Pop*, and the audience appears somewhat passive and apolitical, with the oppositional politics of the counterculture rather downplayed (Schowalter, 2000: 90). These representations are also found in the special Woodstock Music Festival edition of *Life* magazine that was published in 1969. The text of the magazine refers to the event as 'overrun, strained to its limits, [yet] the system, somehow, didn't break … there wasn't so much as a fist fight' (*Life*, 1969: 7). As with the *Monterey Pop* and *Woodstock* films, the magazine focused on the visual style of the hippies, describing their vans as 'gaily decorated old bread trucks' and the audience as 'long-haired hitch-hikers wearing beads, headbands, leather vests, tie-dyed T-shirts, and floppy hats' (*Life*, 1969: 7).

Woodstock's narrative is one of success against the odds, yet *Gimme Shelter* (1970), which documents the Rolling Stones' free concert at Altamont Speedway on 6 December 1969, offers a rather different view of the counterculture. Festivalgoers are still represented as colourful and youthful, and there is the same emphasis on free love, nudity, drug taking and so on, yet these are shown to spill over into chaos and violence. Drug users experience bad trips, people are hurt in seemingly uncontrolled crowds, and members of the Hells Angels, hired as security for the event, become heavy-handed in their efforts to control the area in front of the stage. Matters are made worse by a low stage and a lack of fencing and barriers to protect the backstage area from festivalgoers and to prevent them from gaining access to the stage itself. Fighting between Hells Angels and the crowd is clearly documented in the footage of Jefferson Airplane's set (during which a Hells Angel hits singer Marty Balin) and of the Rolling Stones' headlining set. During the latter, a festivalgoer approaches the stage with a gun and is fatally stabbed by a Hells Angel. *Woodstock* and *Gimme Shelter* have since come to represent the best and the worst aspects of festival culture respectively, the first capturing 'innocence triumphant' and the second showing the 'maggoty underside of the acid utopia' (Duncan, 1984: 29). As a consequence, stereotypes and expectations of festival behaviour, both good and bad, have been translated into the popular consciousness of rock and the counterculture.

The first British festival film to gain cinema distribution was *Glastonbury Fayre* (1972), which documented an event held in June 1971 at Michael Eavis's Worthy Farm in the village of Pilton, near the town of Glastonbury. The film was directed by Nicholas Roeg, though initially credited to Peter Neal, who completed the film when Roeg was unavailable to do so. A triple album boxed set was also released, including live performances from the festival together with recordings made at other locations: Hawkwind's track was recorded at the Roundhouse in London, while the Grateful Dead (who didn't perform at the festival) donated a track performed at the Empire Pool, Wembley. The aim of the film and album was to help recoup some of the expenses of staging the festival, which was free to attend. The album's accompanying 32-page booklet is an important document, since it offers a clear indication as to the motivations and beliefs of the organisers. The cover states that the festival 'was a fair in the medieval tradition, embodying the legends of the area, with music, dance, poetry, theatre, lights and the opportunity for spontaneous entertainments' (*Glastonbury Fayre* [album], 1972: 1). The booklet connects the festival to the mythology and legends of Glastonbury Tor, King Arthur, Avalon and St Joseph of Arimathea, as well as to alternative belief systems such as ley lines and astrology, and ancient structures like Stonehenge and the Egyptian pyramids. It refers to the festival as 'A celebration. A gathering of the acid gypsies. A mystical reunion with the earth. An ancient revel to the midsummer sun' (ibid.: 11), and it also raises concerns about environmental pollution. The event's main aims were given as 'the conservation of our natural resources; a respect for nature and life; and a spiritual awakening' (ibid.: 5). As Sandford notes, Glastonbury Fayre 1971 provided a glimpse of 'a community sharing possessions, living with the environment, maintaining their culture with whatever is naturally available, consuming their needs and little else. It was a powerful vision' (Sandford & Reid, 1974: 44). The film sought to present a similar vision of the festival to that found in the booklet, though critical reception at the time was far from supportive. For instance, a review for *Melody Maker* described it as 'a cheapo action replay of all your favourite scenes from Woodstock [the film] ... naked hippies communing with Mother Nature by wallowing in the mud?... The free food tent? The dope smokers? All the clichés are rolled out once again' (Partridge, 1973: 53). The review went on to argue that the film 'failed to capture whatever magic Glastonbury Fayre held' for its attendees, yet the event itself came to be an important touchstone for the free festivals and revivalist fairs (discussed below) that were to follow during the 1970s.

Perhaps most interesting is the film's portrayal of an audience seeking to find meaning for their lives through religion and spirituality. Contemporary advertising posters for the film gave a headlining role to Guru Maharaj Ji (Prem Rawat), whose name was written twice as large as those of the musical performers, even though the film only shows him addressing the crowd for a relatively brief moment. The film spends much more time showing parts of the crowd attending a traditional and rather sombre Christian mass, intercut with footage of a more colourful and noisy service by the Hare Krishnas at the foot of the Pyramid Stage. There is also a scene in which a group of hippies ascend Glastonbury Tor to watch the sunrise which, with other moments and comments throughout the film, is suggestive of transcendental experience (Goodall, 2013; 2015). As Partridge notes, the 'spiritually eclectic' counter-culture of early 1970s Britain soon eclipsed the transatlantic 'fashionable hippie culture' of the late 1960s, and developed its own distinctive subculture with 'idealistic, romanticised notions of love, community, spirituality, and relationship to the land' (2006: 41). Nevertheless, the first Glastonbury Fayre was also an example of long-haired capitalism (Clarke, 1982: 91), since it was only possible to make the event free by selling film rights, releasing a boxed set, and attracting personal donations from its well-connected organisers Arabella Churchill (granddaughter of the former British Prime Minister Winston Churchill) and Andrew Kerr (who had been Personal Assistant to Arabella's father, Randolph).

Free festivals

During the early 1970s, a new form of outdoor music festival emerged in Britain, which perpetuated the aesthetic, spiritual, environmental, utopian, and communal aspects of the counterculture: the 'free festivals'. These events were not organised by commercial promoters or local authorities, but by groups of like-minded volunteers. There were no admission fees or camping charges (though donations were welcomed), and the bands performed for free, including some relatively well-known 'underground' rock bands such as Hawkwind, the Pink Fairies, Here & Now, Gong and Global Trucking Company, alongside folk groups, singer-songwriters and electronic musicians such as Fairport Convention, Roy Harper and Zorch. By the mid- to late-1970s and early 1980s, free festival stages were featuring an even broader range of styles, including punk rock and reggae from bands such as Alternative TV, The Fall and Misty in Roots. The festivals were free of any corporate involvement from the music industries, focused strongly on participation rather than spectacle, and gave festivalgoers and activists the freedom to raise political and social issues. Participation was regarded as an essential component of a successful event, whether in preparing, distributing or selling food and drugs, or in setting up arts and crafts stalls, organising amateur theatre and dances, and encouraging awareness of ecological issues (Sandford & Reid, 1974). A flyer for the Stonehenge Free Festival of 1977 sums up this attitude: 'Bring wot [sic] you expect to find. If you want to contribute in any way, don't wait to be asked: do it' (cited in Worthington, 2004: 135). Political concerns could sometimes overshadow the musical performances: for instance, the People's Free Festivals were deliberately, and illegally, held at Windsor Great Park (1972–1974) in protest at the monarchy's control of 'public land', while the 1973 event incorporated a rally for the legalisation of cannabis. The 1974 event was broken up forcibly by the police after several days, yet government attitudes to free festivals were not as antagonistic at this time as they were to become in the early 1980s.

The organisation of a free festival could be 'inherently and deliberately unstructured and even anarchic' (Clarke, 1982: 31), and was typically based on volunteers providing assistance and services as needed to keep the event running; there were no strict hierarchies and no clear divisions of tasks. However, by the mid-1970s it was common to find volunteer organisations such as Release (legal advice related to drug arrests), the Samaritans (support for emotional issues) and the St John Ambulance (first aid) attending free festival sites. The government formed Festival Welfare Services (1972–1995) to liaise between the various voluntary groups and with local authorities such as the police, local councils, and the Department of the Environment (Clarke 1982). Initially voluntary, FWS acquired state funding for a full-time worker in 1976, and a government committee report of the time described music festivals as 'a reasonable and acceptable form of recreation' (cited in McKay, 1996: 28). It went on to argue that the range of activities found on festival sites, such as theatre, folklore, rural arts and crafts and so on, could offer 'useful experience to young people in living away ... from the facilities of modern society' (ibid.).

The free festival scene became closely associated with a variety of groups which, by the 1980s, had come to be known collectively as New Age Travellers, New Gypsies or the Peace Convoy. These were often, although not exclusively, 'disaffected middle-class dropouts choosing to live an itinerant existence in buses and caravans' (Collin with Godfrey, 1997: 186), and whose mobile lifestyles allowed them to create and travel between numerous free festivals during the summer months. Hetherington suggests that the Travellers used the festivals to enact their lifestyle and beliefs in a spatial and visual way, thereby reinforcing their in-group identity and solidarity, whilst also distancing themselves publicly from mainstream everyday norms (1992: 87; see also Martin, 1998; 2002). The majority of free festivals were held in rural locations. Examples include the Trentishoe Festival, held in the south west of England from 1973 to 1976, the Deeply Vale Festival, held in the north west between 1976 and 1979, and the Meigan Fayre, held in Wales from 1973 to 1975. Many were held near or at ancient sites which fit with the organisers' new age and pagan belief systems – sites such as Avebury Ring, Cissbury Ring and, perhaps most famously, Stonehenge. The Stonehenge Free Festival was held from 1974 to 1984 in farmers' fields near to the Neolithic stone monument, and was timed to coincide with the Summer Solstice, evoking notions of nature mysticism and sun worship. It also provided a fixed calendar point for the nomadic Travellers to congregate. In addition, it became an important opportunity for Travellers to buy and sell goods, both to each other and to the wider public attending the event (Martin, 1998: 741). Clarke calls the latter 'weekend hippies', because they had not dropped out of society, but maintained day jobs or were still in education (Clarke, 1982). For these attendees, free festivals such as Stonehenge were an exciting and somewhat subversive leisure activity that allowed them to express dissatisfaction with mainstream society and music. Hetherington argues that the free festivals were 'conceived as utopian models for an alternative society, often referring to an imagined ethos of freedom from constraints', and as 'carnivalesque transgressions of social norms associated with an ideal of the medieval fair' (Hetherington, 1998a: 330). This connects the free festivals not only with notions of the medieval carnival, but also with other developments in the 1970s, such as the revivalist fairs and Albion Fairs.

Revivalist fairs

The revivalist fairs of the 1970s were in some ways similar to the free festival movement, though more likely to charge an entrance fee and to lay claim to legal authority through reference to medieval Charters and other historical precedents. The Whitworth Fair of 1977, for example, argued that it had been set up under 'a Charter of the Manor of Rochdale of 1251', while the 1976 Bungay May Horse Fair revived a traditional Gypsy Horse Fair that had last been held in the town in 1934 (Clarke, 1982: 154). These revivalist fairs mixed countercultural rural activism with environmentalism, small-scale arts and crafts, and cultural performances such as 'busking, mumming, Morris dancing, folk music and a variety of circus-style acts' (ibid.: 153). In a sense they created alternative forms of the traditional fêtes celebrated in many British villages each year (and typically run by local religious, charitable or volunteer groups). The revivalist fairs emerged in the early 1970s (for instance, the

Barsham Faire ran most years from 1972 to 1976), though the peak period for these fairs was the late 1970s to the early 1980s (Fairs Archive, 2015). It was at this time that the Albion Fairs were staged in East Anglia, and they in turn inspired similar events in the south west of England. The small profits made from stallholder concessions and from entrance/camping fees were often donated to local charities, and they were generally well-organised across the course of a year by a volunteer committee. In this way, such fairs performed 'an alternative capitalism, one which takes ecological values as seriously as it does innovation, customer satisfaction and profit' (Blake, 1997: 191), and they may be regarded as 'a manifestation of the more prosperous and established middle-class aspects of the counter-culture, well-organised on legal sites' (Clarke, 1982: 153). The organisers of the original Barsham Faire even published *Build Another Barsham: A Guide to Faire Making* in 1976, which included advice on matters such as event publicity, site planning, water supply and sanitation, and offered guidance on programming games, theatre, music, dance and craft activities (Barsham, 1976). The non-musical activities were perhaps more important than the music itself, which was often unamplified. This focus on arts, crafts, theatre and dance has also been seen in post-millennial boutique festivals (see Robinson, 2015a), with some of these latter events being linked, historically, to the fairs of the 1980s. For instance, the Port Eliot Lit Fest (established in 2003) is held in the grounds of Lord St Germans' country estate in Cornwall, where he had previously been involved in organising and hosting the Elephant Fayre (1980–1986), which had developed from the pre-existing Polgooth Country Fayre (1977–1979). Since 2009, the Port Eliot Lit Fest has included not just authors and poets, but musical performances, dance groups, fashion designers, chefs and comedians.

Conservative backlash against free festivals

Clarke characterises both the commercial and free festivals of the 1970s as key sites to celebrate en masse the values and feelings of the counterculture, including such matters as 'anti-authoritarianism, sexual relationships without marriage, drug consumption' (1982: 6). The loud music, colourful and outlandish clothing, muddy fields, drugs, alcohol, sexual freedom and so on, many of which are still celebrated in the media portrayal and advertising of festivals in the twenty-first century, offered a temporary liberation from society's norms: a chance for attendees to critique the 'mainstream' society of the 'straights' through a playful and spectacular escape from everyday life. This was true both for the 'weekend hippies', who would gain only temporary release from societal expectations, and for those who sought a more permanent form of escape and social critique through a travelling lifestyle. Yet mainstream media reactions to greenfield music festivals, New Age Travellers, and hippie, 'alternative' or countercultural values as a whole, were far from positive, and festivalgoers attending these events were characterised and judged through the mobilisation of moral fears regarding drugs, sex, squalor and disorder (Clarke, 1982: 27). For example, Clarke notes that the early days of hippie culture were partly defined by experimentation with drugs such as marijuana and LSD, and that music festivals 'quite rapidly became enclaves where it was possible openly to consume, and even to deal in drugs, without fear of police harassment despite their presence' (ibid.: 27–8). He attributes the persistence of drug usage in 1970s festival culture to social criticism and social cohesion, though McKay adds that it might also have formed 'a temporary connection back to the perceived idealism of sixties counterculture: "Turn on, tune in, drop out" for a weekend or a week' (2000: 45). As Hewison notes, for many if not most of those attending, the festival experience 'remained almost entirely personal' (1986: 184), so the advocacy of personal freedoms such as smoking pot, going naked in public, or engaging in sexual activity outside marriage rarely translated into concerted political or revolutionary action.

Nevertheless, condemnation of popular music festivals as havens of promiscuity, rebellion and drug use was prevalent in the mainstream media from the 1960s to the 1980s, and while the government initially gave support to the free festivals by funding Festival Welfare Services, attitudes changed in the late 1970s and early 1980s. At this time, the number and size of free festival events began to increase and the approach of the new Conservative government, which took office in 1979, was rather different from those of the administrations it succeeded. Early 1980s Britain saw mass unemployment, inner city riots, and bitterly-fought trades unions strikes, with the government taking a strong stance on law and order issues. One outcome of Conservative policies in the early 1980s was an increase in the numbers of disaffected and often urban youth responding to an inner-city housing crisis by converting vans and trucks and adopting the nomadic lifestyle of the hippie Travellers (McKay, 1996). Unlike the older Travellers, who were driven by visions and ideals, the new entrants to the scene saw themselves as 'economic refugees' motivated by desperation and a search for a better life (Lowe & Shaw, 1993: 138). The Travellers and free festivals soon became a highly visible anti-authoritarian target to be tackled by the government and police (Martin, 2014). The Stonehenge Free Festival was especially significant since it had, by the early 1980s, become the preeminent free festival in the country, attracting tens of thousands of people across the month of June. Following the 1982 event, a 'Peace Convoy' (as it was dubbed by the press) of more than one hundred vehicles travelled to RAF Greenham Common to hold a Cosmic Counter-Cruise Carnival in support of the anti-nuclear protests of the Women's Peace Camp (McKay, 2000). This Peace Convoy was evidence of the increasing politicisation of the Travellers and made them a target for the Conservative government and press, which demonised the Travellers as an irritant to rural society. For instance, Prime Minister Margaret Thatcher was quoted as saying that she was 'only too delighted to do anything we can to make life difficult for such things as hippie convoys' (cited in Collin with Godfrey, 1997: 201). Interestingly, the organisers of the Albion Fairs in East

Anglia also had issues with newer members of the Traveller community in the early 1980s, arguing that they intimidated other festivalgoers and left rubbish behind them when they left (McKay, 1996). Here we can see contestation over the meaning and purpose of festival-style events by differing groups, with newcomers castigated for failing to follow the unwritten behavioural codes that had developed amongst the Travellers during the 1970s.

In 1985, a concerted effort was made to prevent the Stonehenge Free Festival from taking place, since the annual event had gained not only an important centrality for the Travellers, who congregated to celebrate the summer solstice there, but also notoriety in the press (Hetherington, 2001). A police operation forced the standoff known as the 'Battle of the Beanfield', where Travellers were taken into custody and their vans, buses and belongings destroyed (*Operation Solstice*, 1991; Worthington, 2005). These events fed into the development of The Public Order Act 1986, which included provisions aimed at preventing unlicensed festivals, and enabling the eviction of festivalgoers and Travellers from unlicensed sites. In the following years the Free Festival scene as a whole contracted in numbers and in scale, though some events continued to be staged. For instance, a Peace Camp emerged to protest the building of an anti-submarine torpedo at Waterlooville and led to the annual Torpedo Town Festival that ran from 1984 until the early 1990s.

Outdoor raves and free parties

Outdoor raves, also referred to as acid house raves or free parties, developed when the urban-based Acid House club scene gained broader popularity and was unable to find large enough venues, or long enough licensing hours, to cater to growing demand; instead, the parties moved to disused industrial premises and warehouses, and then to old airfields and rural locations – often near to the newly completed M25 orbital motorway around London (Collin with Godfrey, 1997), though they could also be found in rural areas throughout Britain (Hemment, 1998; Ingham et al., 1999). These sites were usually occupied illegally for a single night, where they were transformed into dance spaces for electronic music and DJ sets. Central to the rave experience was the newly popular though proscribed amphetamine drug known as Ecstasy, which was said to lower social inhibitions, reduce the need for personal space, and induce feelings of wellbeing and friendliness (Malbon, 1999). The acid house scene from which the outdoor raves grew was regarded as a new countercultural form and was soon linked directly to the aesthetic and hedonistic aspects of the 1960s hippie lifestyle, and seen as deliberately reviving its psychedelic imagery, clothing styles, and anti-authoritarian attitudes (Rietveld, 1993: 54–5). This led an initially supportive media to dub 1988 the 'Second Summer of Love' and, like the original Summer of Love in 1967, this counterculture was soon commercialised by entrepreneurs seeking to profit from the new music scene. For instance, a number of event promoters such as Genesis and Biology ran unlicensed raves during this period and used premium rate telephone lines both to guide their audiences to their sites and to keep those sites secret from the authorities for as long as possible (Collin with Godfrey, 1997). Initial press support turned to disapproval as these greenfield raves grew in size during 1989 and 1990. Concerns were raised in the press and government regarding drug-dealing and drug-taking, as well as trespass onto private land, the flaunting of health and safety laws, disturbance to host communities, and the involvement of organised crime gangs (Thornton, 1995).

One of the consequences of this commercially motivated, though illegal, rave scene was that some of the more politically aware and radically minded rave organisers and sound systems, such as Bedlam, Spiral Tribe, DIY and Circus Normal, began to join forces with the remnants of the Travellers and the Free Festival scene during the early 1990s, to attempt to turn the 'purely hedonistic rave scene into a political medium' (Worthington, 2004: 159), and to get involved with anti-road protestors such as Reclaim the Streets (McKay, 1996). These sound systems also adopted the Travellers' belief that 'charging for entry was not only materialist, exclusive and divisive, but destroyed some of the magic of communal celebration' (Collin with Godfrey, 1997: 198). The Longstock Summer Solstice Festival of 1991 is regarded as an important turning point for the relationship between the free party ravers and the hippie Travellers, as it was here that the influential Spiral Tribe sound system began to develop a 'psychedelic spirituality' (Partridge, 2006) and a neo-pagan or techno-pagan approach based around non-stop music and dancing: 'shamanic rites which, using new musical technologies in combination with certain chemicals ... preferably in settings of spiritual significance, could reconnect urban youth with the earth' (Collin with Godfrey, 1997: 204). The activities of Spiral Tribe and other sound systems grew in the early 1990s as the parties merged with the existing Free Festivals and became larger and more focused upon rural sites. Police resistance to the events also grew during this time, and matters came to a head in 1992, when the authorities tried to prevent the Avon Free Festival (held by Travellers since 1988) from taking place. At short notice, the Travellers moved the location of the festival to Castlemorton Common on the Herefordshire/Worcestershire border, where they merged with a number of rave sound systems to create an illegal gathering estimated at between 20,000 and 30,000 people (Reynolds, 2013). Worthington argues that at Castlemorton Common the 'alternative society envisioned by the free festival pioneers was revived' (2004: 163). The event ran for over a week before the site was cleared by the police, and members of Spiral Tribe were subsequently charged with causing a public nuisance. The Criminal Justice and Public Order Bill was moving through Parliament at the time, and the moral panic surrounding unlicensed outdoor raves led to the inclusion of new clauses targeting both unlicensed events and the lifestyles of the Travellers and sound systems that helped to create them.

The Criminal Justice and Public Order Bill was opposed by many involved in what had become known as the 'crusty' subculture of the free festival/free party crossover, which the *NME* jokingly defined as Travellers, urban squatters and 'soap-dodging, army surplus, 16-hole, dreadlocked, folk-punk devils' (*NME*, 1993). Key acts were Spiral Tribe, The Levellers, Ozric Tentacles and Back to the Planet, who performed at the free events and were vocal in their opposition to the Bill. For these acts, the free festivals and raves went 'back to the true spirit of the original festivals. Nobody's making any money. Everyone's there for pleasure, and for the music' (Carl, of Back to the Planet, cited in *Melody Maker*, 1992a: 42). The *NME* couched the arguments surrounding the Bill in class terms, with the Conservative government and property-owning classes portrayed as coming together to outlaw the 'multicultural, empowering, activist lifestyle' of the 'crusties' (Bailie, 1993a: 26). The article went on to associate the events at Castlemorton Common with the 'Battle of the Beanfield' in 1985, the Glastonbury Fayre of 1971, and the ill-fated Isle of Wight Festival of 1970, where Hawkwind and others had staged a free festival outside the official event. The *NME* and other music magazines of the time were supportive of the 'right to party', while the Travellers, sound systems and a range of activists began working together to protest the Bill under the collective name of the Advance Party. One of the Advance Party's newsletters connects festivals, raves and the Traveller lifestyle to Agenda 21 of the 1992 Rio Earth Summit, which offered a blueprint for worldwide sustainability development. The newsletter noted that 'Information about environmental destruction and eco-action is appearing at parties and festivals' and that donations collected at events were being used to support environmental community centres and farms (Advance, 1994). The free parties were therefore deemed to be part of the environmentalist 'back to the garden' agenda of the hippies and the free festival pioneers of the 1970s.

Demonstrators at the Reading Festival in 1994 managed to collect 20,000 signatures protesting the Criminal Justice and Public Order Bill (*NME*, 1994), and in the same year three large-scale protest marches against its introduction were held in London. The final march attracted 35,000 people and ended in violence between the protestors and the police. Despite the opposition of many organisations who saw the Bill as undermining civil liberties, attacking the nomadic lifestyle of both Travellers and traditional gypsies, and criminalising the free festival/free party circuit, it was duly passed into law. As a result, the number of unlicensed music festivals and raves was drastically reduced and dance music largely shifted back into commercial clubs and licensed events (such as Tribal Gathering), though various public protests and raves continued to take place throughout 1995, organised by, amongst others, The Freedom Network and United Systems. Ironically, the newly passed Criminal Justice and Public Order Act 1994 was rarely used to break up these protests, since the police continued to rely on a range of pre-existing laws to do so. Unlicensed raves can still be found in Britain each summer, but they typically have attendance figures of hundreds rather than thousands of people, and are relatively few in comparison to the early 1990s. A more notable outcome of the Act was that the Traveller lifestyle which supported the free festival scene became largely untenable. This led some Travellers to settle in permanent housing or to pursue their alternative nomadic lifestyle in other countries (Martin, 1998: 751–2).

In this first section of the chapter, the history of music events was charted from the transatlantic counterculture of the late 1960s through to the raves and free parties of the 1990s in order to demonstrate the interrelation of various types of event. This narrative of countercultural attitudes, ideas and events naturalises a particular understanding of the social, political and cultural meaning of music festivals in the UK, which McKay has summarised as 'a young or youthful audience, open-air performance, popular music, the development of a lifestyle, camping, local opposition, police distrust, and even the odd rural riot' (2000: ix). To this we may add a preference for greenfield sites, non-commercial values, alternative spirituality, and utopian modes of living, as well as the expression of environmental and social concerns and the tolerance of excessive and transgressive behaviours such as nudity, free love, and the use of drugs. These images and ideas continue to have currency in popular and academic readings of music festivals, even as the music festival sector has become more regulated, professional and commercial over the past 20 years. This will be discussed further in Chapters 2 and 3, while the following section will turn attention to how this countercultural narrative has become associated with Bakhtin's notion of the 'carnivalesque' (1984). We will also discuss how 'countercultural carnivalesque' readings of the music festival phenomenon are commonplace in academia, and will identify the limitations of such readings.

Music festivals and the countercultural carnivalesque

Blake argues that 'Festivals, however genteel and well-behaved, have to be seen first and foremost as an aspect of carnival, a time during which normal rules of social hierarchy and acceptable behaviour ... [are] suspended or inverted' (1997: 178–9). In the Christian religion of the medieval era, carnival was the period leading up to the religious observances of Lent. Where Lent was marked by self-denial, fasting and prayer, the carnival period (also known as Shrovetide) was marked by a celebration of excess that featured dancing, role-playing and a host of humorous and often violent customs and activities, many of which had their roots in pre-existing pagan celebrations (Kinser, 1999). Carnival participants would indulge in 'fattening food, intoxicating drink, sexual promiscuity, altered ego-identity, the inverse and the heteroglot' (Stallybrass & White 1986: 189). It was a time of conspicuous consumption and waste; of grotesque masks and costumes; of bawdy songs and religious irreverence. In *Rabelais and his World*, the Russian literary critic and philosopher Mikhail Bakhtin argued that carnivals acted as a 'temporary liberation from the prevailing truth and from the established order': it represented a time when the world was 'turned inside out' and a new 'second world' was created in which the religious and social norms, ranks and privileges of the Christian Church and feudal lords were ignored, inverted or mocked (1984: 10–11). Carnival was about living in the moment and for the moment, and there was 'no sharp distinction between actors and spectators' (Burke, 1994: 182). For Bakhtin, the carnival was 'invested with exclusively positive values', while the official culture that it overturned was described 'in wholly negative terms' (Flanigan, 1990: 56). Yet this inverted world of excess, mockery and critique was only temporary, since the social structures and strictures of the time were soon restored with the onset of Lent. Carnival and Lent were, therefore, 'mutually defining and supporting elements in the calendar of the church year' (Lindley, 1996: 17), with the excesses and freedoms of carnival acting as a societal 'safety valve' through which the tensions and contradictions of an unequal society could be publicly raised, whilst ultimately maintaining the status quo or affording only gradual change over time.

Bakhtin argued that a 'spirit' of carnival (its behaviours, activities and discourses) was to be found not only in the pre-Lenten period but also in the many other celebrations and events of the medieval era, which led him to coin the term 'carnivalesque'. In the twelfth century, for instance, the British peasantry celebrated over 50 days of what were nominally Christian holidays yet included 'an immense agglomeration of sacred and secular customs, in origin almost wholly idolatrous, but from an ecclesiastical point of view, in theory if not in practice, largely redeemed' (Whistler, 1947: 5). These carnivalesque celebrations were not without their opponents and, following the Reformation in the sixteenth century, such customs and behaviours were increasingly condemned by an emerging English Protestantism. The Protestant lords and clergy, fearing the potential of carnival traditions to upset the social order, began to suppress or even abolish them: in the early seventeenth century, for example, a number of saints' days were 'expelled' from the Church calendar to prevent their celebration (ibid.: 13). The influence of leading Elizabethan Puritans and authors such as Philip Stubbes led to the suppression of theatre and music at this time, and the indulgences and excesses of the carnival and similar events were considered to be 'idle, wasteful, sinful pleasures of the flesh' (Bauman, 1987: 97). A major consequence of these Puritan ideas was the 'ferocious hatred of everything which smacked of superstition, of all survivals of magical or sacramental salvation' (Weber, 1992: 168), as well as the repression of 'the material pleasures of the body and the pleasures of role-playing in public' (Blake, 1997: 180). The public mockery and criticism of authority, which had previously enjoyed limited sanction in carnivalesque celebration, was effectively suppressed, causing the erosion of the socially-stabilising pairing of Carnival and Lent.

Weber argues that there was a mutually supportive relationship between the Protestant work ethic and the development of capitalist industrial society in eighteenth- and nineteenth-century Europe (1992). In many cases, the industrial entrepreneurs were strongly Protestant, and therefore had both economic and religious reasons for their antagonism towards public festivity. They valued frugality, duty to work and abstinence from self-indulgence, while carnivalesque events and behaviours were deemed both wasteful and immoral. To combat this, they sought to 'rationalise' recreation so that the discipline required by their machine-driven factories could be better instilled in their workforce (Ehrlich, 1985; Russell, 1987). As part of this, the industrial working week was introduced, and the traditional calendar of religious festivals was reduced. The fortnight-long festivities of May, for instance, were cut back to the solitary occasion of May Day, and the fields of London's Mayfair were built upon to prevent the celebrations from being held there. However, festival holidays and their associated carnivalesque behaviours did not disappear completely. They were instead transformed, fragmented and marginalised (Stallybrass & White, 1986; Shields, 1991). There was a separation of functions, producing events that specialised in particular aspects of festival, such as feasts, processions or the eighteenth-century masquerade. The more obviously carnivalesque behaviours found alternative outlets and, in tune with the capitalist and modernist drives of the time, were often commodified: the nineteenth-century music hall and pantomime, for example. The outdoor music festival of the late twentieth century can be viewed in a similar light: as a contemporary commodification of the carnivalesque, though, as will be seen shortly, this is only one way to view these events.

Bakhtin's concept of the carnivalesque does not draw directly from social history, but from the representations of carnival behaviours found in the literary texts of the Renaissance. A range of customs and events are conflated to make his arguments, which has led some commentators to argue that his ideas are an 'exercise in myth-making and covert allegory' and 'as much a program for subverting Stalinism [under whose regime Bakhtin was writing] ... as it is a commentary on late-medieval literature and culture' (Lindley, 1996: 17). Furthermore, it has been suggested that he over-privileged the radical potential of the carnivalesque and failed to consider the ways in which official and popular culture interacted and complemented each other (Flanigan, 1990). For example, there is evidence to suggest that carnivalesque occasions were considerably less radical in their nature: that they were riven with local politics and offered ambivalence and plurality rather than chaos and inversion (Lindley, 1996; Humphreys, 2001). Nevertheless, Bakhtin's work clearly posits a dialogic opposition between the hedonistic, free and utopian spirit of popular festive culture (symbolised by the carnival), and the repressive control of official culture (symbolised by Lent), and variations on this dualism can also be found in other theories of the social role of festivals. These include cultural anthropologist Victor Turner's theory of anti-structure (1969) and anarchist theorist Hakim Bey's description of the Temporary Autonomous Zone (1991). These theories relate strongly to the festive use of space and to the behaviour of festivalgoers within those spaces and will be discussed in further detail in Chapters 4 and 5.

Carnivalesque behaviours could be regarded as a celebration of the peasantry and an open critique of the society in which they lived, yet they were also an important support for that society. At one time in history carnivalesque events were embraced as fulfilling a useful role in decreasing or diffusing tensions brought about by inequality between social classes, yet these behaviours later came into conflict with the religious doctrines of Protestantism and the emergence of industrial capitalism (and the bourgeois middle classes that industrial capitalism created). It could be argued that the contradictory aesthetics of the carnival foreshadow the moral panics and fears that have surrounded popular music festivals since the 1960s, whilst also underpinning their potential for subversive social commentary, utopian alternatives and the public display and enjoyment of life beyond the everyday world of work. Carnivalesque events and behaviours have become a symbolic resource for those looking to critique capitalist society, and a source of fear for those seeking to maintain it.

It is partly within this context that the carnivalesque has been drawn into academic understandings of the contemporary music festival, with several authors, such as Hewison (1986), McKay (2000) and Hetherington (1998a, 1998b, 2001), explicitly connecting the 'transgressive, emancipatory rhetoric and imagery' (Booker & Juraga, 1995: 1) of the medieval carnival with the major pop and rock festivals of the late 1960s and 1970s and the free festivals movement of the 1970s and 1980s. These authors apply Bakhtin's ideas of the carnival in their descriptions of late twentieth century festivals as experiences that overturn everyday life, offer transcendence and, temporarily at least, create an idealised utopian vision of a world in which social hierarchies are irrelevant and a better 'second world' (Bakhtin, 1984: 11) can be forged by the festivalgoers themselves. One of the earliest authors to identify this was Cox, who compared the influential late 1960s hippie festivals of the US to the Feast of Fools, a medieval festival held on 1 January each year, which is also discussed by Bakhtin (1984). For Cox, the hippie festivals mimicked the Feast of Fools because they embodied '(1) conscious excess, (2) celebrative affirmation, and (3) juxtaposition' (1969: 22). These countercultural events were described as a public reaction against the secularism, rationality and work ethic of capitalist modernism, and Cox argued further that the festivals allowed people to envision 'new forms of social existence … without first asking whether they are "'possible'"' (ibid.: 82).

In the British context, Clarke argued that the music festivals of the 1970s were playful and spectacular critiques of mainstream society which involved carnivalesque excesses and inversions of societal norms and morality (1982). In addition, we can recognise how the imagery and concerns of the late 1960s hippie counterculture became associated with the festivals of the era: from the psychedelic, Day-Glo and ethnic clothing of its participants to its critique of the violence, materialism and consumerism of capitalist society, and from its preference for New Age and alternative spirituality and beliefs to its interest in environmental and social concerns. These countercultural beliefs and styles were, as noted earlier, transmitted through media coverage of events such as the Isle of Wight, Glastonbury and Stonehenge festivals in the UK, and the Monterey, Woodstock and Altamont festivals in the US (Peterson, 1973; Bennett, 2004). The mythology surrounding the 1969 Woodstock festival has proved to be particularly powerful, as its idealistic and countercultural elements have been persistently recycled by event organisers, academics, media and public, while the sharp business practices of its entrepreneurial organisers have often been downplayed (Street, 2004). Indeed, this is one of the main concerns with the academic literature on music festivals: that it has tended to preference the transgressive qualities and utopian potential of the music festival without giving enough consideration to the economic realities of staging events, or to those events which are more mainstream or commercial in nature. In so doing, the literature has often presented only partial narratives (such as those offered in the first part of this chapter) that focus on those events which are already characterised as countercultural, or which critique mainstream society through their marginal or liminal status. The remainder of this chapter begins to redress the balance by presenting a range of other histories of the music festival in the UK.

Other histories of the music festival in the UK

This section will discuss a range of festivals that pre-date the emergence of pop and rock festivals in the 1960s, including competitive, charitable, folk and municipal festivals. It will also chart an alternative history of commercial popular music festivals from the late 1960s to the 1990s which adds to, and contrasts with, the countercultural narrative presented earlier. There are often crossovers between these festival types, yet the categorisations are useful for drawing out key themes and for demonstrating their ongoing influence on the contemporary music festival market. The competitive, folk and municipal sectors have their origins in the eighteenth and nineteenth centuries and can be recognised as the earliest flourishing of festivals devoted specifically to music. Some of these events may be compared to Bakhtin's notion of a societal safety valve, yet they were created from above, rather than below, and show how the middle and upper classes harnessed or co-opted the festival form and channelled it in ways which served to discipline the behaviours of the working classes into socially acceptable forms. The commercial sector has its roots in the entrepreneurial events of the nineteenth century, though it only began to focus on popular rather than orchestral music in the 1950s. Other music genres have also developed festival events and markets, yet they have arguably had less influence on broader conceptions of outdoor rock and pop music festivals than the event types discussed below.

Competitive music festivals and the first folk revival

It was noted earlier that the traditional calendar of British festivity and carnival was suppressed and fragmented with the coming of Puritanism and the rise of the Industrial Revolution. By the early nineteenth century, the safety valve provided by the traditional festivals of the past had been severely weakened, while a newly emerging capitalist bourgeoisie were becoming increasingly fearful of the large working-class communities developing in the industrialised cities. The working classes were regarded as 'intemperate, ill-educated and ill-disciplined' (Russell, 1987: 29), and there was great anxiety about their perceived cultural, moral and physical degeneracy, as well as their potential to cause political unrest, such as the large-scale disobediences of the Chartist Movement (Pearsall, 1973: 199). Puritan suppression of traditional festivities meant that 'the new social relations of nation, industrialism and class ... had relatively little outlet for public expression' (Blake, 1997: 28), hence there was a need to establish new forms of celebration that would provide a controlled outlet for public expression and energy, while being acceptable to a bourgeois middle class with Puritan values and ideals. Examples include the newly invented and formalised ceremonies associated with royal weddings, jubilees and coronations, and the State Opening of Parliament.

Russell (1987) argues that one of the greatest achievements of the philanthropists, industrialists and reformers of this era was to make music both acceptable and respectable as an art form and spectacle for all social classes. He argues that 'to most middle-class Victorians it was axiomatic that music should be more than a mere artistic experience or a form of amusement' (1987: 23): that it had an educational value and moral force. Accordingly, amateur music-making amongst the working classes, particularly choral singing, brass band music and classical music, was promoted in 'the belief that by bringing together people from different backgrounds music could act as a social cement, a bridgehead between antagonistic social classes' (ibid.: 19). Amateur choral and musical societies began to blossom from the 1850s onwards, with competitive music festivals appearing in the 1870s, where these societies would perform and compete against each other for prizes (Pearsall, 1973). Especially prominent were the brass bands of northern England, which were usually linked to, and even sponsored by, specific workplaces and companies. The competitive festival movement can still be found today, with many events registered by the British and International Federation of Festivals (see www.federationoffestivals.org.uk/).

The nineteenth century also saw the development of a folk revival, typified by song collectors and enthusiasts such as Cecil Sharp, Francis Child, Sabine Baring-Gould, Frank Kidson, William Chappell and Lucy Broadwood. These collectors sought to preserve the oral traditions, folk songs and dances of a rapidly disappearing rural peasantry, and their writings, organisations and public events demonstrated fears of urbanisation, industrialisation and capitalism: factors deemed responsible for the loss of England's cultural heritage and greatness (Russell, 1987). For such collectors 'folksong and dance [were] a powerful regenerative prescription for modern culture. By the adoption of an older, more authentic form of music ... society could experience a musical, cultural and spiritual reawakening' (Brocken, 2003: 5). By defining urban popular culture as aesthetically and historically inferior to folk culture, the Revivalists positioned 'rural "organic communities" ... as the only valid source of an alternative, uncultivated art' (Boyes, 1993: 3), and introduced notions of purity and authenticity into folk music for the first time (Harker, 1985). This authenticity was highly nationalistic in tone, as it defined folk music as the unmediated expression of a culturally specific group: where an 'authentic song is thought to be one truly belonging to the people who sing it, one that really reflects their spirit and personality' (Nettl, 1973: 9).

Recurrent motifs of this folk revival include the 'cultural and spiritual superiority of rural as opposed to town life, the peasant as opposed to the factory worker, the spontaneous simplicity of the folksong as opposed to the sophistication of art music' (Boyes, 1993: 7). A utopian vision of an imagined rural past was constructed: a notional space presented as fragile and threatened by modernity, as requiring not just preservation, but active revival through re-performance (Boyes, 1993: 18). The imaginative values of this idealised past were to be reasserted through the re-creation and re-incorporation of folk music within the cultural life of the late nineteenth and early twentieth century: the Revivalists sought 'not simply a world as it had been but a world as it could be again' (Boyes, 1993: 4). The dissemination of folk songs, dances and traditions was accomplished by a variety of associations, including the Folklore Society (est. 1878) and the Folk Song Society (est. 1898) (which merged in 1932 to form the English Folk Dance and Song Society), and the Morris Ring (est. 1934). The folk cultures that these organisations constructed and promoted have become 'accepted as accurate representations of working-class culture within and outside the Revival' (Boyes, 1993: 2); it is their representations of folk culture that form the ideological foundation of English folk music today. It is notable that these rather utopian ideas of rural simplicity and authentic culture offer an imaginary escape from the capitalist and industrial present, and are echoed in the beliefs of the counterculture that developed in the UK in the late 1960s and 1970s. For instance, Sir Laurence and Lady Gomme's influential *British Folk-lore, Folk Songs and Singing Games*, originally published in 1916, offers a description of the 'folk' which resonates with the beliefs and lives of the New Age Travellers of the 1970s and 1980s: 'They are stranded amidst the progress. They live in out of the way villages, or in places where general culture does not penetrate easily; they keep to old ways, practices and ideas' (Gomme, 2012: 10). Similarly, the revivalist fairs and Albion Fairs discussed earlier connected to this imaginary 'folk' Britain of the past through romanticised ideas about the medieval period.

Early charitable, municipal and entrepreneurial events

Other developments during the eighteenth and nineteenth centuries stressed the role of spectacle and/or commerce rather than participation. For example, there were classical music festivals and People's Concerts, organised by philanthropists, municipal authorities, charitable organisations and entrepreneurial businessmen (Ehrlich, 1985). The earliest of these were in aid of charitable causes, such as the relief of poor clergymen, their widows and orphans (for instance, the Three Choirs Festival, est. 1724), or for the establishment of provincial hospitals in Norwich, Liverpool and Manchester (Adams, 1986). By the late eighteenth century, London was experiencing a 'rage for music' characterised by a season of Lenten concerts which were often organised on commercial lines, and featured professional musicians (McVeigh, 1993). These musicians sought to amass enough income during the Lenten season to see them through the summer months, when concert life in London contracted; however, many would also perform in Britain's industrialising cities during the summer, as a circuit of municipal music festivals developed to bring music to the provinces (for example, at Birmingham, Leeds, Newcastle and Derby). Such events were sometimes arranged to coincide with other, non-musical, attractions, such as Nottingham's races or York's Assizes Week, so that 'those who found the music rather a bore' would have something to keep them entertained (Fiske, 1990: 21). In addition, the festivals were often associated with municipal development and civic pride, with specially-designed concert halls being commissioned by many urban centres in the mid-nineteenth century (Ehrlich, 1985: 69). Examples include Birmingham Town Hall, Leeds Town Hall, and Bradford's St. George's Hall.

By the middle of the nineteenth century, there were many of these urban-based music festivals, with events typically providing a mix of operatic, choral and orchestral music (Weber, 2000: 301), and with some dedicated to the works of specific composers such as Handel, Bach, Britten and Holst (Adams, 1986: 19). The municipal authorities thought of their events in educational and promotional terms, while entrepreneurs increasingly saw music as a good business opportunity (McVeigh, 1993; 1999). Some festivals were explicitly marketed as tourist events both within the UK and, via railway connections, to Europe: the 1859 Handel Centenary Festival, for instance, was promoted through the distribution of 50,000 prospectuses in European railway offices (Adams, 1986: 18). The majority of these events were held in concert halls, but outdoor festivals could also be found in the eighteenth and nineteenth centuries. The first were held at Vauxhall Gardens in London where, in June 1732, a series of nightly concerts was offered by its entrepreneurial owner, Jonathan Tyers. The performers played on a bandstand, while 'audiences were free to walk about or to take refreshment as the music was being played' (McGuinness & Johnstone, 1990: 70). Copycat venues and events soon followed in Bath, Norwich, Birmingham and Newcastle-upon-Tyne (Fiske, 1990: 23).

It is clear that music festivals expanded considerably in numbers, forms and meanings during the eighteenth and nineteenth centuries, and that musical performance and consumption became not only acceptable as a cultural form and activity but also an important focus for municipal cultural policies. Rolfe has noted two further expansions in municipally organised or supported events (1992). The first came following the end of World War Two, when a range of events was launched that sought to enliven British cultural life, and to cater to a variety of interests, such as music, drama and ballet (McKay, 2015). Examples include the Edinburgh International Festival (est. 1947), the International Music Eisteddfod at Llangollen (est. 1947), and Benjamin Britten's Aldeburgh Festival of Music and the Arts (est. 1948). The second wave came in the early 1980s, when culture was posited as a driving force for economic change in Britain's de-industrialising cities. Publicly-funded music festivals (as well as festivals of literature, drama, poetry, food and so on) were established with the express aims of promoting tourism, encouraging local arts practitioners and audiences, and boosting local regeneration. Economic benefits were expected to accrue through direct and indirect employment, such as the support industries of advertising, catering and accommodation (Rolfe, 1992: 6-8). The 1980s also saw the staging of festival-like benefit concerts such as Live Aid in 1985 and Amnesty International's Festival of Youth in 1988. We can identify a further wave of municipal festivals in the 2000s, which includes large-scale outdoor concerts celebrating the Millennium, the Queen's Golden Jubilee, and the Olympics, and continued growth in events aimed at raising awareness and funds for charities and disaster relief. Many of these events are free to attend or make use of celanthropy – the use of celebrities as 'activists, advocates, organisers, fundraisers and donors' (Rojek, 2013: 71) – which has helped to popularise music festivals, and outdoor music events in general, to a broader, more mainstream, audience demographic.

The second folk revival

Folk music festivals emerged as a distinct type during the 1960s. At the time, a second folk revival was at its height in the UK, and British folk festivals either grew out of, or in reaction to, the burgeoning folk club circuit. Today, these events are some of the longest-running non-Classical music festivals in the country; examples include the Sidmouth International Folk Festival (which ran from 1954 to 2004 and has now become Sidmouth Folk Week), the Cambridge Folk Festival (est. 1965), the Cleethorpes Folk Festival (est. 1968) and the Stainsby Folk Festival (est. 1969).

The second folk revival was rooted in the economically troubled times of the 1930s and was politically motivated. A.L. Lloyd and Ewan MacColl, the folklorists and singers/writers who helped to shape and promote the second folk revival in the UK in the 1950s and 1960s, both had strong socialist and communist sympathies. In contrast to the song collectors of the first folk revival, who had almost exclusively favoured the music of the rural working classes, Lloyd and MacColl were interested in the music of the urban proletariat. For example, Lloyd sought out the expressive culture of coal-mining towns in north east England, and actively encouraged the miners to write new songs in local dialects about their 'experiences of their locality, work and class' (Middleton, 1988: 73). In this way, the second folk revival fostered the writing of new 'industrial' folk songs rather than simply the re-performance of a historic repertoire. In the 1960s, some British folk musicians also began to be influenced by the music of American blues artists, and by the songs and ideas of American folk musicians such as Woody Guthrie and Pete Seeger, whose political sympathies were also markedly socialist. However, this influence catalysed a set of tensions within the second folk revival, particularly as American musicians such as Bob Dylan began to introduce introspective and impressionistic lyrics and to adopt electric instrumentation and stylistic elements drawn from country, rock and pop music. In Britain, a split developed between the traditionalists (generally found in the folk club circuit) and other music fans and musicians who wished to embrace the new sounds, songs, styles and ideas coming from America (Brocken, 2013). Rather than engage in the nostalgic re-creation of an imaginary past through re-performance, or to ape the styles and concerns of the past in contemporary acoustic song-writing, these latter musicians sought an alternative present and future, looking forwards rather than backwards. They embraced the American folk-rock and psychedelic rock of the late 1960s and found their audience in the rock music festivals of the time. Some artists also achieved commercial success in the popular music charts of the late 1960s and early 1970s: Fairport Convention, Steeleye Span, The Pentangle and Lindisfarne, for example, all made use of traditional songs, but also drew on a broad range of other stylistic influences (pop, psychedelia, jazz and so on) to forge what has become known as British folk-rock.

Watson argues that the central problem of the second folk revival was that it struggled to reconcile the twin needs of preservation and adaptation (1983): that to avoid stagnation, there was a need for folk music to adapt to the changing circumstances and tastes of the times, but that this went against the preservationist tendencies of the Revivalists. This helps to explain why the more traditionally-focused folk club scene began to decline in popularity and numbers during the 1970s and 1980s, while the musically eclectic festival scene grew in importance. These events shared certain characteristics with the commercial rock and pop festival circuit of the time. For instance, there was an emphasis on social critique and personal freedoms, on a flattening of social hierarchies, and on a 'back to the land/past' attitude linked to environmental issues and the appeal of handicraft and ethnic goods in the festival markets (Laing & Newman, 1994; Young, 2010). The festivals were also important for folk music performers, as they offered high-profile exposure to a broader audience than that afforded by the folk clubs. Moreover, the scale of these events allowed festival organisers to make artistic choices that would be untenable in the more traditional club circuit, thereby providing a more varied programme of local, national and international artists, and expanding the meaning and scope of folk music (AFO, 2004: 10). Statistical information regarding contemporary folk festivals is relatively scarce, though the ukfolkfestivals.co.uk website listed 349 folk festivals for the 2015 season. This suggests that the folk festival sector remains significant in terms of the overall number of events held each year, though it is notable that the listing includes a number of events which do not self-define as 'folk', such as the Cornbury Music Festival, Larmer Tree Festival and Bearded Theory, as well as events which focus on non-British forms of traditional music such as Cajun, zydeco, blues and bluegrass (UK Folk Festivals, 2015).

The financial health of the contemporary folk festival sector is rather variable, with as many as one-in-six events reporting that they struggled to cover their costs in the early 2000s (AFO, 2004). This may be because there is a public perception of folk music as old-fashioned: 'sessions and singarounds do not belong to the common parlance of young people of the twenty-first century and do not relate to their social mores or everyday social interactions' (Brocken, 2003: 130). This image problem is particularly challenging for English folk music, which is beset by negative stereotypes of 'bearded, Aran-sweater wearing, finger in the ear' performers and fans, while Scottish and Irish folk music are regarded in more positive terms (AFO, 2004: 12). Yet, those outdoor folk festivals which owe a debt to the events of the 1960s have continued to offer a challenge to the musical orthodoxy of the folk clubs. They question notions of folk music purity and authenticity by celebrating both artistic creativity and cultural diversity and are fuelled by a public interest in world music, acoustic music and singer-songwriters. However, like the folk clubs, these events tend to attract a predominantly white and middle-class audience, albeit with a broader cross-section of musical tastes than that seen in the clubs. This has led to claims that such events are simply servicing the entertainment needs of 'mellow, suburban, middle-class people who have literally grown up with festivals' (Brocken, 2003: 127), or that they have become elitist in their attitudes, with high ticket prices and little social relevance (ibid.: 130). Hence, while folk festivals have undoubtedly helped folk music to survive as a genre, they continue to have something of an image and credibility problem beyond their heartland audience of white, middle-class attendees.

Commercial music festivals

The commercial market for outdoor music festivals entered a period of growth in the UK during the late 1960s when, as noted earlier, it was tied to the emergence of a transatlantic hippie and rock counterculture. However, a number of antecedent events can be recognised in the late 1950s and early 1960s, such as the Beaulieu Jazz Festival (1956–1961), the National Jazz Federation festivals (1961 onwards) and the Cambridge Folk Festival (1965 onwards). The Beaulieu Jazz Festival was held in the grounds of Lord Montagu's stately home in the New Forest in the south of England. It was modelled, in part, on the US Newport Jazz Festival (1954 onwards), though Lord Montagu also drew inspiration from the Glyndebourne Festival Opera, which had been held in the grounds of another stately home since the mid-1930s (McKay, 2004: 104). The Beaulieu festival ended in 1961, when fights between traditional and modern jazz fans led to property damage. In the same year, the first National Jazz Federation (NJF) Festival was staged in the London Borough of Richmond. It was organised by Harold Pendleton, who had previously worked on the Beaulieu Jazz Festival and was also the owner of London's renowned live music venue, the Marquee Club. In the early to mid-1960s, The Marquee was pivotal in promoting up- and-coming British Blues bands such as the Rolling Stones, The Yardbirds, and John Mayall's Bluesbreakers, and was later known for supporting pop, rock and progressive rock music. The NJF Festival followed the musical trends identified by the Marquee Club; for instance, the 1969 event at Plumpton Racecourse was named the National Jazz, Pop, Blues and Ballads Festival and saw Pink Floyd, Bonzo Dog Doo Dah Band and The Pentangle headlining across the late August Bank Holiday weekend. The event had to change location on three occasions in the late 1960s due to local political pressures, but found a permanent home in the town of Reading in 1971, where tickets described it as the Reading Festival of Folk and Progressive Music, though the official programme referred to it as the Reading Pop Festival – a difference which reflects the fast-moving music industry of the time, and firmly shifted the event away from its jazz roots.

The late 1960s also saw the growth of commercial pop music festivals which drew explicitly on the emerging trend of psychedelic rock. One of the first was the Festival of the Flower Children at Woburn Abbey in 1967, which was a three-day camping event featuring Jimi Hendrix and Eric Burdon and The Animals (both of whom also played at Monterey International Pop Festival that year), alongside new psychedelic groups from Britain, such as Tomorrow and Dantalian's Chariot. Extant film footage shows an event very much in the style of the Monterey festival, with brightly coloured cars and vans emblazoned with terms such as 'beautiful people', 'psychedelic happening' and 'free love', and young people dressed in hippie fashions and wearing flowers in their hair (Huntley Film Archives 2014). The film footage also demonstrates a rather British aesthetic, with festivalgoers shown riding on a miniature railway and a Victorian carousel and constructing beds from deck chairs and sleeping bags. The live venue network and broadcast media for psychedelic pop and rock music was in its infancy during the late 1960s, so outdoor events provided one of the few opportunities for people to congregate en masse to hear the new bands and musical styles, alongside pirate radio stations such as Radio London, Radio Caroline and Radio Luxembourg. The BBC launched Radio 1 as a response to these stations, and among its earliest disc jockeys were John Peel and Tommy Vance, both of whom compèred at the Festival of the Flower Children. The event received mixed reviews from festivalgoers and press, with complaints that it was a 'cash-in' profiting from the youth culture of the time by charging high ticket and food prices (*Time*, 1967: 32) – complaints that have dogged the commercial music festival sector ever since.

Other outdoor music festivals to be staged in the mid-to-late 1960s include the Uxbridge Blues (and Folk) Festivals of 1965 and 1966 that featured The

Who, Manfred Mann, Spencer Davis Group and Long John Baldry, and the Lincoln Pop Festival, which was held in the grounds of Lincoln City football club in 1966, and presented The Who, The Kinks, The Small Faces and The Yardbirds (amongst many others). These events pre-date the 1967 'Summer of Love', which suggests that outdoor summer music festivals were not a creation of the hippie and psychedelic counterculture, but a reaction to the popularity of the mid-1960s boom in popular music, and the need for larger venues to host events and accommodate demand. 1967 saw not only the Festival of the Flower Children, but also new pop festivals in Hastings Stadium and at Blenheim Park in the English town of Woodstock in Oxfordshire. The following year saw a second event at Woburn Abbey, a festival at Chateau Impney in Worcestershire, and the first of three festivals to be held on the Isle of Wight. From 1969 to 1972, over 50 commercial music festivals were held in Britain, typically in sports arenas, race courses and football stadia, the parklands of country houses, or on parkland/farmland big enough to house ever-growing numbers of festivalgoers. The largest events were the 1970 Bath Festival of Blues and Progressive Music, which was attended by around 150,000 people, and the 1970 Isle of Wight Festival, which attracted up to 500,000 people (though many did not pay for tickets). The latter was probably the first festival in Britain to experience a concerted rebellion by the more radical elements of the hippie counterculture. An organisation calling itself the UK White Panthers (led by Mick Farren of The Deviants) argued that the festival was 'an obvious example of capitalist interests seeking to exploit the energy of the peoples [sic] music' (Farren, 2010, no pagination). A printed 'bulletin', produced and circulated before the event, pointed out the weaknesses of the festival site and urged non-paying festivalgoers to watch the festival from a nearby hill (which became known as Desolation Row) and to tear down the fences (ibid.). A group of protestors, including anarchist radicals from Europe and North Africa did exactly that, forcing the organisers to declare the event 'free' and to bear considerable financial losses as a result (Hinton, 1995).

The trend for multi-day outdoor music festivals petered out in the early 1970s, with few events being held more than once, due to poor weather conditions, inefficient or corrupt security, or a lack of resources and technical infrastructure (Orme, 1977; Sandford & Reid, 1974). Britain was also slow to invest in large-scale arenas at this time, whereas the US market developed rapidly and became highly lucrative for British rock bands and artists who could play to large audiences in the US but struggled to find venues of an appropriate size in the UK (Laing, 2004; Brennan, 2010). Nevertheless, a few large-scale commercial events were staged during the 1970s, including the NJF Festival at Reading (hereafter referred to as Reading Festival) and a string of events at Knebworth House. However, these events were criticised for being overly sanitised and controlled; for instance, a *Melody Maker* review of the 1974 'Bucolic Frolic' at Knebworth House suggested that rock festivals had become 'so highly institutionalised that pretty soon one fully expects the kids to be playing croquet, as well as throwing Frisbees, in between sets' (Watts, 1974: 8). The implication was that festivals should be more socio-political in nature and/or capable of transcendental experience (the countercultural carnivalesque), rather than simply offering a picnic atmosphere. The Glastonbury Fayre returned in 1979, this time as a ticketed event in aid of UNICEF's International Year of the Child campaign. A review of the event in *Melody Maker* describes the festival as an 'eco-reunion', and the field as having 'craft stalls, alternative bookstalls, Sufism and Buddhism texts, activists for the Hunger Project, Greenpeace, Legalise Cannabis and a lecture tent', in addition to an adventure playground, donkeys and inflatables for the children (Brazier, 1979: 9). The review quotes from the official programme, which was written, in part, by headliner Steve Hillage (formerly of Gong). The programme reprises the mysticism of the 1971 Glastonbury Fayre by alluding to nearby Glastonbury's myths of Avalon and the Holy Grail: 'Within our hearts, the Chalice is our receptor for that mysterious force that binds atoms, men, planets, and stars together' (cited in Brazier, 1979: 9). However, the review suggests that the event was 'an enjoyable day, a good festival, but no Happening', and was aimed squarely at hippies and families in their mid-twenties (ibid.). The festival failed to make a profit and was not held again until 1981, when it was renamed the Glastonbury CND Festival, reflecting its fundraising support for the Campaign for Nuclear Disarmament. A review of the 1982 event published in *Melody Maker* describes it as a musical 'time warp' to the 1970s, and as offering the 'sorry sight of people clinging to the vestige of an ideal that's long dead and buried' (Humphries, 1982: 8).

The 1980s saw only modest expansions in the commercial outdoor music festival sector. Large-scale one-day concerts were held at the Milton Keynes Bowl throughout the decade, as well as at various stadia around the country, often with the support of local or national radio. The popularity of so-called 'world music' (defined loosely as the traditional and popular music of non-Anglophone countries) gave a boost to events such as the Cambridge Folk Festival and led to the formation of WOMAD (World of Music and Dance), which launched its first festival in 1982. Since the early 1990s there have been WOMAD events in numerous other countries around the world as the organisation seeks to spread a message of cross-cultural awareness and tolerance. The first artist-managed and artist-curated outdoor festival also became established during the early 1980s: the Cropredy Festival in Oxfordshire. Essentially an annual reunion for the folk-rock band Fairport Convention, which had played at many festivals during the 1970s, it has since grown into one of the longest-running music festivals in the UK (Anderton, 2007; 2016).

Despite the lukewarm reviews noted earlier, the revived Glastonbury Festival continued to grow in size during the 1980s, while a number of new rock music events also began to gain ground. The Monsters of Rock festival (1980–1996) was launched by Paul Loadsby and Midland Concert Promoters at Castle Donington Raceway, where it focused on the resurgent popularity of the heavy metal genre. It was joined by a new heavy metal event at Knebworth House (1985–1986), while the long-running Reading Festival also catered to the genre. This crowded marketplace may be one of the reasons – alongside competition from acid house raves – that the Reading Festival found itself in financial difficulties in the later 1980s, precipitating the involvement of the Mean Fiddler club in 1989. During the 1970s and the 1980s the Reading Festival (and similar commercial 'rock' festivals) forged a very different form of festival from the hippie-influenced free festivals. This reflects a shift in rock counterculture, whereby the hard rock and heavy metal genres and their fans increasingly moved away from the psychedelic and progressive music that had also emerged in the late 1960s. The New Age aspects of the late 1960s counterculture were largely abandoned at these festivals, which developed instead into rites of passage for young rock and heavy metal fans. These rites of passage were fuelled by alcohol rather than cannabis and appealed rather more to the masculine 'cock rock' style identified by Frith and McRobbie (2007). It is notable, for example, that between 1970 and 1990 the only female acts to headline the Reading Festival were Patti Smith (1978) and Girlschool (1981) – a pattern of male domination that is still seen at this and other large-scale events today (for example, see Vincent, 2014). Various festival 'traditions' also emerged at the Reading Festival. For instance, if the crowd objected to the choice of artist booked, they would throw bottles and cans at the stage; in 1988 targets included Bonnie Tyler, Deacon Blue and Meat Loaf (Carroll, 2007: 78). Festival campfires and troublemaking on the final night of the event also became commonplace each year, and these antisocial behaviours can be regarded as carnivalesque inversions of everyday norms, even if the event as a whole was a commercial concern featuring relatively mainstream rock and heavy metal artists.

The 1990s saw the growth of commercialisation and corporatisation within the music festival sector, as large national and international concert promotion companies became involved in staging outdoor festivals as well as venue-based concerts. They were initially capitalising on the loss of the free festival and free party sector following the implementation of the Criminal Justice and Public Order Act 1994; hence we can see the development not just of rock and pop music events, but of commercial dance music festivals in this decade. For instance, Tribal Gathering ran as a co-promotion between the rave promoters Universe and the venue owners/concert promoters Mean Fiddler from 1995 to 1997, before disagreements about naming rights led to the 1998 event being cancelled. Those involved in Universe had previously held unlicensed raves, as had the organisers of The Big Chill (1996–2011) who, like Universe, began to host licensed events after the passing of the Criminal Justice and Public Order Act. Other leading dance music festivals which began in the late 1990s were Homelands, which was created by Mean Fiddler and ran under various names until 2006, and Creamfields, originally an outgrowth of the Liverpool club Cream. The

Creamfields festival launched in the UK in 1998, but since the early 2000s has extended its brand to multiple locations around the world. In 2012 Live Nation Entertainment acquired Cream Holdings Ltd, which it operates as a wholly owned subsidiary.

The legacy of the countercultural carnivalesque is evident in reactions to the involvement of Mean Fiddler and other businesses in the legal rave sector. An article on the *Urban75* website refers to Tribal Gathering as 'shamelessly cashing in on anti-CJA [Criminal Justice Act] squat rave culture' (*Urban75*, 1998). It goes on to quote a Mean Fiddler press release from 1996 that, ironically, describes the festival as a 'strike back against the establishment and clubland's evil empire of mediocrity, commercialism, and the creeping corporate capitalisation of our cosmic counter culture'. The *Urban75* article also criticises the high price of Mean Fiddler's Homelands Festival and claims that festivalgoers' own bottles of water were confiscated in order to push water sales in the festival arena. Other articles in the late 1990s and early 2000s take a similar stance, criticising not just the commercialisation of raves, but the very involvement of companies such as Mean Fiddler in rock and pop festivals. For journalists such as Slocombe (1998), Michaels (2002) and Osler (2005), who were typically writing from an activist perspective, festivals and raves had become naturalised as sites of countercultural and environmental critique, as a way to publicly enact alternative ways of living that connected with a deeper history. The commercialisation of festivals and raves was therefore antithetical to their political stance and seen as co-opting a cultural form away from its true or intended purpose.

In addition to Mean Fiddler, the 1990s saw other concert promoters moving into the summer festival market, such as DF Concerts in Scotland (T in the Park, est. 1994) and both SJM Concerts and Metropolis Music in England. These three companies even banded together with the Irish promotion company MCD Productions to create the first V Festival in 1996 where they were able to capitalise on their strong working relationships with Britpop bands (Anderton, 2008). Britpop is broadly regarded as a form of British alternative rock, though *Melody Maker*'s review of 'the best of Britpop 93' actually included coverage of heavy metal, dance, industrial, hip hop, chart pop, ragga, avant-rock and ambient techno (1993: 40–1). Later in the 1990s, Britpop narrowed in scope and became connected with the broader notion of Cool Britannia and its association with the economic and cultural renaissance of London and Manchester, as well as renewed pride in British art, fashion and music. The V Festival tapped into this cultural zeitgeist by focusing strongly on Britpop acts: Pulp, Prodigy, Blur, The Verve, The Charlatans, Massive Attack and the Manic Street Preachers all headlined in its first four years, and many more British acts featured lower on the bill or on the second stage. Over the same period, the Reading Festival included headlining performances from many of the same acts, though there were also headlining performances from several American acts including Red Hot Chili Peppers, Beastie Boys and Metallica. These festivals, and others, also added 'dance' music tents or stages to their overall offering in order to capitalise on the suppression of the unlicensed rave sector.

The first ten years of the twenty-first century saw consistent growth in popular music festivals, with many existing events expanding by adding extra days and/or stages, introducing longer running times, or increasing their maximum attendance figures. Multinational businesses such as Live Nation Entertainment and AEG Live have now become firmly established in the British market. These US-owned event promotion companies, which also act as bookers, organisers, ticket sellers and even band and tour managers, now have a strong presence in the UK live concert and festival sectors, either directly or through financial relationships made with British and Irish promoters. Other genres and types of festival also expanded, with entrepreneurs and local authorities launching events and attempting to cater to the needs of sustainable niche markets. As the next chapter will show, there has been considerable diversification in the outdoor music festival market, which has transformed dramatically in the first decades of the twenty-first century and is continuing to develop.

Conclusion

This chapter has discussed how a countercultural version of the carnivalesque has been used by authors to characterise and theorise the outdoor rock, pop and dance music festivals of the late twentieth century. The imagery and ideology of this countercultural carnivalesque has become a cultural, aesthetic and political resource used by festivalgoers, festival organisers and journalists to validate festivals as an expression of rock and youth cultures, and to authenticate them as sites of opposition and critique: as places where environmental, social, political, and religious concerns and alternatives can be discussed in an atmosphere of personal freedom and collective hedonism. One response to this has been for local and national legislators to introduce increasingly strict regulations and laws to control who is able to organise events, how organisers should manage their events, and how festivalgoers can experience and engage with them. However, as shown in the latter part of the chapter, there is no imperative for music festivals to be viewed as either countercultural or carnivalesque, since their history in the UK is much broader and incorporates charitable, municipal, commercial and other events which pre-date the emergence of the transatlantic hippie counterculture. Some of these earlier events created occasions for a 'moral' or musical education that sought to promote national identity and relieve social tensions. Others presented opportunities for entrepreneurs to make profits, for charities to raise funds for good causes, and for municipal authorities to enhance local economic and cultural development. In many ways, the concept and meaning of any particular music festival is rooted in the social and political milieu of its own time and place, as well as in the specific purposes for which its organisers staged it. The issues that may be raised or promoted through festivals are therefore chronologically and geographically contingent. In this sense, it can be argued that the hippie and rock counterculture of the late 1960s and 1970s co-opted the festival format for its own purpose, as did the free party sound systems of the late 1980s and 1990s. The associative power of medieval models of carnival and festival may have given these countercultures an ideological justification for criticising those who sought to profit from their events, yet the deeper history of music festivals in the UK shows that commercialisation was already present in the festival sector.

Nevertheless, music festivals always retain the *potential* to be carnivalesque – particularly the larger outdoor events – since there is always a risk that festival excesses may spill over into violence and trouble (Clarke, 1982): for example, the Carling Weekend in Leeds and Reading experienced small-scale riots and arson in the late 1990s and early 2000s. Overall, though, the more violent, anti-social and anti-structural aspects of modern large-scale outdoor music festivals, which caused such anxiety amongst the media and government during the 1970s, 1980s and early 1990s, have become increasingly sanitised and controlled through the use of legislation and regulation, and through the professionalisation and corporatisation of those organising them. These factors are discussed in the next chapter, which examines the growth and characteristics of the music festival sector in the twenty-first century.

2 The proliferation, professionalisation and mainstreaming of outdoor music festivals

During the summer months, Britain plays host to hundreds of outdoor music festivals, and there may be over 40 events happening simultaneously on peak weekends during June, July and August. The sector has experienced a 'boom' period during the first two decades of the twenty-first century, alongside enhanced media coverage and marked improvements in customer service quality. This chapter will examine the post-millennial music festival sector through three broad and interrelated topics. First, the proliferation and diversification of the outdoor music festival industry will be explored using data collected over a ten-year period from 2005 to 2014 (inclusive). The data will be used to discuss developments in event programming, the rise of the 'boutique' festival, and the relatively high volatility of the sector as a whole. Second, the market structure of the festival industries will be examined in terms of business types and ownership, before exploring issues of professionalisation, environmental sustainability and regulation. The final section will focus on the notion of 'mainstreaming' and relate contemporary developments in the market to the deeper history and narrative of the countercultural carnivalesque introduced in the first chapter. For instance, some commentators, event organisers and festivalgoers regard the proliferation, diversification and professionalisation of the sector as an erosion of the utopian ideals associated with music festivals and raves from the mid-1960s to the mid-1990s. As a result, festivals are negatively perceived as having lost the cultural and political meanings that were originally ascribed, or believed to be inherent, to them. From this perspective, contemporary music festivals are regarded as commercial simulations trading on the imagery of the past. This has led various organisers to launch smaller and/or 'alternative' events which reconnect with aspects of that past history or challenge the perceived hegemony of the commercialised present.

Proliferation, diversification and volatility

Comprehensive information regarding the size and characteristics of the outdoor music festival sector in the UK is difficult to obtain, since there are no centralised systems for collecting and managing such data for all festivals. Many are registered as members of the various festival associations discussed in the later section on professionalisation, but there is no requirement that they become members in order to manage events. Outdoor festivals are required to have a license, but licensing data does not clearly differentiate between outdoor and indoor events, or provide further detail regarding whether or not the events were actually staged. To overcome these difficulties, an initial survey was conducted between 2003 and 2005 to identify all music festivals, whether indoor or outdoor, using the information available from a broad range of festival listings (Anderton, 2007). The survey identified over 600 music festivals catering to numerous genres in 2005, of which over 40 per cent could be classed as outdoor events (though some also incorporated indoor stages as part of their offering or hosted their main stages in covered marquees). The data on outdoor events have been subsequently updated on a number of occasions, tracking the fortunes of existing festivals and adding new ones to the data set. It is likely that there are more festivals in existence than have been identified here, since smaller festivals in particular often maintain a relatively localised presence. When these smaller and previously unlisted festivals gain a listing, they have been researched further to find out if they were held in previous years, and then the data set amended as a whole to reflect this. While perhaps not entirely comprehensive, the data set does offer a strongly representative coverage of outdoor music festival events held in the UK between 2005 and 2014 (inclusive). Earlier versions of the data set have been used to provide preliminary analysis in Anderton (2008) and Anderton (2011), while this chapter analyses trends and developments across the full ten-year period.

Proliferation and saturation

Figure 2.1 charts the expansion of the outdoor music festival sector from 2005 to 2014. It shows that, in terms of the overall numbers of events staged, the sector doubled in size between 2005 and 2011 (from 261 events to 521 events), with a slight drop and a levelling out in the following three years. This is broadly in line with the findings of the market research company Mintel, which reported a 69 per cent increase in sales turnover and a 29 per cent increase in attendance figures for the period from 2005 to 2010, though these figures include all forms of live music event, including data received from the National Arenas Association, which represents the country's arenas and stadia (Mintel, 2010). Mintel's *Music Concerts & Festivals* report for 2014 argues that, after a dip in 2012, the market 'bounced back', with further expansion predicted in the final years of the decade (Mintel, 2014). However, this has yet to be demonstrated in the overall number of outdoor music festivals which, as Figure 2.1 shows, has remained relatively static since 2011.

The rapid rise and continued resilience of total festival numbers shown in Figure 2.1 has been accompanied by concerns that the market has become

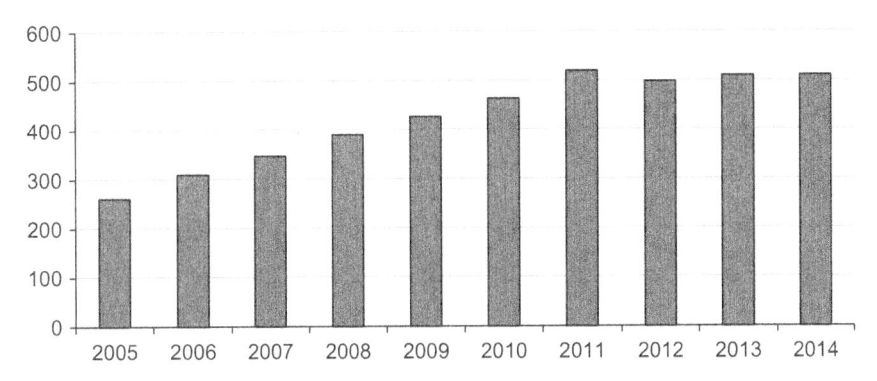

Figure 2.1 Total number of outdoor music festivals in the UK, 2005–2014
(Source: author)

oversaturated with events: that there are too many festivals chasing a proportionately diminished pool of suitable headline performers and audiences. These concerns reached a peak in 2011 and 2012 (Cochrane, 2011; Salmon, 2011; Corner, 2012; Fellowes, 2012), but were also expressed in several previous years. For instance, articles in *Music Week* and *The Times* claimed that the festival and live music markets were saturated in 1998, 2006 and 2009, with high failure rates cited as evidence that the festival 'bubble' had burst (*Music Week*, 1998; Sherwin, 2006; Barrett, 2009). Yet as Figure 2.1 shows, the upward progress of the sector during the 2000s was only halted in 2012 – a year of uncommonly wet weather, and one which saw considerable competition from the London Olympic and Paralympic Games, as well as from the Queen's Diamond Jubilee celebrations. Festivals cancelled due to bad weather included new entrants such as MFest (due to take place at Harewood House in Leeds) and long-running events such as Liverpool's Africa Oye and the dance music festival Creamfields (which was forced to cancel its final day due to on-site flooding). Many other events had already followed Glastonbury Festival's lead in announcing a year off to avoid competing with the Olympics, but the loss of momentum led to over two-thirds of these events failing to reappear in the festival calendar of either 2013 or 2014. Of the many smaller events that took the year off, less than a dozen reappeared, though this is perhaps indicative of the broader issue of market volatility discussed later. However, it also supports the notion of a 'structural inertia' (Getz & Andersson, 2008: 5) among events that, due to a lack of resources and other organisational factors, find it difficult to adapt to, and cope with, market changes. Several high-profile events organised by major UK promoters such as Festival Republic (The Big Chill) and MAMA & Co. (High Voltage) also failed to return in 2013 or 2014, though this likely reflects the portfolio business models of these promoters, who are able to spread their overall risk profile across a number of events, and thus adapt to changes in the market more readily than smaller-scale companies.

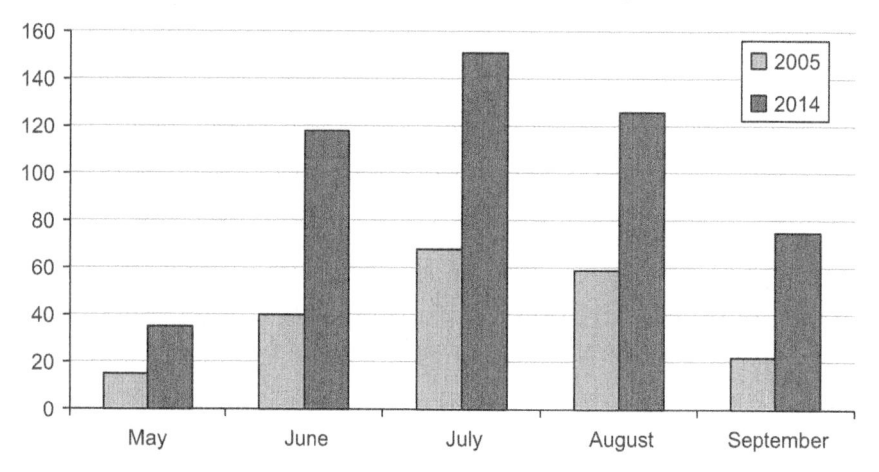

40 *Proliferation, professionalisation and mainstreaming*

Figure 2.2 Number of outdoor music festivals in the UK, by month, 2005 and 2014 (Source: author)

A more detailed analysis of the festival market across the 2005–2014 period finds some interesting trends. Figure 2.2 illustrates a clear festival 'season' of outdoor music events, which peaks during the month of July. While this is to be expected, due to weather and holiday patterns in the UK, comparison between 2005 and 2014 shows that there are proportionately more events in the months of June and August in 2014. In addition, September has become a much more important month for festivals than it had been in 2005, while May saw only moderate growth in comparison. This may be explained by weather patterns in the UK which lead to drier and sunnier conditions in September than in May, but may also be related to changing audience demographics and the dynamics of market competition. For instance, school holidays typically finish at the start of September, while the majority of university terms begin at the end of that month, creating a period in which university-age festivalgoers are available to attend events while families are more restricted by schooling. In addition, the historically busy festival months of July and August are more 'saturated' with events than September, so September is less competitive for the staging of both one-day concerts and weekend events.

Figure 2.3 shows that there are also variations in the duration of events. One- and two-day events demonstrate steady growth across the ten-year period, with one-day events increasing by 82 per cent and two-day events increasing by 110 per cent. However, a steeper gradient is shown for three-day events, which grew by 126 per cent between 2007 and 2011 alone. In addition, a comparison of 2005 and 2014 finds that while events of all durations have increased in numerical terms, there are differences in terms of market share. Events of one and two days have seen a fall in market share by 27 per cent and 15.7 per cent respectively. Over the same time period, three-day events have increased their share of the market by 41.4 per cent, which suggests that more

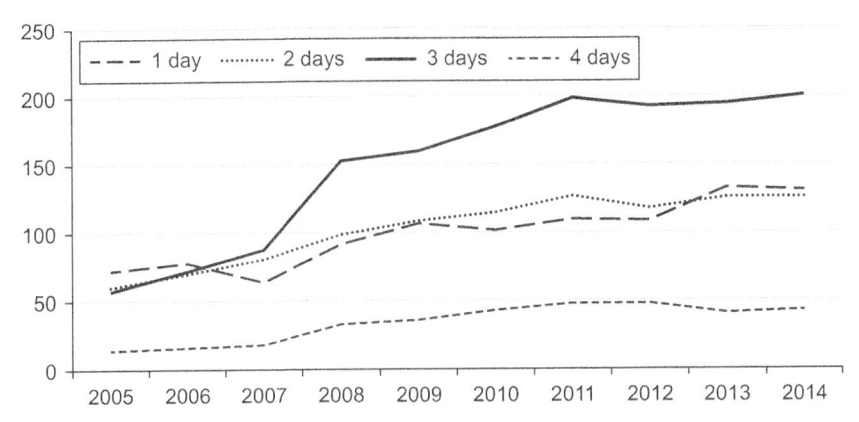

Figure 2.3 Number of outdoor music festivals in the UK, 2005–2014, by duration of event
(Source: author)

weekend-long festivals have become established. As these weekend festivals predominantly offer camping or other temporary accommodation on-site or near to the festival arena, so a corresponding increase in camping events can be discerned across the ten-year profile. Further examination of the data also showed that the increase in camping events was spread more or less evenly across the entire festival season. This growth in the popularity of camping events reflects changes in a number of key areas. For instance, there has been enhanced coverage of outdoor music festivals in the music and broadcast media during the 2000s and, as we will see later in the chapter, continued enhancement of customer service quality. This has changed the public image of festivals, shifting them away from the carnivalesque associations of the past and towards a higher quality and more consistent summer leisure experience. In turn, this has broadened the potential market for festivals, and opened up new opportunities for entrepreneurs and businesses to establish new events. The expansion of brands and sponsors into the festival market has also assisted in this mainstreaming process, as has the development of specialist firms catering to specific aspects of the festival experience, such as pre-erected tents and luxury accommodation, gourmet food outlets, and the brand sponsored 'experiential' areas that will be discussed further in Chapter 3.

The period also saw a change in the dynamics between the recorded and live music industries, with the year 2008 identified by PRS for Music as the year in which revenues from the live music industries first exceeded those from the recorded music industries (Page & Carey, 2009). As revenues from recorded music have dropped, so artists have sought to enhance their income through live performance, and to tie their releases to the summer festival season rather than the traditional late summer/autumn release schedule that had been common since the 1970s. For instance, Björk released the album *Volta* at the start of May 2007, where it acted as a calling card for her upcoming live shows, as well as merchandise for sale at those shows. After a month of theatre performances in the USA, Björk headed to Europe to complete a tour of music festivals, beginning with the Glastonbury Festival in June and proceeding through Rock Werchter in Belgium, Roskilde Festival in Denmark, and numerous others, before ending the summer at the Connect Festival in Scotland; she then returned to North America to continue her world tour. It is now common for major acts to follow a similar pattern, with festival performances offering a relatively risk-free revenue opportunity. This is because artists will earn a guaranteed fee irrespective of the festival's turnout and will also avoid the costs and risks involved in traditional venue tours. A good example of a festival-specific tour is that by the group OutKast, who reunited to play over 40 festivals around the world in 2014, including both the London and Birmingham Wireless Festivals and Bestival on the Isle of Wight. Exclusivity deals are an important factor in the international circuit, since headlining artists are often contractually prevented from playing more than one major festival in any given country in order to give the promoter a competitive advantage over other events. This has been further facilitated by major international promoters such as the American company Live Nation Entertainment, which owns festivals worldwide and controls the touring schedules and routing of many potential headliners. The market dominance of this company makes it difficult for other festival promoters to gain access to suitable headliners and produces a market which has a relatively small number of very large events attracting the biggest global stars, and many hundreds of smaller events where the fame of the headliner is less important as a driver of ticket sales.

The shift in revenue streams affects all levels of the music industries. For instance, the summer festivals offer up-and-coming and nationally touring bands the opportunity to earn additional income and media exposure, as well as for chart pop acts to demonstrate their live performance credibility. In some cases, this can lead to a sense of déjà vu, as the same artists may appear on multiple festival programmes around the country. However, there has also been a move towards exclusivity deals at all levels of the market (not solely headliners), meaning that artists may be prevented from playing events within a particular geographical radius, or within a specified time period. This can make it difficult for smaller festivals to book an attractive and competitive programme, thus affecting their chances of making a profit. One response is to book 'heritage' or 'evergreen' acts as headliners rather than contemporary rock and pop stars. These are artists who have achieved a level of national or international acclaim at some point in the past and continue to appeal to older festivalgoers who grew up with them, as well as to younger festivalgoers who listen to their parents' record collections or have seen the acts canonised by the media. In some cases, entire festivals have been created around heritage acts and nostalgic themes – for instance, the Reload, Rewind and Let's Rock festivals focus on pop stars of the 1980s. Another response is to create events which add significant non-musical attractions alongside their music stages, so that a competitive advantage can be achieved without a high-profile line-up. These are typically identified as boutique festivals – a term and sector that will be examined shortly.

The rise of camping festivals in the late 2000s may be related to the global economic recession sparked by the US financial crisis of 2007–2008, with financial insecurity and raised unemployment levels in the UK encouraging the growth of staycations: more affordable holidays taken in a home country rather than abroad. Outdoor music festivals offer good value in this context as they offer a mix of camping and entertainment, while smaller festivals in particular are often reasonably priced in comparison to the major events. In some cases, festivals have offered 'extended stay' tickets: the Green Man Festival in Wales sells 'Settlers' Passes' which permit festivalgoers to camp for the week leading up to the festival, while the promoters of the staunchly non-corporate Shambala Festival have opened a five-day spin-off event called Starry Skies near the Welsh borders, which trades not on its music acts (though it does offer performances and interactive shows), but on providing a holiday atmosphere and a range of activities suitable for families with younger children. A similar concept is found at Somersault Festival in North Devon, though this event was created by MAMA & Co. (now known as Mama Festivals), which was the second largest live venue operator in the UK at the time the festival was launched in 2014, and also ran or had stakes in the Lovebox, Wilderness, Godskitchen and Global Gathering festivals. However, while staycations may appeal to those on a budget or those with families, a counter-trend has also been seen: overseas events that replace the 'traditional' overseas holiday with a festival. East European events such as Serbia's Exit Festival and Croatia's Outlook Festival, have become especially important in this context as they are relatively inexpensive destinations and offer large-scale events similar in their programming to the major events of the UK.

Boutique festivals

Another important trend in the 2000s was the emergence of the so-called 'boutique' festival, though definitions and usage of the term vary considerably. The term was first employed by the media in relation to popular music festivals in June 2003 when *The Observer* and *The Guardian* newspapers used it in their short previews of that summer's events. *The Observer* defined them as 'compact, stylish and intimate', and offered three examples: a series of outdoor events at London's Somerset House, which the authors claimed as 'one for the family' and which maintained 'the current trend for concerts in historic settings'; The Big Chill festival, which was described as 'anti-corporate'; and The Green Man festival, which was characterised as 'Another case of disheartened music fans taking matters into their own hands' (Knight et al., 2003). *The Guardian* also listed the Somerset House concerts, describing them as 'Possibly the most civilised event of the summer', and referred to The Big

Chill as 'civilised' before noting that its programme 'resembles a thirtysomething former raver's dinner party soundtrack' (Petridis, 2003). Two other events were included in *The Guardian* article: the Eden Sessions in Cornwall which, like the Somerset House concerts, was a series of one-day events without camping; and the folk-rock band Fairport Convention's 'annual get-together', the Cropredy Festival, which was described as 'Heavy on the real ale and facial hair, but there's a lovely atmosphere and you're unlikely to be woken by a 24-hour rave tent' (ibid.). Robinson argues that early definitions such as these tended to focus on events that were 'small, arty and relatively unknown', and cites a Mintel report from 2008 which claimed that boutique festivals had a capacity of up to 5,000 people (2015b: 170, 179); yet the Cropredy Festival regularly attracts between 13,000 and 20,000 attendees, and is not an 'arty' event. Instead, it is much like the greenfield festivals of the 1970s and 1980s (a single main stage and field surrounded by campsites), crossed with an outdoor CAMRA (Campaign for Real Ale) meeting and a village fête (Anderton, 2007).

Over time, the definition of a boutique festival has expanded, and it is not uncommon to find the term used in reference to luxury camping and premium options, or in relation to more interactive and participatory events that engage festivalgoers in a creative and active way (Robinson, 2015b). The term has come to denote a diverse range of events of markedly different sizes, beliefs and motivations, yet a review of Ireland's Electric Picnic perhaps best sums up the underlying discourses of the term 'boutique' in a festival context, as it suggests that the term was used by the organisers as a shorthand for 'special, unique and not mass market ... implying that they are aiming at the discerning punter, who has an authentic sense of taste and style' (McWilliams, 2006). The review goes on to argue that the organisers have targeted a particular age group and type of person: the wealthier 'middle youth' of 35 years and upwards. This 'middle youth' market may also have helped foster developments in luxury camping and other premium ticket options, which have grown in significance since the late 1990s. Drawing on the above, we can see that expectations and characterisations of boutique festivals include exclusivity, broad-based participatory and curated content, an older, family-focused audience, and higher quality facilities. Even a large-scale festival such as Bestival, which grew from a few thousand attendees in 2004 to a mega event of nearly 80,000 daily capacity in 2015, continues to seek a boutique atmosphere because it caters to this 'middle youth' market. This can be seen in the numerous small-scale activities, stages, tents and spectacles that are booked for the event for festivalgoers to enjoy: a range of activities that meet the demographic and psychographic needs and interests of its target audience and reinforce its image as boutique despite high attendance figures and a large site.

One way to consider the development of the boutique sector is through the application of Urry and Larsen's notion of post-Fordist leisure consumption (2011), since emphasis is typically placed on boutique events' unique style in contrast to mass consumer events such as the Reading and Leeds Festivals or the V Festival. Post-Fordist consumption is characterised by market segmentation and specialisation, and Urry and Larsen offer as an example the 'Campaign for Real Holidays' launched by the *Independent* newspaper in the late 1980s. They argue that the campaign defined 'real' holidays as those where holidaymakers visit places not included in cheap package tours or promoted by mass market travel companies and suggest that it drew upon a 'romantic tourist gaze' to create a 'pleasure periphery' of exclusivity and individual experience (2011: 108). Travel companies subsequently responded to the campaign by creating packages that emphasised individual choice, travel rather than tourism, avoidance of the package holidaymaker and their interests, and the inclusion of educational value (ibid.). Such a pattern can also be identified in the music festival market, where boutique events are often smaller, themed and participatory, and emphasise their non-corporate nature, pro-environmental stance or arts and crafts interests. However, here too we can find commercial promoters taking note: for example, Festival Republic (which operates the Reading and Leeds Festivals) launched the Latitude Festival in 2006, and later purchased a majority stake in the Electric Picnic.

The 2014 festival season included a number of small-scale boutique-style festivals, such as Something Else in the Dean, OutCider Festival, and Also Festival, all of which had audience capacities of 500 people. Something Else in the Dean was described as 'the way festivals were "way back when" before much of the festival scene got corporate sponsors and became a massive money making machine' (Tayler, 2013), while the OutCider Festival website stated that it was creating a 'ragged community of free-thinkers, drinkers and music lovers' with 'No tribute bands. No X-Factor. No Carling lager. No hipsters. No tossers' (OutCider, 2015). These two events hark back to the countercultural carnivalesque of the free festivals and hippie festivals of the past, while the Also Festival offered something rather different. It was curated by Salon London, a series of intellectual 'club nights' founded by writer Helen Bagnall and musician Juliet Russell, which 'explore a subject from three points of view: artistic, scientific and psychological' (Also, 2015). The club nights are held in various London venues, while the Also Festival extended the concept to an intimate outdoor setting featuring talks, live performances and DJ sets.

Hybrid festivals

Some boutique festivals might also be described as 'hybrid' festivals, which merge two or more distinct entertainment elements. One long-standing example is the music and real ale festival, where festivalgoers can sample from a huge range of independently-produced real ales, lagers and ciders and enjoy live music on outdoor and marquee stages. Examples include the Blackdown Hills Music & Beer Festival in Devon (established in 1996 as a charitable venture to support local schools and music groups) and the Silloth Music and Beer Festival in Cumbria (a not-for-profit event established in 2000). There are also events which blend the music festival format with food, adventure sports and literature. For instance, Farm Feast in Merseyside is an expanded version of the original Wirral Food and Drink Festival: since 2014 it has hosted live music stages in addition to locally-sourced food and drink exhibitors and stalls, and demonstrations by chefs and artisan producers. Base Camp Festival in the Peak District was established in 2014 to offer a variety of adventure sports such as river tubing, mountain biking, abseiling and white-water rafting, alongside a line-up of guest talks from adventure sports professionals, plus live music in the woods at night-time. Adventure sports-based activities, talks, demonstrations and exhibitors can also be found at the Somersault Festival, and at the NASS Festival near Bristol (established in the late 1990s), with the latter focusing on skateboarding and BMX biking, and including competitive events. There are several festivals which mix literature and music alongside comedy, poetry, theatre and other attractions, including the Port Eliot Festival in Cornwall and the Dinefwr Literature Festival in Wales.

Some events have been deliberately created with a mixed arts and activities agenda, while others have evolved to incorporate music as an important new strand of their offering. This diversification and hybridisation of the events sector is indicative of increased competition in the festival marketplace, and of the need to cater to a range of interests associated with specific target audiences: the music programme itself is often not enough to drive ticket sales. This trend can also be seen in a number of mid- and large-scale events which seek to offer a boutique-style atmosphere by incorporating a range of specialist activities. In this they follow the lead of the Glastonbury Festival, which has had a mixed arts agenda since it reactivated in 1979 and has been named the Glastonbury Festival of Contemporary Performing Arts since 1992. However, its mediated image on television and radio typically focuses on musical performances from its various live music stages, alongside interviews and acoustic sessions with festival artists. This mediation reinforces Glastonbury Festival's position within the broader music industry as a route for artists to gain recognition, kudos and exposure, and to help promote sales and future concert performances, while the festival's cultural, social or ideological significance is often reduced to stereotypical imagery of festivalgoers in unusual costumes, covered in mud or behaving in outlandish ways (Flinn & Frew, 2013: 425). This imagery is to be found on the Glastonbury Festival website alongside sections which highlight the 'Glastonbury spirit'. This 'spirit' is ultimately derived from the event's countercultural history and the behaviours of festivalgoers on-site, yet Flinn and Frew have suggested that it may act as a smokescreen to obscure the rationalised consumption (Ritzer, 1993) on offer at the event, which stands in contrast to the 'casual and chaotic past' that it romanticises (Flinn & Frew, 2008: 428).

Volatility

The data presented in Figure 2.1 suggested that the outdoor festival market experienced smooth growth from 2005 to 2011. However, this picture is misleading, and belies considerable market volatility. Over a thousand different music festivals were held during the period covered by the data, and of those events established since 2005 the average lifespan was three years, though more tellingly the median was two years and the mode one year. There is, therefore, a high failure rate within the sector, with only a relatively small number of festivals achieving longer-term success. For instance, only 25 per cent of the events held in 2014 had been in existence for ten years or more, while only 14 per cent were established prior to the year 2000. Longer-lived events are even rarer, with only 5 per cent established prior to 1990 and 2 per cent prior to 1980.

Figure 2.4 shows the total number of new events established each year and the total number of festivals that were either cancelled during the planning stages or were no longer present in the festival calendar despite having been held the year before. An overall growth trend is discernible, yet it is also clear that the number of festivals cancelled increased from 2005 to 2009, prior to stabilising in 2010 and 2011, and then rising sharply in 2012. The sharp rise in 2012 is to be expected since, as noted above, many existing events took that year off; yet over 80 new events were launched in that same year, no doubt hoping to capitalise on the absence of those pre-existing festivals from the market. 2013 and 2014 show consistently high failure rates, suggesting that market conditions have become tougher and that newly launched festivals have found it difficult to survive.

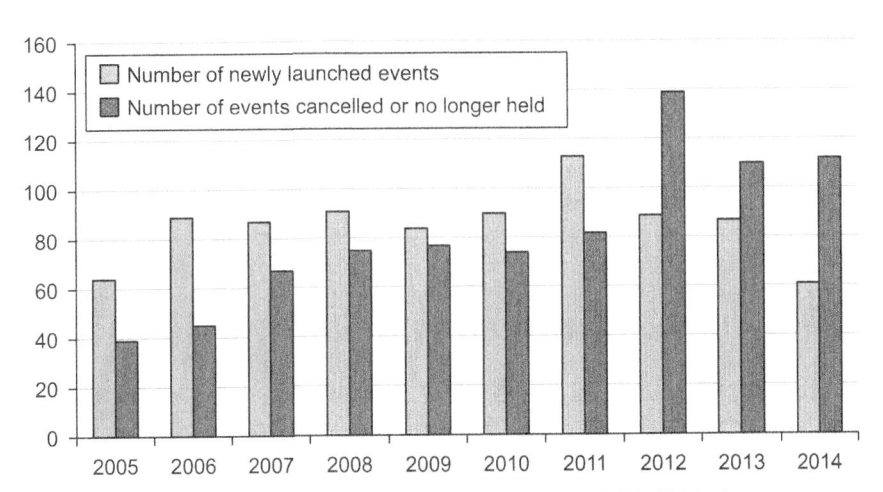

Figure 2.4 Number of outdoor music festivals in the UK, 2005–2014, that were newly launched in each year, and the number of events that were cancelled or no longer held in each year
(Source: author)

Analysis of the 61 events launched in 2014 gives a useful insight into the kinds of events being created. Attendance information is only available for half of these events, but of those, half could be classed as 'small' since they had audience capacities of less than 5,000 people, and eight had capacities of less than 500. The remainder had capacities in excess of 15,000 people, with several of these larger events being promoted by companies who were extending their existing brands into new sites or adding new festivals to their existing rosters. For instance, Live Nation Entertainment launched Wireless Birmingham, AEG Live added East Coast Live and South West Live to its UK Live brand, and the dance music promoter Found launched a second event, named Ceremony, to its Found Series brand. Impresario Events launched two new sites for its existing Rewind brand, while the promoters behind Let's Rock the Moor added a third Let's Rock event in Southampton, alongside those held in Bristol and Berkshire. Other events were launched by national promoters such as SJM Concerts, MAMA & Co., DHP Family Ltd, Harvey Goldsmith, and UK Events and Production.

At least 20 further events were planned and publicised for 2014 but failed to be staged. Where information was available, the reasons given for this were primarily financial. In some cases, sponsor support was withdrawn (whether from commercial companies or local authorities), while in others poor ticket sales meant that the events became commercially unviable. The latter is one of the reasons that underpinned the failure of Alt-Fest, a heavy metal and alternative rock festival which launched a crowd-funding campaign through Kickstarter in an effort to raise the funds required to hold the event. The campaign raised over £61,000 (more than double the target listed at Kickstarter) but poor ticket sales meant that there were insufficient funds to cover mounting costs estimated by the organisers to be £1.7 million. The event was cancelled just two weeks before it was due to be held, with many creditors (including ticket holders, bands and concessions) unable to obtain refunds from the failed business venture. Four other festivals failed because they were unable to secure a public entertainment license due to concerns over health and safety issues, noise pollution or objections from local residents.

Almost a third of the new events which were staged in 2014 were not held again in 2015. Ten per cent were only ever intended as one-off events, such as the Rapha Tempest festival which celebrated the first ever visit of the Tour de France cycling race to the north of England. Several promoters faced financial difficulties after their 2014 events. These include LMF Leisure (which ran the poorly attended Leicester Music Festival) and UK Events and Production, which had launched a new version of the Hop Farm Festival with no involvement from the original promoter Vince Power. UK Events and Production also staged the Flashback Festivals at Nostell Priory and Clumber Park, but cancelled three events planned for Chelmsford's Hylands Park. Major international promoters are not immune to market conditions either: Live Nation Entertainment's Wireless Festival (Birmingham) did not return in 2015, nor did AEG Live's East Coast Live, South West Live or

North East Live. Market volatility appears to have increased since 2012, with more events cancelled or no longer held in comparison to new events established. Whether this marks a transition to a sustained period of market contraction is yet to be seen, but the data suggests that the era of rapid growth has now ceased. In addition, the trend towards boutique and hybrid festivals indicates that the form and style of the sector is diversifying as organisers seek sustainable and innovative niches, and it is likely that this trend will continue.

Market structure and issues

Cloonan distinguishes three main kinds of live concert promoter: enthusiasts, professionals and state (2012). Enthusiasts promote concerts because they like the music, excitement and sense of fulfilment that comes from doing so and, because of this, are less concerned with making profits from their events. In contrast, professional promoters are businesses which need to make money from events in order to survive and grow. The word 'professional' is used to denote full-time workers or businesses operating in the live concert sector, and this notion of a 'professional' as working full-time is commonly used within the events management sector as a whole (Freidson, 1994; Harris, 2004). Between, or to one side, of these poles are the state promoters: typically, local governments, but with funding also coming from development agencies such as the Arts Councils (which have separate branches covering England, Scotland, Wales and Northern Ireland), or organisations such as the National Lottery. The work of state promoters is 'underpinned by a sense of the public good' (Cloonan, 2012: 154), hence the success of an event may be determined not simply through financial profits, but through the provision of positive benefits with regard to, for example, social inclusion, community cohesion or local economic development (see Mirza, 2006).

All three kinds of promoter defined by Cloonan (2012) may also be identified in the outdoor music festival sector, though some variations must be considered. For instance, we may differentiate between events in terms of their goals, especially with regard to enthusiast promoters. Some may be explicitly music-centred, with the aim of promoting and supporting local talent or particular music genres. Others are based around matters of lifestyle, where the music provides a soundtrack and a focus for an event which promotes or satisfies the needs and interests of particular audiences. This is especially clear in the hybrid events discussed earlier, but can also be found in those events which, for example, seek to recreate the atmosphere and ideals of the hippie counterculture of the 1960s to 1980s, or of the free parties of the late 1980s and early 1990s. Other festivals' principal aims may be charitable or relate to the enhancement and support of local community life. At the other end of the spectrum there are sponsor-led events which aim to capitalise on the marketing potential of outdoor events in order to promote their products or to align themselves with a particular audience profile. These events are typically promoted by events management companies on behalf of a sponsor, and so form another category of event where profits are desirable, but marketing and public relations impacts are also of importance. In this respect they are comparable with state promoters, though it is not the 'public good' that is being served, but the needs of the sponsor. An example from the 2014 and 2015 season is Corona SunSets, which is a sponsor-branded event staged on beaches around the world by the Mexican beer brand Corona (owned by the transnational brewery company Anheuser-Busch InBev). A final variation to consider is what might be termed the 'entrepreneurial amateur' or 'entrepreneurial semi-professional': event organisers who host events as part of a portfolio of business relationships or alongside the full-time jobs they do for the rest of the year. These are not 'professionals' in the sense of earning a primary income from events, yet they do organise at least one annual event with the aim of making profits (though many will also donate to charities). In a way, this category is a form of 'enthusiast' promoter, yet their aims will have commercial outcomes of one kind or another and relate in some way to the other businesses they run: they may, for example, be diversifying the potential revenue streams of land that they own, as many farmers and owners of country estates have done, or they may be charitable organisations who use annual events as part of their awareness and fundraising campaigns.

The 2014 and 2015 festival market provides examples of each of these different types of organiser, and will be used here to briefly explore the breadth of the sector in Britain. Commercial festival promoters (or 'professional promoters' in Cloonan's taxonomy) can be found at international, national and local levels. The majority of large-scale events with audience capacities in excess of 50,000 are managed by a small number of national and international promoters, some of which are integrally connected to each other through shareholder relationships, as discussed below. Live Nation Entertainment Inc. (LNE) has the dominant market share of music festivals in the UK, including a majority stake in LN-Gaiety Holdings – a joint venture with Gaiety Investments Ltd which, in turn, is the parent company of the Irish concert promoter MCD Productions (Mintel, 2014). LN-Gaiety wholly owns Festival Republic (the promoter of the Reading and Leeds Festivals), in addition to majority shareholdings in the companies which stage T in the Park and the V Festivals in Essex and Staffordshire. In 2015, LN-Gaiety acquired the MAMA group, which incorporates the Lovebox, Wilderness and Citadel festivals. Separately from LN-Gaiety, LNE owns, manages or has stakes in the Download, Wireless, Calling and Creamfields festivals. In recent years, Anschutz Entertainment Group Inc. (AEG) has begun to challenge Live Nation in the UK, having won the contract, previously owned by Live Nation, to stage major outdoor events in London's Hyde Park. This led to the creation of the British Summer Time festival in 2013, which ran alongside a number of regional festivals staged under the UK Live name in 2013 and 2014. However, the company has not expanded any further into the British festival market; instead, it focuses on the now annual British Summer Time festival in Hyde Park, and its portfolio of large-scale concert arenas, including two in London (the O2 Arena and the SSE Arena Wembley) and one in Glasgow (the SSE Hydro). A further international player to move into the UK market is the German entertainment company Deutsche Entertainment AG (DEAG), which bought a controlling stake in Kilimanjaro Live (which stages the Sonisphere and Wakestock festivals) in 2014 and took full ownership of classical music promoter Raymond Gubbay Ltd (which co-promotes Kew the Music festival with Kilimanjaro Live) in 2015. It is likely that DEAG will continue to expand its British music festival portfolio through the purchase of controlling stakes in further independent festival production companies.

National level promoters include SJM Concerts and Metropolis Music, which promote many events together as gigsandtours.com, and control minority stakes in the company which owns the V Festivals (having jointly founded the V Festival with Scotland's DF Concerts in 1996). In 2014, SJM Concerts launched Summer in the City, based at the Castlefield Bowl in Manchester, which extended to four concerts over ten days in 2015, while Metropolis Music runs the Summer Series at Somerset House in London. However, these promoters are more concerned with their venue and concert promotion businesses and are, alongside Live Nation, co-owners of the Academy Music Group which manages numerous O2 branded venues across the UK. Other significant promoters operating at a national level are Global and DHP Family Ltd. Global is a commercial radio, music and entertainment company that entered the outdoor festival market in 2015, when it acquired the event portfolios of Broadwick Live and Impresario Festivals. It now controls over a dozen British festivals including Kendal Calling, Field Day, Festival No. 6, Truck Festival, Y Not and Rewind. DHP Family Ltd is primarily a venue operator (for instance, Nottingham's Rock City and Bristol's Thekla) but also runs a number of indoor and outdoor festivals, including Splendour Festival (est. 2008) and No Tomorrow Festival (est. 2014). A range of smaller promoters operate festivals across the country, sometimes extending their brands into multiple events across different locations, such as the Let's Rock and Flashback festivals, or in particular cities, such as the Found Series of events across a number of London's parks (under the names Found, Born & Bred, Ceremony and 51st State in 2015).

The outdoor music festival sector includes many events which are organised by enthusiasts or by entrepreneurial semi-professionals, and this may in part explain why there is such a high turnover or failure rate for festivals in the UK, and why event longevity is not common. These promoters will often lack the marketing, public relations and events management experience and knowledge that the national and international companies have at their disposal, or may simply not have the funds required to afford a consistently compelling programme of acts for their events. It can be difficult for novice promoters to be taken seriously by booking agencies, and they lack the bargaining power available to promoters who regularly book bands for concerts or operate an existing portfolio of festivals. For this reason, smaller events of this kind are more likely to book local acts, to be held on land owned by one of the organisers and to rely on volunteers to make the event happen. Together, these factors reduce the overall cost and risk profile of an event and may allow it to become cost-effective and grow over time. A good example is The Beacon Festival in Oxfordshire, which is run by volunteers and held on farmland owned by one of the organisers. It is a not-for-profit event aimed at raising funds for local charitable causes, and books local, up-and-coming and lesser-known acts. Another is Blissfields in Hampshire which began as a small-scale event on the owner's farm in 2001, before growing steadily in both attendance figures and ambition. In 2008, the event moved to a site which could accommodate three to four times as many attendees as the original farm, but this proved to be a step too far, as ticket sales were insufficient to cover costs and the event had to be cancelled. Returning to its roots on the owner's farm in 2009, the event consolidated its early success before moving to a neighbouring farm site in 2011 where it has gradually expanded its attendance figures to 4,000 a day.

State involvement in the outdoor music festival sector is often in the form of subsidies or in-kind support for festival organisers, although local and municipal authorities are also involved in staging events of various kinds themselves, or with the support of volunteers. An example of the latter is the North Wales Blues and Soul Festival (est. 2014), held at Kendricks Fields in the town of Mold – a not-for-profit festival organised by volunteers with funding from Mold Town Council and Flintshire County Council, alongside another 20 sponsors and collaborators. A longer-lived event is the Cambridge Folk Festival, which was organised by Cambridge City Council and volunteers from its inception in the mid-1960s (Laing & Newman, 1994), prior to the Council establishing a charitable trust, Cambridge Live, in 2015, to manage the festival and other assets such as the Cambridge Guildhall and the Cambridge Corn Exchange. Many events benefit from state support of this kind, or from charitable organisations such as the British Council, the PRS for Music Foundation, or the Arts Council, yet public sector funding has reportedly reduced in the 2000s due to restructuring and cost-cutting exercises (Palmer & Thelwall, 2013).

Professionalisation

The professionalisation (or otherwise) of the events management sector has been a topic of interest since the early 1990s, with Getz & Wicks proposing that, at that time, the events industry as a whole was emerging as a 'quasi-profession' (1994). Later papers by Harris (2004) and Thomas and Thomas (2013) argue that events management has yet to achieve the formal status of a profession and is unlikely to do so in the future. However, there are differences in how the term 'profession' is defined, as well as what is meant by 'professional' and 'professionalism' (Harris, 2004), and the concept of professionalisation has not hitherto been applied specifically to rock, pop and dance music festivals. While some parts of the outdoor music festival sector have become more professional in approach, there is considerable variation dependent on business type and approach. Furthermore, there are significant pressures driving organisers and other festival workers towards a broadly defined notion of professionalism, and these pressures may be traced to the activities, expectations and recommendations of trade associations, insurance companies and sponsors, as well as the requirements of the British licensing system.

According to Goldblatt, there are three basic requirements for a field of work to be regarded as a 'profession' (2011: 9). First, there must be a unique body of knowledge specific to that field of work. Second, there must be standards and systems of certification in place to test that knowledge. Finally, there must be 'an accepted code of conduct or ethics' to which members of the profession adhere. This is clear, for example, when looking at the medical and legal professions, yet the outdoor music festival sector struggles to meet these criteria to any great extent. However, an emerging body of knowledge can be recognised in the broader events management sector. For instance, EMBOK (Events Management Body of Knowledge) splits events management into five management 'domains' (design, administration, marketing, operations and risk) and gives advice on the specific activities and project planning phases involved in creating an event (embok.org, 2015). These areas are also covered in academic programmes aimed at producing graduates with the knowledge necessary to work effectively in the events management sector. A range of festival and events associations and organisations now provide reports and guidance on best practice, which adds further to the EMBOK project. Nevertheless, it remains a work-in-progress, and there are considerable crossovers with other industry sectors, such as tourism, leisure and hospitality, regarding the domains and processes that it tackles; it therefore has yet to develop a thoroughly defined and distinct body of knowledge that is specific to events management.

Goldblatt's second and third elements of professionalism are also poorly formed within both festivals and events management: for instance, there is no clear consensus regarding certification or ethics, though there are (as noted later) some moves towards this. Festival organisers do not need certification or to be registered with any professional associations prior to setting up events, which is one of the reasons there are so many entrepreneurs and enthusiasts in the sector. Nevertheless, those who achieve success or longevity within the sector find their knowledge base increasing year on year as they gain stronger working relationships with stakeholders and suppliers and develop their events in response to customer feedback. Knowledge management is therefore an important aspect of professionalisation, and festival organisers and workers need to disseminate knowledge effectively about their events in order for them to run smoothly and successfully. This may be achieved by documenting knowledge in the form of manuals and checklists, or through the training of volunteers (Stadler et al., 2014).

Harris (2004) and Thomas and Thomas (2013) discuss the 'traits' model of professionalism, which seeks to identify the characteristics that a 'professional' may evince in their role. The tripartite model of the 'profession' which Goldblatt (2011) refers to sits comfortably within this approach, since the traits identified include demonstrative expert knowledge, validation or certification by existing members of the profession, and the safeguarding of ethical behaviour (Thomas & Thomas, 2013: 9). However, as noted earlier, it is more typical for the term 'professional' to be used in the sense in which Cloonan (2012) uses it, and which may be defined as someone working full-time in an occupation from which they derive their principal source of income, and which requires specialist knowledge (Freidson, 1994: 133). This knowledge may, in the case of music festivals, be taught through relevant academic courses, but will almost certainly be continually enhanced and developed through on-the-job learning. However, this use of the term might imply that the many volunteers and enthusiasts who are involved in launching, managing and working at festivals are not 'professional', though they may well be acting in a professional manner with regard to their events (Brown, 2014: 17). These volunteer workers might be said to be 'professionalised amateurs' or 'semi-professionals' in the sense that they do not rely on festival work to provide their principal source of income.

Thomas and Thomas (2013) reviewed the literature on professionalisation and argued that it gave insufficient attention to the processes through which professionalisation may be fostered within a particular sector. Arguably, it is these processes which may lead to the perception that a particular field of work, such as that of the music festival, is becoming more professional in its approach. For instance, as shown in Figure 2.5 there has been a rapid expansion in the numbers of trade associations and pressure groups related to live music and festivals as well as to event management more generally, both in Britain and internationally. These associations help to promote the various elements which make up the events and festivals industries, to offer best practice advice, information, training courses, conferences and networking opportunities to members, and to carry out or commission research into matters pertaining to the industries, such as health and safety and policing. However, with such a large number of associations it is difficult to achieve a consensus regarding issues, and these organisations can be seen as competing for membership (Getz & Wicks, 1994; Harris, 2004). Nevertheless, common to most organisations is a commitment to supporting educational measures within the sector through updating their members on contemporary issues which may affect them and encouraging them to develop relevant knowledge and skills. Conferences, research reports and awards ceremonies are just some of the ways in which these associations drive this agenda forward and help to give the impression of a legitimate and professionalising sector (Arcodia & Reid, 2008). Related to this is the notion of corporate social responsibility,

Name of association	Website address
AEO – Association of Event Organisers	http://www.aeo.org.uk/
AEME – Association for Event Management Education	http://www.aeme.org/
A Greener Festival	http://www.agreenerfestival.com/
AIF – Association of Independent Festivals	http://aiforg.com/
BAFA – British Arts Festivals Association	http://www.artsfestivals.co.uk/
BIFF – The British and International Federation of Festivals	http://www.federationoffestivals.org.uk/
EFA – European Festivals Association	http://www.efa-aef.eu/en/festivals/
EPA – Event Planners Association	http://eventplannersassociation.com/
EIF – Events Industry Forum	http://www.eventsindustryforum.co.uk/
IEM – Institute for Event Management	http://iem.institute/
IFEA – International Festivals and Events Association	http://www.ifea.com/
IFF – International Festival Forum	http://iff.rocks/
ILMC – International Live Music Conference	http://www.ilmc.com/
NAA – National Arenas Association	http://www.nationalarenasassociation.com/
TESA – The Events Services Association	http://www.tesa.org.uk/go/
UK Festival Awards & Conference	http://www.festivalawards.com/
Yourope	http://www.yourope.org/

Figure 2.5 Selective list of festival and event management related trade associations, pressure groups and conferences
(Source: author)

whereby organisations operate a form of ethical self-regulation by adhering to best practice ideas that are seen to extend beyond the organisation's basic needs and drive towards profit. With regard to festivals, the clearest example of this is the adoption of environmentally sustainable practices (discussed below) which have an effect on local communities and host locations, as well as the broader natural environment.

Sponsors are another important driver for professionalisation, since they want to work with events that run smoothly and provide positive associations with their brands. As Chapter 3 will show, corporate hospitality – where the sponsor provides selected clients or suppliers with free tickets and access to a backstage hospitality or VIP area – is a significant aspect of sponsorship at many of the mid- and large-scale festivals, so sponsors want these events to provide a consistently well organised and high-quality hospitality area. They also want to avoid any negative publicity associated with, for example, problems caused by poor weather, violence, drugs or event cancellation, so need to be assured that the risks have been properly considered and appropriate contingencies put in place. Similarly, broadcast partners need festival performances to run to schedule and for the production of those performances to be of a high standard, creating pressure on event organisers to enhance the quality and consistency of their organisation and planning. Furthermore, event insurance companies will also want to see that contingencies, systems and paperwork are fit for purpose, and may request copies of venue contracts, risk assessment documentation, health and safety policies and so on. There may be knock-on effects to the cost of insurance based on the quality of the documentation provided and the track-record of the specific festival under consideration. Sponsors are also relevant here as they may demand, for example, that a festival purchases cover against event cancellation and/or postponement or for the non-appearance of a headlining performer, in order that the sponsor's interests are protected (Lloyds, 2013).

Environmental sustainability

Outdoor music festivals may have significant environmental impacts. Within a festival site there are issues related to potential land damage and the management of water, waste and power, while broader impacts include noise pollution and traffic management in host locations (Hannam, 2009), as well as carbon emissions from power usage and travel, whether by suppliers, performers or festivalgoers (Mair & Jago, 2010). As ecological and environmental concerns have become more mainstream over time (for instance, regarding climate change, genetic engineering, resource depletion and so on), so the 'green' agenda has been applied to music festivals, for they represent highly visible activities taking place on greenfield sites. It is therefore important for festivals to be seen to be doing something about the environmental impacts of their businesses, since research has shown that festivalgoers have a high awareness of environmental issues and believe festival organisers must take responsibility for their events (Moore, 2013). In the broader event management context, Mair and Jago note that a company's 'green' credentials may promote competitive advantage, image enhancement and corporate social responsibility (2010). In addition, there is a belief that festivals offer a good opportunity for sustainability campaigners to spread their messages and educate festivalgoers about environmental concerns, and that this may perhaps lead to attitudinal and behavioural changes in the future (Moore, 2013). Some festival organisers use their events to promote environmentally sustainable messages as part of their overall ethos. For example, Shambala Festival and Sunrise Celebration are both committed to achieving what Brooks et al. (2007: 11) call the 'strategic goals' of sustainability, which include: 100 per cent reliance on renewable energy, working with sustainable stakeholders, zero production of waste, and educational outreach about sustainability challenges and solutions. However, others may be said to have adopted environmental policies in order to fit with prevailing societal expectations: that they wish to be seen to be doing something for the environment. Where this occurs, there is the possibility of 'greenwashing', where organisations appear to be following environmentally sustainable policies but are actually offering exaggerations, unsubstantiated claims, or are publicly promoting one policy in order to obscure another, environmentally unfriendly, one (TerraChoice, 2010).

Furthering environmental sustainability is an important way for festival organisers to be seen as taking a professional approach to their events and meets another commonly cited aspect of a 'profession': that 'the skills of members of the profession are deployed in the public interest' (Thomas & Thomas, 2013: 9). Organisations such as A Greener Festival publish reports and advice regarding sustainability measures and goals and have also run a Green Awards scheme in association with the specialist music industry insurance firm Robertson Taylor W&P Longreach. This firm offers a 10 per cent discount on public liability insurance for those festivals which demonstrably implement at least five 'green initiatives' from a given list of possibilities (RT Worldwide, 2015). These initiatives include on-site recycling provisions, the use of sustainable energy sources for at least 25 per cent of power used (biodiesel, solar, wind and so on), and strategies to reduce carbon emissions such as enhanced public transport, car-pooling schemes and car parking charges. However, the provision of such initiatives does not necessarily mean that festivalgoers will engage with them. For instance, Webster (2014: 3) reported on six years of audience research carried out for the Association of Independent Festivals (AIF), finding that there had been a 13.1 per cent rise in the proportion of people travelling to festivals by car, and a reduction in the numbers of respondents using public transport, despite an expansion in provision over the same period. While this may be a statistical anomaly, it may also reflect the fact music festivals are increasingly attended by families with children, and by those who see them as a mini-break with camping: it is simply more convenient to transport large tents, disposable barbecues, clothing and so on by car than by bus or train.

The adoption of green initiatives may not only aid the impression of professionalism and care for the environment, but also enhance the 'triple bottom line' of an event, defined by Gration et al. as: planet (environment), people (society) and profit (economy) (2011). Green practices naturally meet the sustainability needs of the environment, yet they may also meet economic objectives. For example, landfill charges for the removal and disposal of waste can be reduced through recycling schemes, while recyclable waste may actually provide an additional source of income. The Love Your Tent campaign, launched in 2012 by Eco Action Partnership and A Greener Festival, is aimed at reducing the landfill waste created by festivalgoers leaving tents and related campsite equipment at festivals, and has expanded successfully across a number of events. Actions have also been made to reduce the amount of on-site power used by festivals, and these may benefit both environmental and economic objectives. For instance, best practice advice regarding both sustainable power sources and power reduction strategies has been produced by the Powerful Thinking campaign, which is organised by a consortium of music festival related businesses and associations (known as the Green Festival Alliance) which includes the AIF, A Greener Festival, Julie's Bicycle (a global sustainability charity that works with creative arts organisations), Festival Republic, Kambe Events (which manages the Shambala and Starry Skies events), and the 'cleantech' innovation company Firefly. These initiatives support the professionalisation and positive public image of the sector as a whole, as well as of individual festivals. This is bolstered further by Industry Green Certification, which is available from Julie's Bicycle.

Licensing and regulation

In the 1970s, successive British governments decided against the introduction of a festival licensing system, though the troubles encountered at the 1970 Isle of Wight Festival did lead to the localised Isle of Wight County Council Act 1971. The festival was a commercial venture organised by Fiery Creations, who had held previous events on the island in 1968 and 1969, but it was overwhelmed by unexpectedly large numbers of visitors in 1970, including anarchists intent on disrupting it. The 1970 event became a free event on its last day when five thousand people ripped down the perimeter fencing and invaded the festival site (Hinton, 1995). The festival highlighted the 'glaring contradictions between the commercial values of organisers seeking a profit and the anti-materialist and cooperative philosophy which dominated the counter-culture' (Clarke, 1982: 41). Local opposition to the festival grew in its aftermath, leading local MP Mark Woodnutt to propose legislation aimed at preventing future problems. The Act was passed in 1971 and imposed a local licensing system which required land owners and festival organisers to give at least four months' notice of an intended event and allowed the council to set conditions regarding water supply, sanitation and public order. An attempt was later made to introduce a stricter version of this system across the UK as a whole: the Night Assemblies Bill 1972 could have imposed licensing conditions upon any event of 1,000 people or more, but was vigorously opposed by civil liberties groups who saw it as an attempt to erode Britain's historic right to assembly, and feared that it could be used to prevent not just music festivals but other forms of assembly, including union meetings and political rallies (Beckett, 2009). Clarke (1982: 32) notes that larger, commercially-run festivals tended to show quite rigorous attempts at organisation, with Great Western Festivals (GWF) even proposing a Charter for Festival Administration in 1972 as part of its opposition to the Night Assemblies Bill. In the same year, GWF encountered considerable local opposition from potential host locations for its late May bank holiday festival, with three different villages blocking plans, before confirming a site at Bardney, near Lincoln (*Billboard*, 1972: 20). Evidently, local opposition could be mobilised to prevent festivals from occurring, and new legislation was not needed.

This line of thinking is also to be found in the three working party reports published by the Department of the Environment in the 1970s. The first proposed a code of practice which was advisory rather than statutory and sought to ensure public safety and minimise public nuisance to the host location (DoE, 1973). The second looked specifically at free festivals (DoE, 1976), while the third largely repeated the findings of the earlier reports by arguing that new legislation was unnecessary because existing powers related to 'planning, food and drugs, public health, control of pollution, and public nuisance...could be or have been used to obstruct or prohibit pop festivals' (McKay, 2000: 32; DoE, 1978). However, a concerted effort to regulate rock, pop and free festivals re-emerged in the early 1980s, when the Local Government (Miscellaneous Provisions) Act 1982 was passed. This gave local authorities the power to grant public entertainment licences for a fee and to demand compliance with various provisions, such as maximum attendance numbers, limited performance times, and health and safety requirements. The Act affected all greenfield music festivals and was the first attempt by the Conservative government to control people such as the New Age Travellers and other free festival organisers, whom it had cast as 'enemies within', alongside other groups such as urban squatters and trade unionists (Halfacree, 1996a: 45). Some free festival organisers decided to ignore the Act and continued to hold events on unlicensed sites; the government's response (as discussed in Chapter 1) was to take direct action against them with 'an almost militarised police' (Blake, 1997: 191), and to add further provisions to the Public Order Act 1986. Section 39 of this later Act criminalised trespass for the first time in British history, thereby undermining the right to free assembly which had been used as an argument against legislation in the 1970s (NCCL, 1986; Fenwick, 2007). As free parties grew in importance in the late 1980s, it became apparent to the government that further action was needed to bolster the Conservative government's commitment to law and order (Halfacree, 1996a: 45). The first step was the Entertainment (Increased Penalties) Act 1990, which raised the fines applicable under the Local Government (Miscellaneous Provisions) Act 1982 from £2,000 to £20,000, and added a maximum prison sentence of six months. The second was the Criminal Justice and Public Order Act 1994. Section 61 of this Act significantly extended the terms of criminal trespass, while Section 63 specifically targeted outdoor raves. Under certain conditions, the police now had the power to impound vehicles and equipment and to seek custodial sentences for those accused of trespass (Smith, 1995). The Act was widely regarded as an attack on free festivals and free parties as well as on the traveller lifestyle that was associated with them (Press, 1994; Halfacree, 1996b; Rietveld, 1998).

This political history of legislation and regulation has led to the contemporary British licensing system, which promotes a managerial attitude to the planning of events (Brown, 2014: 22). It focuses on supplying paperwork intended to reassure the local emergency services, population and licensing authority (usually a local or municipal council) that all relevant risks have been accounted for and mitigated against. In so doing, the licensing system promotes a professionalised approach to event creation and management for organisers at every level, from the smallest events to the largest. For instance, site plans, emergency response plans, traffic management plans and risk assessments are all required in order to demonstrate the responsible and professional manner in which the proposed event will be managed. If the documentation fails to convince the licensing authority that due care and attention has been taken with regard to event planning and safety, and to managing the event with minimal impact upon the local host community, then licensing approval may be withheld. As public consultation is an element of the licensing process, local complainants may also stop events from taking place, which why events sometimes support local charitable causes or offer discounted tickets to residents within a certain distance of the event. Once a license has been granted, the organiser will need to ensure that the terms of that license are adhered to, otherwise future licenses may be jeopardised, and fines may be imposed for failure to comply. A key document for assisting event organisers is the 'Purple Guide', now published online by the Events Industry Forum (EIF, 2014). This guide is an updated version of guidance previously published by the Health and Safety Executive (HSE, 1993), which was developed from a *Code of Practice for Pop Concerts* introduced in the mid-1970s by Greater London Council (GLC, 1976). These guides all give step-by-step advice regarding every aspect of managing events safely, including: initial planning, management and site design; emergency, fire safety and medical planning; the management of crowds, transport, noise and waste; stage and barrier construction/needs; sanitary provision; communication strategies; and advice regarding electrical installations. The Purple Guide references over a hundred British Standards and pieces of legislation, bringing together a diverse range of advice which serves to regulate the work undertaken in staging outdoor music festivals. The original version, published in 1993, resulted in part from investigations following the Monsters of Rock Festival in 1988, where lateral crowd surges and crowd-surfing in muddy conditions led to the deaths of two festivalgoers in front of the main stage (Kemp et al., 2007: 19–28). Further guidance on crowd management, noise management, and occupational health has been produced by the Health and Safety Executive, as well as by festival industry trade associations and organisations. In addition, specific areas of festival management have become further regulated and professionalised. In particular, the Private Security Industry Act 2001 led to the creation of the Security Industry Authority (SIA) which licenses private security firms such as those providing security at outdoor music festivals; people working for those firms must be individually licensed through formal SIA-endorsed qualifications (PSI Act, 2001). Advice regarding the licensing procedures and the implications of the PSI Act 2001 is available in the SIA's *Security at Events* booklet (SIA, 2008).

Mainstreaming

Chapter 1 showed how popular music festivals have drawn upon counter-cultural associations since the mid-to-late 1950s, and how moral panics and questions of commercial co-optation have been present since at least the mid-1960s. By the early 1970s complaints about over-commerciality were commonplace amongst festivalgoers, yet commercial organisers continued to coexist alongside the growing free festival movement, and arguments about commercialisation and corporatisation only really came to prominence again in the early 1990s, during the height of the outdoor rave scene. For instance, The Levellers (a commercially successful rock group which drew influences from both folk and punk music and was strongly associated with the travelling community and free festivals) became one of a number of bands who publicly criticised the Criminal Justice and Public Order Bill. An article published by *Melody Maker* quoted The Levellers as claiming that: 'Since time began, festivals have taken place for a variety of reasons: celebratory, annual or seasonal, historical, or connected with pagan ritual. Most important was the realisation that festivals are a way of life' (1992b: 4). They contrasted this way of life with the introduction of laws which attacked it, and with events such as Glastonbury Festival which in their view 'purport to advocate the same way of life as ancient festivals, but by their very size and nature become commercial ventures' (ibid.). Indeed, by the mid-to-late 1990s, and following the implementation of the Criminal Justice and Public Order Act 1994, commercial festival promotion became the norm as unlicensed events such as free festivals and free parties became 'outlawed' and subject to police surveillance, regulation and criminalisation (St John, 2009: 12).

For St John, the transgressive potential of the outdoor raves and free festivals was recuperated into authorised and commercialised leisure activities that offered domesticated and routinised experiences (ibid.). One of the key developments during this process was the increasing support of the corporate music industries (both recorded and live) as well as the mainstream media and commercial sponsors. For instance, an article in *Marketing Week* from August 1998 decries the fact that too many people have jumped on the festival 'bandwagon' and argues that sponsors are 'desperate to use trendy tools to target trendy audiences, and they have made budgets available for promoters to drive supply upwards' (Nazerali, 1998: 14). The end result: too many events and festivals which 'have become much of a muchness. The same bands, the same sponsors, the same levels of personal hygiene' (ibid.). Such complaints continue to resonate through the music press, with *The Telegraph* [UK] writing of 'corporate domination' (Corner, 2012) of *The Guardian* [online] arguing that while some contemporary festivals trade on the sector's 'alternative roots', there is 'nothing alternative about a multi-million pound industry whose products are only affordable to wealthy consumers' (Proud, 2015). Audience surveys also reflect these views to an extent. For instance, a pre-season report by the market research company YouGov published in early 2014 found that 35 per cent of those surveyed believed festivals to be 'too expensive', while 28 per cent found them 'too corporate' and 14 per cent felt that 'the same acts were going around the festivals' (Tobin, 2014). As noted earlier, the development of 'festival touring' and exclusivity deals have had a major impact on the ability of events to secure distinctive line-ups, while artist fees have been rising year on year. These rising fees, together with other escalating costs associated with the staging of outdoor events, have increased the average ticket prices of major festivals considerably, yet the shifting demographic of music festivals towards the 'middle youth' market has supported this. In acknowledgment, festivals such as Bestival and Reading have offered payment schemes aimed at younger festivalgoers who cannot afford to pay for a ticket outright or prefer to budget the cost over a number of monthly payments.

Commercialising and sanitising the countercultural carnivalesque

As the UK festival sector has become more commercial, professional and mainstream, so it has adapted and sanitised various aspects of the festival experience and the countercultural ideas and expectations associated with it. This is not simply something which has happened because of festival organisers, sponsors and marketers, but is related to the ancillary industries which have emerged to service the festival industries or are making the most of the commercial opportunities that changing audience perceptions, behaviours and needs have brought. It was noted earlier how corporate social responsibility (CSR) and the 'triple bottom line' (Gration et al., 2011) focused attention on environmental issues, and the concept of CSR is often used in discussions of the external actions taken by companies (McWilliams & Siegel, 2000). Important justifications for CSR schemes include moral obligations towards environmental sustainability and host locations, and the potential to improve the public and media reputation of a business (with knock-on effects for its continued success) (Porter & Kramer, 2006: 80–1). In music festivals, the external environmental, social and economic impacts are only part of the picture with regard to positive public relations and CSR. There are also factors internal to the running of a festival which should be considered. A useful way to examine these factors, and to demonstrate how festivals have become increasingly commercialised and sanitised, is to refer back to the cardinal points of outdoor festivals as defined by Clarke. He argued that moral panics were created by and perpetuated though the mainstream media of the 1970s, and that these were mobilised around four key elements: sex, drugs, squalor and disorder (1982: 27–34). The changes which have occurred regarding each of these elements will be discussed below.

Sex and nudity

The classic pop festival films of the late 1960s and early 1970s all included scenes of nudity and public expressions of sexuality that illustrated the prevailing hippie attitudes and mythology of free love and a return to nature (Bennett, 2004). In the 1970s, these films helped to normalise both nudity and free love as part of the festival phenomenon, though in the UK, moral outcries about shared sleeping marquees had been reported in the press as early as the mid-1960s (McKay, 2000). Nudity can still be found at festivals, though this varies from event to event, and is certainly not commonplace. However, there are concessions such as Sam's Magic Hat Sauna and the Lost Horizon Sauna and Solar Stage (which can be found at events ranging from Glastonbury Festival to Secret Garden Party to Reading Festival), where naturist-style nudity is an accepted part of the experience. Sam's Magic Hat Sauna works on a donation system, while day and weekend passes can be bought for Lost Horizon. While these concessions provide festivalgoers with an alternative to the showers on-site (see the section on 'squalor' below), they also hook into the festival imagery and mythology of the past and demonstrate how the carnivalesque can become commercialised and controlled. Today, concerns related to festivals are more likely to be raised regarding sexually transmitted diseases and personal safety. For instance, advice on the V Festival website states:

> Meeting new and exciting people goes hand in hand at V Festival, but remember you can't tell just by looking at somebody what they are really like or if they have a sexually transmitted disease. Don't put yourself in a situation where you are not in full control. If you do feel the time, place and person is right, then always let your friends know where you are going and with whom and always use a condom.
>
> (V Festival, 2015)

At some festivals, welfare tents offer free condoms and advice regarding emergency contraception, while there have been many promotional gifting campaigns aimed at festivalgoers arriving on the sites of large youth-centric events which have seen condoms included in a free 'goody bag'. Festivals have also been targeted by sexual health campaigners who see outdoor events as valuable occasions to offer advice and to communicate safe sex and personal safety messages to younger attendees. Such campaigns are not only found at the larger commercial events. For instance, the Leicestershire Teenage Pregnancy Partnership (which included participation from the local council and NHS Trust) ran an on-site sexual health clinic at the 5000-capacity Strawberry Fields festival in 2013. By allowing campaigns such as this, a festival enhances its CSR by being seen to care about the sexual health and wellbeing of its audience, while the condom companies providing the handouts will also gain in terms of marketing. However, the stereotypical image of the festival as a place to experiment with sex or find partners has not diminished, and advice regarding sex and festivals abounds on the internet, where it is sometimes used as marketing 'click-bait' to attract browsers towards retailer websites. For instance, an article published online by *Cosmopolitan* (2012) purports to be giving advice, but actually links through to a number of camping- and hygiene-related accessories.

A rising number of reported sexual assaults has been seen at UK festivals since the late 2000s (Sanghani, 2015), and while the numbers are relatively low, it is important that personal safety messages as well as safe sex messages are publicised: the relative anonymity provided by a large site, with often poorly lit campsites and young, intoxicated festivalgoers is a potentially dangerous combination. A visible security presence on campsites as well as in arenas is therefore important, as is making it easier to report suspicious activities through, for example, the anonymous text message service provided by Crimestoppers. A more concerted approach has been adopted by White Ribbon Campaign UK, established in 2005 to tackle violence against women at festivals and live music concerts. In 2016, White Ribbon UK launched its Safe Music report and guide at the Boomtown Fair. The guide offers festivalgoers advice for taking action if they see something happening that gives them cause for concern, while the report specifies a ten-point plan for festival organisers and staff (Boardman, 2016). In 2017, White Ribbon UK worked with a number of other organisations, including Safe Gigs For Women, Girls Against and Rape Crisis England & Wales to formulate the Association of Independent Festival's 'Safer Spaces' campaign, which includes a Charter of Best Practice. More than sixty festivals have signed the Charter which commits festival organisers to staff and volunteer training, confidential welfare services for victims, and a zero-tolerance approach to any form of sexual harassment at their events (AIF, 2017).

Drugs and legal highs

Clarke suggests that in the 1970s the use of illegal drugs was part of a countercultural lifestyle strongly associated with music festivals, and that festivals became important venues for the open use of drugs (1982: 27–8). Festival films of the time showed musicians and festivalgoers smoking and sharing marijuana and using other drugs on-site, while coverage and discussion of drug use by the music press has often been contradictory or ambivalent. For instance, Glastonbury Festival was described by the *NME* as a 'cannabis coming-out party' in 1993, in an article that suggested that it was a 'socially acceptable drug once more', yet also noted the dangers involved in using it (Bailie, 1993b). Similarly, an *NME* reporter travelled to an unnamed music festival with a drug dealer in 1994 to see how easily he was able to bypass police and security to sell drugs on-site (Neslen, 1994). The dangers of drug use are tackled in this article too, but the overall impression given by articles such as these is that drug use at festivals is accepted, even expected, as part of a cat-and-mouse game between festivalgoers and the police. Another example comes from a special festival edition of *Melody Maker* in 1998 that included a full-page interview with an American rock band which focused directly on drugs. The band admitted to smoking cannabis and opium and were asked about so-called 'legal highs' (typically made from legitimately available chemicals that produce similar effects to illegal drugs) and whether they thought they were any good. Their consensus was that they were not, and the author of the article included the phrase 'just say no kids' (a reference to an anti-drugs campaign) a couple of times in his copy (Roland, 1998). Yet, once again, the use of drugs seems to be trivialised by the article into a simple comparison between different types, while at the same time making it seem like an acceptable or cool thing to do, because it is a popular rock band discussing it.

In 2012, the *Guardian* newspaper used the Freedom of Information Act to compile statistics for drug seizures made at music festivals, using data collected by police forces around the UK (Quinn & Burn-Murdoch, 2012). The bulk of the seizures (which had declined since 2009) were from major festivals such as Glastonbury, Isle of Wight, Bestival and V Festival, which offer a mixed bill of popular music styles. Interestingly, seizures at hard rock festivals such as Download, Reading, Leeds and Sonisphere were lower in comparison, despite having similar attendance figures. This may reflect the focus on alcohol consumption at these events, while the higher seizures at the other events may be due to an older and wealthier audience reliving their youth. The most common drugs to be seized were cannabis, cocaine and ecstasy, with ketamine and BZP (Benzylpiperazine) (often seen as cheaper alternatives to cocaine and amphetamines) also showing strong totals for Glastonbury Festival. Legal highs are not referred to in the *Guardian* report, though there was a category in the data for 'others/unknown'. Legal highs have been available since the 1990s but grew in popularity during the 2000s. For instance, the V Festival in Staffordshire had sixteen market concessions selling legal highs (also referred to as 'natural highs' or 'herbal highs') in 2004, plus street team distribution of marketing leaflets directing festivalgoers to visit websites where they could purchase them once the festival was over (Anderton, 2008: 45). The event's official information guide warned festivalgoers that possession of illegal drugs could lead to fines and prison sentences and stated clearly that 'We [the V Festival] do not condone drug use. Please heed the following advice: unfamiliar surroundings and large crowds are not the place to experiment with drugs' (V Festival, 2004: 6). This was seemingly at odds with the commercial activity happening in the festival's market village, although the various compounds of *Sida cordifolia* and *Salvia divinorum* (the active ingredients of the legal highs on offer) were not subject to any UK legislation at that time.

Since 2012, the issue of legal highs has become an important one for festival organisers to tackle. In that year a festivalgoer at Bestival took some

'Magic Crystals' and suffered a paranoid attack that led him to slash his arms fatally with a kitchen knife. The 'Magic Crystals' were later found to contain the Class B drug 4-Methylethcathinone (also known as 4-Mec) (BBC, 2013a). In 2013, the T in the Park Festival was subject to intense media attention due to a spate of deaths in the west of Scotland in the weeks running up to the festival. These deaths were linked to fake ecstasy tablets known as Green Rolex, and it was feared that these might be circulated at the festival (BBC, 2013b). The organisers of T in the Park worked with the police to launch a publicity campaign aimed at those attending the festival, with the issue covered by local and national media. The police also used sniffer dogs at entry points and encouraged festivalgoers to dispose of any drugs and legal highs in their possession using amnesty bins, with the consistent message that drugs of any kind should not be used. One result of these news stories was the launch of a new anti-drugs campaign led by the AIF and the educational charity Angelus Foundation. On 4 May 2014, a 24-hour 'digital blackout' was organised by more than twenty festivals which saw their websites and social media replaced with the message 'Don't be in the dark about legal highs' and a link to a website naming and describing the chemical compounds and their effects (whynotfindout.org, 2015). The campaign was repeated in 2015 with the involvement of over forty festivals, and the message 'You could lose the lot on legal highs'. As part of the campaign, all participating festivals have since banned legal highs, including nitrous oxide (so-called 'laughing gas'), from their grounds. In 2016, the UK government passed the Psychoactive Substances Act which targets those who produce or supply any chemical compound 'intended for human consumption that is capable of producing a psychoactive effect' (PSA, 2016), though not the possession of any such substances. The maximum penalty if convicted is seven years' imprisonment and/or an unlimited fine.

Another recent development has been the work of The Loop, a community interest company that has helped the police with behind-the-scenes drug testing for a number of years and has now launched a 'front of house' testing service similar to that already available in a number of European countries. The service allows festivalgoers to bring in samples of drugs and to have them confidentially tested (and subsequently destroyed) while they wait. They are then given information about the purity of the drugs that they bring in, which may have been mixed with a range of other substances such as caffeine, table salt and phenacetin (a carcinogenic analgesic commonly mixed with cocaine), so that they can make informed decisions about whether or not to take the remainder of the drugs they still have in their possession. Fiona Measham (2016), Professor of Criminology at Durham University and co-founder of The Loop, says that the service can also highlight wide variability in the strength of drugs, with testing at Manchester Parklife Festival showing that ecstasy tablets could contain between 20 and 250 milligrams of the active ingredient MDMA. She argues that the drug-checking service has a number of benefits. First, that on-site dealing can be reduced via social media warnings given by event organisers about the drugs tested. Second, that by making festivalgoers aware of the drugs' variable content and strength, experimentation by new users may be reduced. And finally, that it can assist the emergency services in dealing with drug-related issues in a more timely fashion, and thus reduce drug-related harm. In contrast, critics such as David Raynes of the National Drug Prevention Alliance think that it 'will simply normalise drug taking amongst the young and will reinforce the attitude that taking drugs is an integral part of the festival experience' (cited in Evans, 2017). Nevertheless, after a successful launch at events such as the Secret Garden Party, Kendall Calling and Parklife in 2016, drug testing looks set to expand its coverage in the future, with Melvin Benn of Festival Republic working with the West Yorkshire Police and the National Police Chiefs' Council to support the initiative at the Leeds Festival and other events promoted by Festival Republic.

Squalor

Common perceptions of music festivals include muddy conditions, poor quality toilets and unhygienic festivalgoers. These have been persistently reinforced by media representations of music festivals since the 1960s, with the news media using scenes of mud-stained festivalgoers as a visual trope to represent festivals as a whole, alongside imagery of stages, wellington boots, and people dressed in unusual outfits. The imposition of thousands or tens of thousands of festivalgoers onto a site not designed for such use inevitably leads to difficulties regarding sanitation, waste and land degradation, and these will be aggravated by persistent rain. The particular issues faced by festivals will differ from event to event in line with site conditions and the needs of different site owners, yet all should have contingency measures in place as part of their licensing application or terms. These might include alternative campsite spaces should fields become waterlogged, and details of suppliers should additional trackway or materials be needed to protect commonly walked routes on a site.

Since the late 1990s there has been a noticeable trend amongst festival organisers towards improving the overall quality of their camping and arena facilities. This has partly been in response to changing audience demographics (older, wealthier, more families) and the rising expectations of that demographic, though there are other factors contributing to the trend. For instance, increased competition within the sector has led to event organisers differentiating their events by enhancing the non-musical aspects of their programming, and there has been a growth in entrepreneurs seeking to commercialise different elements of the festival experience. Many festival organisers now routinely add VIP packages to their usual ticketing options. These packages sell at inflated prices and offer festivalgoers access to enhanced facilities such as flushing toilets, a dedicated food/bar area, parking next to tents or preferential viewing platforms. In addition, festivals have become increasingly reliant on income received from commercial sponsors and brands who seek to entertain clients and impress existing and potential customers with their on-site experiential marketing activities: activities which often target the customer service needs of festivalgoers and will be discussed in more detail on Chapter 3.

Research by Mintel (2013) suggests that festivalgoers find toilets to be more important to their overall festival experience than showers, and at a level of importance similar to that of a festival's line-up. Entrepreneurs have already recognised this, with numerous companies now offering 'luxury' toilet facilities at festivals, such as When Nature Calls, Comfy Crappers, Club Class Events, VIPees Ltd, and PTL Portable Toilets. These companies (and many more) charge attendees a fee for the use of their facilities which may include flushing toilets, luxury fittings, complimentary perfumes and deodorants, regular cleaning and warm water hand wash facilities. In 2004, the Kotex feminine hygiene brand ran luxury toilet facilities at the V Festival which were specifically for the use of female festivalgoers, thereby targeting what was then a rising demographic for outdoor music festivals, while also promoting their products. In the same year, the hair care and cosmetics company Wella launched a 'hair rescue centre' at the V Festival, demonstrating that female festivalgoers were perceived as those most likely to place a premium on personal appearance and hygiene. Numerous personal grooming and hygiene brands now routinely run marketing campaigns that draw on the 'buzz' of the festival experience each summer, showing how the old perceptions of festivals as places where you had to 'rough it' are being supplanted by increased commercial activity.

Another key area for this is the provision of accommodation for those staying on-site during a festival weekend. Mark Sutton of boutiquecamping.net (cited in Norwood, 2007) sees his target market as older, wealthier festivalgoers who may have attended festivals in their youth but are now returning in the 2000s with a desire for greater comfort, luxury and convenience. Instead of struggling to erect tents in the pouring rain, or accepting the privations of basic level accommodation, festivalgoers have turned to suppliers such as Boutiquecamping, Tangerine Fields and The Luxury Tent Company for an alternative. At the most basic level this may be a pre-erected tent with an inflatable mattress, but there are many other options. Those with a greater disposable income can, for example, hire pre-erected and furnished tepees, yurts, podpads, beach huts, camper vans and converted buses. At the top end of the market is Camp Kerala (found at Glastonbury since 2005) and Camp Kerala-Mademoiselle (launched at the Isle of Wight Festival in 2015): here, large Indian Shikar tents house king-size beds with Egyptian cotton sheets and Rajasthani furniture, together with gourmet food, cocktail mixologists, spa treatments, and 24-hour customer service. This is a long way from the canvas tents of the 1970s and 1980s or the festivalgoers seen sleeping rough in the festival films of the late 1960s and early 1970s.

Disorder

Concerns regarding public disorder at greenfield music festivals have been common since the late 1950s and reflect societal 'anxiety about large gatherings of people without clear structural divisions' (Clarke, 1982: 31). In part, this relates to political fears, since events in the 1970s and 1980s saw pro-cannabis rallies and protests against nuclear weapons, though disorder can also refer to fears of lawlessness and the potential for this to spill over into host localities. As we saw in Chapter 1, the crackdown on the Stonehenge Festival in 1985 was in part a result of Travellers offering their support to the anti-nuclear protesters at Greenham Common and other sites. Since the passing of the Criminal Justice and Public Order Act, it has been rare for commercial festivals to play host to this sort of political agitation, and while some musicians spoke out against the Iraq War from the stage, commercial festivals appear to have become largely de-politicised in the twenty-first century, at least in terms of issues that might threaten the state and lead to the sort of police actions seen at Stonehenge Free Festival or Castlemorton Common.

Beyond politics, the influx of thousands of people to a temporary site can lead to a variety of public order-related concerns; consequently, we see greater measures taken each year to deal with issues such as drug dealing, pickpocketing, and thefts from cars and tents, as well as issues related to arson, small-scale disturbances or riots, and assaults on other festivalgoers. A report by the AIF argues that festival crime is at relatively low levels in comparison to that found in the wider population, and a survey of festivalgoers reported a fall in crime between 2012 and 2013 (Webster, 2014: 34). This is in line with a 2011 *Music Week* report which argued that there had been a fall in crime at major events since 2009 (Masson, 2011). 2009 is a significant date, since it was the first year that the AIF ran its Security Task Force initiative, and also the first year that Melvin Benn of Festival Republic organised the now annual Crime at Major Music Festivals Conference. Both these initiatives bring together representatives from the police, security companies and festivals to discuss ways to reduce festival crime and to coordinate information. It is now common to see CCTV used at music festivals, both to monitor crowd flow and to aid police investigations. Undercover police are also active at festival sites, though it is more common for the police to remain in a compound outside the main arena. Security teams and stewards can quickly respond to incidents within the arena and call police if necessary, while the police may send uniformed 'reassurance patrols' through the arena from time to time in a non-threatening way, to remind festivalgoers of their presence. The police also patrol outside the festival site and have been known to undertake stop-and-search activities at motorway service stations as well as at festival entrances, where they are looking for drugs and offensive weapons. Some festivals, such as the V Festival, have used targeted letter campaigns aimed at those who have been arrested for offences at festivals in the past, and may even impose bans against offenders to prevent them from attending other festivals (Anderton, 2008: 46). Photographs of these 'known offenders' are circulated and used by police and CCTV operators (who may also have access to face recognition technology), and Automatic Number Plate Recognition (ANPR) is used to flag up any vehicle owned by them. Increased surveillance, policing and security has been accompanied by an increase in costs, with John Giddings of the Isle of Wight Festival stating that he had spent around £1 million in 2015 (Forde, 2015). As long ago as 1995, the Glastonbury festival was labelled as a 'police-benefit festival' by the libertarian communist journal *Aufheben* (*Aufheben*, 2005), while the Glade Festival blamed rising security and police costs for its cancellation in 2010 (Glade Official, 2010). Nevertheless, the police are an important part of the licensing process for festivals, and their input is a key driver towards both professionalisation and the growth of events which cater to a family market, since the latter are deemed lower risk than those aimed primarily at the 18–30-year-old demographic.

An interesting case with regard to festival policing is the Reading (and Leeds) Festival which saw final night riots throughout the 2000s. Festivalgoers (principally teenagers and young adults) lit campsite fires fuelled by tents, toxic plastics and explosive gas canisters, as well as tipping over or setting fire to portable toilets, and destroying festival infrastructure. In 2010, the organisers brought in new measures aimed at controlling these behaviours, which included a ban on campsite fires of any sort after 8pm on the Sunday night and stewards (soon nicknamed 'ghostbusters') patrolling the campsites with portable fire-extinguishing equipment. In addition, aerosol and gas canisters are now banned from both sites and alcohol restrictions have been introduced: only two cases of lager or beer per person are allowed onto a site before 6pm, and none after this time. Since these measures were introduced, there has been a sharp reduction in public order issues and fires at these festivals (Thames Valley Police, 2014). One of the implications of the measures is that alcohol consumption is behind the problems these festivals face, which has led to interventions by the Advisory Council for the Misuse of Drugs (ACMD), the British Medical Association (BMA), and Alcohol Concern, each of which has called for bans on alcohol sponsorship at music festivals. For instance, the BMA has argued that alcohol sponsorship and advertising serves to 'normalise alcohol as an essential part of everyday life' (Cassidy, 2009), while Alcohol Concern's report *Stick to the Facts* has argued that there are 'high levels of alcohol brand recognition amongst children' and that sponsorship of music events should be phased out (2013: 2–3). However, the Department for Culture, Media and Sport (DCMS) has resisted making changes to legislation, in part because of the necessity of sponsorship revenues to the economic sustainability and profitability of music and other events (McCabe, 2013). In addition, the Portman Group, which represents the leading alcohol producers in the UK, has worked to create a voluntary Code of Practice which states that alcohol is to be 'promoted in a socially responsible manner and only to those over 18' (Portman Group, 2014: 3). Signatories to the Code, including the major British music festivals, agree to display 'responsible drinking' messages on their websites, including a Drinkaware logo and a link to Drinkaware's educational website (www.drinkaware.co.uk). Alcohol sponsorships are only allowed where an event can show that at least 75 per cent of its intended audience comprises festivalgoers over the age of 18, and there are various other guidelines regarding advertising. Most festivals also follow the Challenge 25 retailing strategy (originally introduced as Challenge 21 in 2005) which encourages anyone over the age of 18 (but who might look younger) to carry identification that proves their age; failure to do so permits bar staff to refuse service to that person (WSTA, 2015). By following these codes and guidelines, music festival organisers demonstrate that they are taking action on an issue that contributes to public order offences and may adversely affect the health of festivalgoers. They also avoid more stringent legislation which might remove a key source of sponsorship funding.

Alternatives to the 'mainstream': the persistence of the free party scene

Campaigns against drugs, alcohol, disorder and so on could be regarded as a domestication or sanitisation of the festival experience, and as a shift away from the utopian, anarchic freedoms that have been ascribed to outdoor music festivals via the countercultural carnivalesque. The same is true of the on-site presence of cash machines, internet cafés, Wi-Fi towers, and branded stages, bars and restaurants. These disrupt the utopian 'second world' (Bakhtin, 1984) of a festival by bringing the everyday world into it, while the social norms of that everyday world are only overturned or transgressed in increasingly regulated and licensed ways (St John, 2009). For some organisers and festivalgoers, this shift is unwelcome, and the 'true' festival experience remains exemplified by the free festivals and raves which flourished from the 1970s to the mid-1990s. As noted above, some boutique-sized events might be regarded as a manifestation of the 'true' festival experience, but it is perhaps most clearly seen in the contemporary free party scene of small and unlicensed events (also known as raves or teknivals), whose organisation, promotion and management involve cat-and-mouse games with the police. Some are held in abandoned industrial warehouses, while others are staged in out-of-the-way rural locations. Their illegality means that reliable statistics are unavailable for these events, but they do appear to have increased in number since the early 2000s. They typically have attendances of only one or two hundred people, though larger events, such as the annual UK Tek, can attract more than a thousand. In addition to lacking relevant licensing (a Temporary Event Notice (TEN) for attendances of fewer than 499 people, or a Premises License for attendances in excess of this), these Unlicensed Music Events (UMEs), as they are called by the Metropolitan Police, lack 'fire safety accreditation, health and safety certification, Security Industry Authority staff (SIA), [and] professional medical support', and so place attendees at risk

(Met Police, 2015: 2). Using available intelligence sources, the police policy is to try to prevent UMEs from getting started; failing that, they may seek to contain the event in order to prevent any public order risks. The Criminal Justice and Public Order Act 1994 is one of a range of laws that the police can use, and they are empowered to evict event attendees, arrest organisers and confiscate equipment such as sound systems and generators. This happened at UK Tek 2015 in Twyford Woods in Lincolnshire, which saw altercations with the police and 43 arrests, despite calls from the sound system to follow the rave credo of PLUR (peace, love, unity, respect) (*Mixmag*, 2015). Information about free parties used to be readily available through internet sites such as *Guilfin*, *Squall* and *Urban75*, but as the police have become more adept at internet-based intelligence, so free party organisers have returned to the use of flyers, telephone hotlines and word-of-mouth marketing as their main promotional routes.

Conclusion

In this chapter the contemporary UK music festival market has been explored and found to be highly varied, highly volatile, and characterised by a mix of event organisers from multinational corporations to locally-based amateurs. The last 20 years have seen considerable consolidation, with Live Nation Entertainment and associated companies now dominating the market for medium- to large-scale events. In the past five years, Global and DEAG have emerged as significant new rivals to this domination by purchasing existing independent festival production companies, but this wave of consolidation and corporate control is likely to be opposed by the Association of Independent Festivals. This is because the bargaining power and exclusivity deals enjoyed by national and multinational corporations make it difficult for the independent sector to book the calibre of headline artist they need to stage profitable events.

Large-scale festivals, such as Glastonbury, Reading/Leeds, Isle of Wight, Creamfields and V Festival tend to dominate the music and lifestyle press and broadcast media, yet smaller events are much more numerous. One response to the consolidation and proliferation of the sector has been the increase in smaller, independently-run, boutique and hybrid festivals that cater to niche markets and are less reliant on big name artists to drive ticket sales. Another has been the growth of a customer service orientation that has broadened the demographic characteristics of festivalgoers. Both of these responses will continue in the near future as event organisers compete in a crowded market to build loyalty and achieve financial sustainability. However, market volatility will also continue, and future waves of consolidation are expected as the larger corporate promoters compete to buy out struggling events and expand their own portfolios. The data show that the outdoor festival market struggled to recover from the competition and disruption of 2012, and early indications are that Mintel's (2014) prediction of continued growth through the second half of the decade will not prove to be true, at least in terms of the overall numbers of events being held.

Festival organisations of all sizes have, to varying degrees, become more professional in their approach as they seek to meet the needs of local authorities, emergency services, regulators, sponsors, media and insurers. As a result, the countercultural carnivalesque characteristics which previously led to moral panics in the press and government have become increasingly suppressed, controlled or commercialised, though may still be found, to varying extents, in what remains of the free party scene. This finding is discussed in further detail in the following chapter, which examines the commercialisation and mainstreaming of music festivals through the lens of sponsorship and branding.

3 Branded landscapes

Sponsorship, marketing and mediation

Branding, sponsorship, experiential marketing and mediation have all grown in importance for outdoor music festivals since the early 1990s. They are now essential to the commercial and aesthetic image, success and longevity, or otherwise, of many events, yet they have been subject to much suspicion amongst 'traditional' festivalgoers: those who began attending festivals in the 1970s and 1980s, and those who hold more highly politicised views of music festival culture. This chapter will explore how corporate sponsorships, experiential marketing, event branding and media coverage have changed the image and management of the outdoor music festival sector, including shifts in genre expectations and line-ups. It will also discuss the influence of the countercultural carnivalesque on the marketing of contemporary music festivals, alongside changes in consumer society and audience demographics since the 1990s. A variety of festivals is considered, including the Glastonbury Festival (which does not publicise its sponsor partners even though it has them), the V Festival (one of the first festivals to fully embrace the possibilities of corporate sponsorship in the mid-1990s), and the Hop Farm Festival (which operated without headline sponsorship). In addition, a range of other events and brand campaigns are studied in order to examine the changing nature of festival sponsorship activities, and the attitudes of festivals and audiences towards them.

The 'brand matrix'

Branding refers to the name, symbol, logo or other recognisable mark that allows one business, service or product to be distinguished from others operating in a similar market. This denotative function of branding is accompanied by a connotative function, in which the brand name or mark becomes a shorthand way for brand owners to communicate their brand values: a broader collection of social, cultural, political and economic meanings relating to, for instance, quality, trust, value-for-money, inclusivity, fun and so on. The ideal situation for a brand-owner is that consumer perceptions of its brand values will match its own, though this is not always the case; hence brand-owners are always looking for ways to reinforce or realign consumer

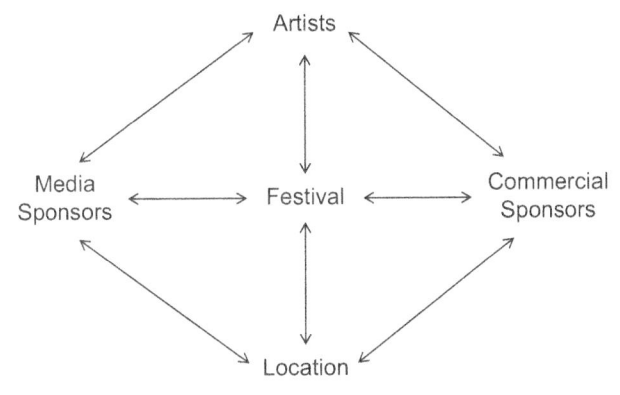

Figure 3.1 The 'brand matrix' of music festivals
(Source: author)

perceptions. It is during the consumption and mediation of a business, service or product that its brand connotations are forged, challenged or reinforced, and this is especially important for music festivals, since they are time-limited annual events that act as focal points for a wide variety of branding activities. A brand matrix (see Figure 3.1) can be recognised in the music festival sector that includes, but is not limited to: the brand of a festival; the brands of the artists performing; the brands of any commercial or media sponsors supporting and mediating the event; and the place-branding of the specific locations in which they are held. Place-branding will be discussed in more detail in Chapter 4, while the focus of the current chapter is on the other main aspects of the brand matrix.

Festivals as brands

Music festivals may be considered as brands since the name of a festival will, over time, become associated with a range of musical, social, cultural, geographical and behavioural meanings and expectations. For longer-lasting events, these associations and expectations will reassure festivalgoers about the experience they will have when they attend. This may then translate to the purchase of 'early bird' tickets prior to the announcement of the following year's headlining acts, which is very useful for the forward planning of individual events. Good examples of this are the Glastonbury Festival, whose tickets typically go on sale prior to the headliners and programme being publicised, and Scotland's T in the Park festival, which was one of the first to offer early bird tickets. Other events have created brands around specific styles of music or particular types of experience. For instance, both Download Festival and Bloodstock Open Air focus on the heavy metal genre and subculture, while Boomtown Fair and Secret Garden Party offer surreal, otherworldly experiences based around unusual design, audience participation and attractions that downplay the need for big name artists.

New entrants to the festival market have to work hard to build their brand associations, especially as the market has become increasingly crowded with competitor events. In branding terms, the key issues for these new entrants are how to differentiate their offerings from the competition, and how to build a set of positive associations that will attract repeat business and foster word-of-mouth marketing. The latter is crucial for creating a 'buzz' around the festival that can draw further interest from potential attendees without the expense of an advertising campaign. These factors have, in part, helped to drive the emergence and success of the boutique festival market, since the emphasis is on providing distinctive and varied experiences or on creating themed events that act, in marketing terms, as unique selling points and brand-builders.

Brands not only define a business or product; by implication they also define their intended markets. This is particularly important for music festivals, as other brands may wish to be involved as sponsor partners in order to gain access to the intended markets represented by those festivals. For the sponsoring brand, the aim is to align its product or services with both the brand of the festival and its intended target market. For this to work effectively, the audience attracted to the festival must match the sponsor's own preferred market in terms of demographics (age, class, gender, geographic location) and psychographics (attitudes, interests, beliefs). Similarly, it is necessary for the festival organiser to ensure that the intended market of the sponsor brand matches that of the festival, and that the brand activities of the sponsor tally with the festival's brand identity and ethos. This is referred to as 'brand fit' or 'congruence' in the events and marketing industries, and problems may arise should the sponsorship activity or brand associations of the sponsor brand fail to fit with the expectations of the festival audience. Hence, the 'fit' between a brand and a festival is evaluated by both the festival organiser and that festival's particular audience. Drengner et al. (2011: 27–8) argue that festivalgoers evaluate 'fit' through reference to their individual subjective knowledge, which includes pre-conceived ideas regarding an event and its sponsors that may be influenced by marketing, mediation and word-of-mouth about them. Further to this, we can argue that festivalgoers will be guided by any prior experience of an attending that event, and by the broader cultural positioning of music festivals discussed in Chapter 1.

A good example of a brand campaign where 'fit' came into question is the Show Me Your Sloggi campaign at the Hylands Park site of the V Festival in 2007 and 2008. The underwear brand Sloggi used the festival as part of a global contest to find new male and female models to star in an advertising campaign. In addition to in-store competitions and promotions, there was a branded stage at the festival which featured DJ sets, fashion shows, dancers and skateboarders, with models parading in Sloggi underwear. There was also a photo booth area where festivalgoers could enter the brand's competition to find 'the world's most beautiful bottom'. Reactions to this brand activity were mixed. Lingerieblog.co.uk (2007) reported that hundreds of people had entered the competition on-site, suggesting that festivalgoers were engaging with the campaign, while a review for Virtualfestivals.com branded the stage 'leery, cringey and unnecessary, but somehow it captures V's feel in a nutshell' (Fahey, 2008). The Sloggi campaign was, for this reviewer and others, indicative of a broader issue with the V Festival brand, which has consistently been criticised for not meeting the 'traditional' expectations of a music festival, and for being overtly commercial in its nature (Anderton, 2008). Linked to this commerciality is a denigration of its attendees, with an article in *Sabotage Times* referring to the festival as a 'chav paradise' perfect for 'people who don't actually like music but still want to say they've been to a music festival' (Waller, 2013). Sloggi's on-site brand activity may be said to have 'fit' with the V Festival brand to a certain extent, yet it also reinforced a view of the festival as failing to comply with broader conceptions of how festivals should be, and who should be attending them. Arguments about the style and audience of the V Festival reflect broader social, cultural and political changes in the festival sector since the mid-1990s, with older conceptions of festivals as countercultural rock events being supplanted by numerous alternatives. Yet, it is interesting to note that when the V Festival first launched in 1996, plans to name it the Virgin Cola Festival after its principal sponsor were blocked by headlining band Pulp, whose roots in the independent and alternative rock scene of the late 1970s and 1980s had given them anti-commercial and anti-establishment views (Holden, 2001; Sturdy, 2003). 'V' was the eventual compromise which, perhaps ironically, has allowed other Virgin Group brands to become more easily associated with the event over the years (including Virgin Radio, Virgin Trains, Virgin Mobile and Virgin Media).

Artists as brands

The notion of 'brand fit' can also be applied to the musical programming of festivals. Headlining artists are themselves brands, and so offer the organisers of large events in particular direct access to dedicated fan bases and the marketing and publicity required to maintain a high public profile. The brand power of specific artists may bring a festival a degree of kudos, since they can be seen as validating or endorsing the festival through their presence as headliners. This may then lead to enhanced media coverage and act as an important driver for ticket sales. In turn it may boost the reputation of the festival with sponsors, agents, managers and audiences, allowing the event to expand in size or ambition in future years. The opposite is also the case, since a festival that fails to book acts of sufficient brand power may make a loss or be forced to cancel. For instance, Sonisphere UK was cancelled in 2015 due to a lack of suitable headliners being available on a date that would not clash with other major rock events.

Once a festival has become well-established and well-regarded, the relationship between artists and festivals may become inverted, with artists seeking to be booked by high-profile and well-respected festivals so that they can increase their own brand value (and future artist fees). This brand value is enhanced further if the artist performs on the main stage of a large event or achieves headliner status. Indeed, it is possible to track artists across their festival performances to see how their brand power has waxed or waned over time. A key trend since the 1990s has been rising artist fees, and this is partly in response to the relatively limited number of acts that have sufficient brand power to promise sell-out attendances in comparison to the rapid growth in the number of festivals seeking to book them. As a result of this increased competition, festival organisers are paying higher fees for their headlining acts and, as discussed in Chapter 2, demanding exclusivity clauses. In contrast, smaller or more established festivals that offer a mixed programme of arts and entertainments, or which attract regular repeat visitors and foster loyalty to their events, are less reliant on booking big name acts. Instead, they concentrate on developing their own festival brands by emphasising the attendee experience as a whole, or by fostering niche genres and markets where acts can be booked at more affordable prices.

A good example of a conflict surrounding the brand 'fit' of an artist with a festival is the case of Glastonbury Festival and audience reactions to the bookings of the American rappers and business entrepreneurs Jay-Z and Kanye West. When Jay-Z was announced as headlining the event in 2008, the decision was met with an unfavourable response on some internet message boards, and Oasis' Noel Gallagher suggested that it had led to poor ticket sales for the festival that year (Swash, 2008a). In a BBC interview that was widely reported, Gallagher further stated that: 'Glastonbury has a tradition of guitar music [...] I'm not having hip-hop at Glastonbury. It's wrong' (cited in Paterson, 2008). This position was echoed in 2015, when Kanye West was announced as headlining the Pyramid Stage. An online petition termed the booking a 'musical injustice' and amassed over 130,000 petitions. Online debates about the announcement either criticised Kanye West himself as a poor role model or argued, as Gallagher had in 2008, that Glastonbury is a rock festival and should be headlined by a rock band (Freeman, 2015). Yet, as Glastonbury's Emily Eavis (2015) and others have noted, the festival encompasses much more than rock music, and it may be that the mediation of the event is the cause of the issue, since the festival has become, in Street's terms, a 'media event' that is largely consumed through broadcast and online media due to its long-standing partnership with the BBC (2005). The event is also covered by the major rock music magazines in the UK, and many headlining performances by rock bands have been held up as career peaks or turning points, such as Pulp's performance in 1995 or Radiohead's in 1997.

The Pyramid Stage is the largest and most highly mediated of the many stages at the festival, and the headliners who play it are the most visible of all the acts at the event. Analysis of the headliners from 1995 to 2015 (see Figure 3.2) shows that over 80 per cent were rock or crossover rock/pop

Year	Friday	Saturday	Sunday
2015	Foo Fighters	Kanye West	The Who
2014	Arcade Fire	Metallica	Kasabian
2013	Arctic Monkeys	Rolling Stones	Mumford & Sons
2011	U2	Coldplay	Beyoncé
2010	Gorillaz (replaced U2)	Muse	Stevie Wonder
2009	Neil Young	Bruce Springsteen	Blur
2008	Kings of Leon	Jay-Z	The Verve
2007	Arctic Monkeys	The Killers	The Who
2005	The White Stripes	Coldplay	Basement Jaxx (replaced Kylie Minogue)
2004	Oasis	Paul McCartney	Muse
2003	R.E.M.	Radiohead	Moby
2002	Coldplay	Stereophonics	Rod Stewart
2000	Chemical Brothers	Travis	David Bowie
1999	R.E.M.	Manic Street Preachers	Skunk Anansie
1998	Primal Scream	Blur	Pulp
1997	The Prodigy	Radiohead	Ash (replaced Steve Winwood)
1995	Oasis	Pulp (replaced The Stone Roses)	The Cure

Figure 3.2 Headlining performances on the Pyramid Stage at Glastonbury Festival for the Contemporary Performing Arts, 1995–2015
(Source: author)

artists, ranging from vintage acts such as Neil Young, The Who, The Rolling Stones and David Bowie to more contemporary performers such as Oasis, Kings of Leon, Coldplay, Muse, Arcade Fire, Arctic Monkeys and Foo Fighters. It can be argued that Glastonbury Festival has been primarily mediated as a rock music festival even though other genres are represented on the programme of the Pyramid Stage, and the event as a whole features numerous stages and genres. The iconic performances and televised coverage of the festival have helped to construct it as a rock music event – one reason for the objection of rock fans to headlining artists from other genres. It might also be argued that hip hop music, rooted in the struggles of urban America and associated (at times, and especially in the media) with images of gang violence and conspicuous consumerism and excess, is out-of-place in the rural hippie arcadia (as it is often mythologised) of the Glastonbury Festival. A similar case might also be made for heavy metal bands, with Metallica being the only heavy metal band to headline the Pyramid Stage. That decision was also subject to considerable criticism, with artists such as Mogwai, Alex Turner of Arctic Monkeys and Jarvis Cocker of Pulp all expressing their concerns that Metallica was not appropriate for the festival (Denham 2014). The question of 'appropriateness' in terms of location, ideology and mythology will arise again in Chapter 4, but it is worth reflecting here that the booking decisions discussed above were astute moves for the organisers. The mediated 'brand' of Glastonbury Festival is linked to two key tropes: access to the biggest artists in the world, and the mythology of the festival's countercultural past. It is important for the festival to remain 'fresh' and 'relevant' to a changing media audience by avoiding accusations of repetitive programming and deliberately extending its offering to draw in new audiences and maintain media interest. Controversial booking decisions, therefore, help to promote news stories in the media, provide free publicity for the event, and communicate the musical repositioning of the festival to a broader audience. Meanwhile, the festival makes use of the photo gallery pages of its official website and photo-centric social media such as Instagram and Twitter to reinforce its countercultural carnivalesque heritage by focusing on the weird and wonderful people, art installations and performance artists found at the festival. This simultaneously reflects some of the more unusual and unique aspects of the event, while also helping to create a sense of community amongst festivalgoers, and a sense of 'missing out' amongst those who are unable to attend.

Commercial sponsorship

Since the early 1990s, the brand matrix of the outdoor music festival sector has become increasingly dominated by the sponsorship and mediation of companies and organisations that aim to benefit from their association with a growing live events industry. For example, a 2013 report produced by PRS for Music and the marketing agency Frukt suggested that sponsorship of British festivals, tours and venues totalled just over £33 million in 2012 (PRS for Music/Frukt, 2013). This is likely to be an underestimate of brand spending since it excludes the costs of festival-related advertising and of online and physical media campaigns. For many festivals, sponsorship is a vital source of financial and other support (Drury, 2013) because it can offer a level of financial stability to an event and offset the risks of a highly volatile market. It can also allow festival organisers to book more expensive artists that may enhance the image and appeal of an event, while sponsors themselves provide publicity and marketing tie-ins that help drive attendance and reduce the need for direct (and often expensive) festival advertising.

Sponsorship has been defined by the International Events Group as 'a cash and/or in-kind fee paid to a property [such as a festival] in return for access to the exploitable commercial potential associated with that property' (IEG, 2000: 1). This definition focuses on the financial agreements made between the contracting parties: agreements that are intended to lead to mutually beneficial outcomes and from which the sponsor expects a 'return on investment' of some kind. The definition provided by the International Chamber of Commerce (ICC) goes further:

> any commercial agreement by which a sponsor, for the mutual benefit of the sponsor and sponsored party, contractually provides financing or other support in order to establish an association between the sponsor's image, brands or products and a sponsorship property [such as a festival] in return for rights to promote this association and/or for the granting of certain agreed direct or indirect benefits.
>
> (ICC, 2003: 2)

The ICC definition suggests that sponsors are seeking to benefit from the semiotic associations of their involvement with music festivals, and so reinforces the importance of alignment or 'fit' between the needs of the sponsor and the brand image of the sponsored event, as well as to elements of the broader brand matrix within which the event is situated. For instance, it may be important to the sponsor that the festival is held in a specific location, or that it gives access to a certain type of music, calibre of artist, or audience demographic.

A number of motivations may be proposed for the commercial sponsorship of music festivals. Sponsors may be seeking to build brand awareness and visibility that can help to promote sales, or they may hope to differentiate their brand from their competitors' and thus enhance market share. Festivals can also be used to launch and demonstrate new products and services, or to reinforce or realign the social, cultural, economic or political meanings associated with a brand. For instance, a brand may use its festival sponsorship as part of a broader campaign to demonstrate corporate social responsibility, whether through links to charities or through ecological solutions such as recycling initiatives or alternative energy use. Sponsors also request VIP ticket allocations so that they can foster business-to-business relationships with key suppliers or clients or offer rewards schemes for their employees. They may even create and manage their own backstage VIP areas or provide product gifting opportunities aimed at influencing journalists, celebrities and other tastemakers. Central to each of these motivations are three main assumptions. First, it is assumed that the festival will offer a good opportunity for the brand to connect with a demographically relevant target market (or aspirational market), though it should be noted that the brand may well be in competition with others on-site, and there is a high potential for the target market to be distracted by the other activities the festival offers. Second, it is assumed that the positive feelings and goodwill associated with festival attendance will make festivalgoers more receptive to a well-planned and engaging on-site campaign; that it will establish a credible link between the brand and a specific event and audience. This is, of course, reliant not only on the campaign in question, but also on the festival itself running smoothly and providing a positive experience in the first place. Furthermore,

Meenaghan has argued that where an event attracts regular attendees, the intensity of their goodwill towards that event may be enhanced, and that this may also reflect positively on the sponsors associated with it (2001). Third, it is assumed that festival sponsorship activities can be translated into brand awareness and conversation (such as word-of-mouth marketing and social media engagement by festivalgoers), and then into future brand preference and intention to buy or use the product or service (Wakefield, 2012). Several reports provide support for this, since they show high levels of social media usage and acceptance or support of sponsorship activities. For instance, the *Festival Awards Market Report 2013* found that 92 per cent of respondents used Facebook, and 33 per cent used Twitter (Drury, 2013), while a report by Havas Sport & Entertainment found that 36 per cent of festivalgoers thought they would be 'more likely to purchase a sponsor's product after the event' was over (Havas, 2012). However, this latter report also found that nearly 32.9 per cent of festivalgoers found sponsor activities 'imposing', while 19.2 per cent found them 'tasteless', which further reinforces the need for sponsors to make their brand 'fit' with the festivals they work with.

Commercial sponsorships differ from other funding arrangements that festivals may benefit from. In the UK there are a number of organisations who provide funding to music festivals in the form of non-repayable grants that may or may not be renewed on an annual basis. For instance, the In the Woods festival created by the Laurel Collective has received funding from both the Arts Council England and the PRS for Music Foundation, while the Green Man Festival in Wales has been supported by the Arts Council, the Welsh Assembly, the National Lottery and the Bevan Foundation. This financial support is somewhat philanthropic, since there is no overt commercial return on investment for the sponsor organisations. However, the funding sources that these organisations rely on (such as state funding support) may require that the organisation meets particular socio-cultural, economic or touristic goals; hence, whilst not a directly commercial return on investment, there is an indirect financial benefit for these organisations in the form of continued funding. As a result, there are also implications for festivals in terms of how these organisations make decisions about which events, genres and activities they will work with and what expectations they may have of recipients. This may lead festival organisers to adapt their artistic programmes and service provision in order to meet the expectations of funders in the hope of securing investment.

Typical business sectors acting as commercial sponsors of British outdoor music festivals are telecommunications (such as O2 and Virgin Mobile), financial services (such as Barclaycard), alcoholic beverages, energy drinks and soft drinks (such as Carlsberg, Red Bull and Volvic), broadcast, print and online media (such as the BBC, the *NME* and Yahoo), and a whole range of lifestyle-related products, from cars to hair-care. Sponsorship arrangements of various kinds can be recognised, from reciprocal agreements through to pouring rights, media rights, naming rights and other event marketing activities. There are also pseudo-sponsorship activities, such as ambush marketing, which seek to associate a brand with an event without actually paying for official sponsor status. These various forms of activity are discussed in the following sections.

Reciprocal and in-kind arrangements

Many smaller festivals make use of relatively informal reciprocal arrangements through which in-kind benefits (services, goods or assistance, rather than cash payments) are received without a detailed sponsorship contract being in place. These arrangements may therefore occupy a grey area between philanthropy and sponsorship, since the commercial benefits of involvement may be quite different from those of a formal sponsorship. In some instances, they are akin to favours in which services or equipment are provided to a festival organiser for free or at a discount. Such goodwill agreements may later translate into business opportunities for the supplier, whether from the festival organiser or from others. In this sense, such arrangements may be regarded as loss-leading business activities through which suppliers seek local community and business contacts and kudos as a result of their participation. In some cases, these reciprocal agreements take on a pseudo-sponsorship form in that advertising space may be given for free in the festival programme, or links added to the festival website. An early example of in-kind sponsorship activity is found at the Bath Festival of 1970. In the run-up to the event, costs began to escalate, leading festival promoter Freddy Bannister to seek sponsorship from recording companies and multinational firms. The only company to respond positively was Coca-Cola, which provided 'a large number of cans free of charge and ... further stock at a heavily discounted price' (Bannister, 2003: 91). In addition, Coca-Cola agreed to subsidise the cost of a charter flight from New York that brought a number of American acts to the UK, saving Bannister a considerable amount of money (ibid.: 85). Coca-Cola did not seek a formal sponsorship agreement or brand presence on the festival's stage, posters or programme, but the deal placed a large amount of Coca-Cola cans in the festival arena, thereby creating brand exposure and awareness during the event.

Badging and leveraging

Badging is the most passive form of sponsorship arrangement, through which a company secures rights for its name and/or logo to be included on a variety of 'touch points' where festivalgoers and the wider public are likely to see it. Touch points may be many and varied, ranging from brand-centric advertisements in the media to the official posters, website, social media and souvenir programme of the sponsored event. The brand's logo may also be found when purchasing tickets online, on the tickets and wristbands issued by the festival, and on any festival merchandise that may be available.

A slightly more active form of sponsor activity is leveraging, where the sponsor creates its own marketing and promotional campaigns that link to its badging activities, and so gains added value (a leveraging of its investment) from its association with an event. For instance, the sponsor may run ticket competitions, offer product sampling on-site, or use a festival's logo in conjunction with its own products, in-store displays, websites and social media. It is not uncommon for music festivals to have multiple sponsors, or for different sponsors to gain different levels of reward based on the amount of financial support given; thus some sponsors may have branded concessions in the backstage area, while others may have naming rights for stages or simply an acknowledgment on the festival programme and website.

In all of these various activities (whether on-site or off-site), the sponsor seeks to benefit by linking its brand with that of the festival, while the festival gains from what is effectively free advertising, which serves to reduce its own promotional costs while expanding its marketing reach. In addition, sponsors are able to engage with potential and existing customers via social media applications which offer the added benefits of data-mining and an ongoing relationship between the brand and its customers before, during and after the festival itself. Data-mining allows marketing and branding agencies to quantify the effectiveness and reach of their campaigns and to learn more about the interests and behaviours of users, while the social media applications and campaigns help to publicise both the brand and the festival to non-attendees who might be inspired to find out more about a brand and its products/services, or to purchase a ticket for future events sponsored by the brand.

Title rights

A brand's name and/or logo will be especially visible when a company has secured 'title', 'naming' or 'presenting' rights for a festival, since this allows the brand's name to be incorporated within the official name of the event. This is also termed 'co-branding', since the brand of the sponsor and the brand of the event form a strategic brand alliance (Rao, 1997) which names and defines a specific festival in the minds of consumers. In the UK, a good example is T in the Park, where the 'T' refers to Tennant's Lager and the branding of the event includes the Tennant's logo. In addition to title rights, there are also a number of other 'naming rights' available at larger commercial festivals, where individual stages, tents or areas within an event may be named after different brand sponsors. For instance, the V Festival has had various stage sponsors since it began in 1996, including JJB Puma, Strongbow, MTV, *NME*, Volvic, Channel 4, and Nissan Juke. Title sponsorships have been seen at British festivals since at least the early 1980s, initially with a strong preference for breweries. For instance, in 1982 Theakston sponsored an event at Nostell Priory in West Yorkshire (the Theakston Music Festival), and in the same year the long-running Cambridge Folk Festival secured its first title sponsorship with Newcastle Brown Ale. The name of the beer was incorporated into the title of the latter festival, as were later title sponsorships from Greene King (with its Abbot Ale brand) and Charles Wells. The 1980s also saw the Guinness Brewery launch its *Harp Beat* campaign to promote its Harp lager brand, which led to a title sponsorship of the Monsters of Rock festival, and the addition of the words 'Harp Beat Presents' to the event's title in 1987. However, branding and sponsorship were relatively underdeveloped at festivals during the 1980s, with on-site brand presence and leveraging minimal.

Brand involvement accelerated through the 1990s. Between 1993 and 1995, the Heineken Music Festival was staged at a number of locations, while T in the Park began in 1994 and V Festival launched in 1996 (initially sponsored by Virgin Cola, then later by Virgin Mobile and Virgin Media). The early 1990s also saw a variety of stage sponsors at the Reading Festival, though its first title sponsorship was not granted until 1998, when the Mean Fiddler organisation brokered a ten-year deal with the brewer Carling. The festival was renamed The Carling Weekend, and a second event of the same name and line-up was added in Leeds from 1999 onwards. When the deal came up for renewal in 2007, the promoters decided not to renew it or to seek a replacement. Melvin Benn of Mean Fiddler was interviewed at the time by BBC 6 Music and stated that the decision had been made to allow the events to 'return to their roots' and be 'slightly less corporate' (cited in Swash, 2008b). This decision helped to re-connect and re-affirm the Reading Festival name with its long history, thus enhancing a sense of credibility, yet, as argued later, it might also be related to changing perceptions regarding the effectiveness of both title rights and badging activities at festivals. Nevertheless, the Reading and Leeds Festivals have continued to make use of stage sponsorships since that time, with the *NME* and the BBC being key players alongside a variety of other sponsors each year: in 2015, for instance, the festival featured sponsorship deals with Smirnoff, Relentless, Pepsi Max, Black XS and Firestone. The Isle of Wight Festival was, from 2004 to 2006, known as the Nokia Isle of Wight Festival but, like Reading Festival, now operates without title sponsorship. In contrast, large-scale non-camping and one-day events continue to make use of them: examples from 2015 include the New Look Wireless Festival in London's Finsbury Park (named after the clothing retailer New Look), and Barclaycard Presents British Summer Time, in London's Hyde Park. It is also notable that sponsors are now often referred to as 'partners', 'friends' or 'supporters', which is perhaps aimed at making corporate or commercial involvement and support seem less overt, and thus more in keeping with the history of British festival culture explored in earlier chapters.

A less common variation on the title rights approach is the brand-owned festival, where the brand itself takes on responsibility for managing the event rather than simply purchasing title rights and creates a brand-themed immersive experience. Examples include Ben & Jerry's Sundae on the Common, which was staged on London's Clapham Common from 2005 to 2011 and saw an additional event at Manchester's Heaton Park in its final year. Another long-running event of this type was Fruitstock, staged by fruit juice and smoothies brand Innocent. Launched in 2003, it ran under the Fruitstock name for four years in London's Regent's Park. It was a two-day free event which eventually reached attendance figures of over 120,000. However, the increasing scale of the event meant that the brand's message was becoming lost, so it was re-branded as the Innocent Village Fete in 2007 and 2008. These latter events were ticketed, though still not-for-profit, and limited to 60,000 attendees; in addition, there was a shift towards a more family-friendly demographic, and activities which 'fit' the brand's fun and ethical message more closely.

Pouring rights

Exclusive contracts for the provision of alcoholic or non-alcoholic drinks to a festival are referred to as 'pouring rights'. In the past, pouring rights and title rights were often one and the same, as a brewery would pay to be the headline sponsor and then become the on-site supplier for the event. However, it is now common for pouring rights to be arranged separately with, perhaps, parallel deals for alcoholic drinks, energy drinks, and soft drinks. One of the most significant pouring rights deals since the turn of the millennium was that signed by Carlsberg UK with the festival promoter Live Nation UK. Carlsberg UK now has exclusive pouring rights for its Tuborg lager and Somersby cider brands at the many large-scale festivals owned or managed by Live Nation UK. The on-site monopolies produced by this wide-reaching deal have perhaps helped to reinforce a perception of Britain's major rock and pop festivals as becoming overly similar: as offering a standardised experience with the same drinks brands on offer at nearly every event, and a lack of real choice. This has been partly offset by the presence of other drinks brands offering specialised experiential areas or 'activations' at these same festivals, thus adding a degree of diversity to the festival's drinks offering.

Sponsor activation and experiential campaigns

In the early 2000s, the term 'sponsor activation' began to appear in the marketing literature. This term acknowledged that 'badging' and 'leveraging' activities were a largely ineffectual form of marketing because they did not actively engage with festival attendees (Wakefield, 2012: 146). It was argued that badging activities acted much like traditional advertising, so were subject to the same criticisms regarding cost-benefit ratios, the high probability of distraction and competition between brands on-site, as well as the unproven ability to translate attention and brand recall into purchase-making decisions (De Pelsmacker et al., 2010). To tackle this, sponsors began to offer 'added value' activities and services that could tie in to the festival-going experience and so help the sponsor's products appear relevant, useful, exciting and engaging. In this sense, the sponsorship is 'activated' within the lives and minds of festivalgoers and therefore more likely to be remembered favourably and discussed with others since they have invested their own time in participating with the brand in a co-created experience (Ritzer & Jurgenson, 2010). Lanier and Hampton refer to this as experiential marketing and argue that the experience being offered must fit the 'sign system' and audience expectations of the festival concerned (2009). In essence, this is another form of 'brand fit', and focuses attention on how an activity meets the specific needs of a festival audience and can best engage them.

Early activations focused on providing 'added value' in quite instrumental terms. For instance, mobile phone companies and internet service providers created free on-site phone charging areas and free internet cafés or lounges in the early 2000s, while Virgin Mobile introduced its *Text the Fest* and *Foto the Fest* campaigns in 2004. These latter campaigns permitted festivalgoers to send messages and photos to the stage-side screens of the festival's main stage, which not only created interaction between the event and the audience, but also brought a financial return, since messages were sent at standard network rates. Messages were also available to view on a dedicated website after the event, which added an element of post-event extension that is now common for sponsors working with festivals. Similar activations can be found at many other large festivals and are often linked to social media applications such as Instagram rather than websites, since these are optimised for smartphone usage. Sponsor activations have continued to advance in sophistication and reach, with campaigns now tapping into other aspects of the festival experience or linking to charitable causes or environmental sustainability.

The winners of the UK Festival Awards' 'Best brand activation' category are a useful barometer for looking at developments in sponsorship activity. The category is decided by an industry panel and was introduced to the Awards in 2009. The first winner was Schuh's *Welly Exchange* campaign, which was launched at the RockNess Festival in summer 2009. Here, festivalgoers could exchange their old shoes for a free pair of Schuh wellington boots, with those exchanged shoes then being resold or recycled by the Newlife Foundation for Disabled Children. The campaign was extended across a number of festivals in the following years, but in 2015 a new approach was adopted: £10 discount codes and a chill-out area where wellington boots would be gifted to lucky festivalgoers. This more recent campaign was linked to a broader range of shoe styles marketed as part of Schuh's *Festival Lookbook 15*, which also illustrates a growing trend in the marketing of 'festival fashion'. Several other fashion and accessory brands and retailers have also launched festival 'style' ranges or have made use of festivals to help market their products. This is particularly the case for women's fashion and includes dedicated style ranges at online stores such as Boohoo, ASOS, Missguided, New Look, River Island and Top Shop.

The 2010 winner was Coca-Cola with its *Keep it Going* campaign. For this activation, Coca-Cola created a 'Recycle Garden' at several large summer festivals, and operated a 'Swap for Swag' scheme where festivalgoers could swap their used drinks bottles for merchandising items made from recycled polyethylene terephthalate (PET), such as rain ponchos and caps. The gardens were decorated and furnished with items made from recycled PET and grew as more waste bottles were recycled on-site. The scheme made use of volunteers from both Coca-Cola and local youth organisations who managed the gardens, conducted litter-picking of PET bottles in the arenas and handed out free cups of Coca-Cola to festivalgoers. The company claims to have recycled over 90,000 bottles in 2010, thus preventing more than 18 tonnes of waste entering landfill (*The Manufacturer*, 2010). Subsequent winners of the 'best brand activation' award include Bacardi (2011), Southern Comfort (2012) and Virgin Media (2013), each of which illustrated a further development in festival activations. Rather than simply branding an area with an activity, as seen in Coca-Cola's 'Recycle Garden', these later brand activations created increasingly immersive themed experiences. These experiences sought a deeper engagement with festivalgoers by creating playful, imaginative, interactive and multi-sensory leisure spaces that could add value to the festival experience as a whole, and so be perceived by festivalgoers as part of the festival's overall entertainment offering. This included in-house DJs and/or performers providing music (as had been seen earlier in the 2000s at branded tents such as the Bacardi B-Bar and the Strongbow Rooms), but also a high degree of creative design, theatre, play and interaction – to provide both a themed visual spectacle and interactions between festivalgoers and the brand.

Drengner et al. (2008) refer to these branded entertainment areas as 'event marketing' in order to distinguish them from simpler forms of event-based sponsorship activity. The Southern Comfort Juke Joint is a good example of event marketing. In 2012 the Southern Comfort liqueur brand worked with marketing and brand agency Frukt Communications and the company Get Lost And Found (described as 'interactive nonsense facilitators' on their Facebook page) to build an experiential area whose external appearance was designed to look like a run-down old-fashioned and semi-legal New Orleans drinking den (or 'juke joint') of the early twentieth century. The rough-looking wooden and corrugated iron exterior fronted a bar and performance area serving Southern Comfort-based cocktails. Music was provided by DJ sets and a New Orleans style traditional jazz band, while Get Lost And Found provided actors to play a variety of eccentric characters. These characters mingled with the audience and engaged them in conversation, games and dancing, as well as parading with the band around the site to entice more festivalgoers into the bar. Numerous other activations of this general style can be seen at festivals, where brand-specific bars and quick-serve catering brands have created 'concept' areas of one kind or another to connect with festivalgoers in imaginative ways. Examples include Tuborg Town, the Wagamama Lounge, and Nando's Rule the Roost. Other sponsor categories have also created similar campaigns, including the fashion brand

Diesel and the online retailer Very.co.uk. Diesel partnered with BluePeg Agency and Festival No. 6 to hold an invitation-only Secret Woodland Rave at a normally out-of-bounds area of woodland near to the Festival No. 6 site in Portmeirion, North Wales. The campaign was supported by festival-themed in-store events at the brand's Manchester, Liverpool, Leeds and Birmingham retail stores, with key fashion bloggers curating a 'Festival No. 6 capsule collection' (BluePeg, 2015). Immediately prior to the event, Diesel's Facebook page offered ticketholders the chance to apply for a limited number of invitations to the rave, thus enhancing its exclusivity. Very.co.uk has worked with V Festival since 2012, where it initially offered a pampering and makeover area called the Very Fashionable Tent, aimed at female attendees. Giant letters placed outside the tent spelt out #very to encourage festivalgoers to interact on the social media site Twitter. The Ear to the Ground agency, who worked on the campaign with Cow PR, reported that '15,000 consumers experienced the consumer interaction with 80,000 more aware of the activation' (Ear to the Ground, 2012). In 2014, Very worked with retail technology specialists One iota to develop a smartphone app that allowed attendees to order festival-related goods while on-site at the V Festival, and to collect those goods an hour later from Very's branded on-site tent. This enabled the brand to achieve on-site sales from its brand activation in addition to social media conversation and press coverage from the *Daily Mail* and *Grazia* (One iota, 2014).

Carù and Cova (2007a: 41) argue that on-site sponsor activations work best when the brand has complete control of a specific area and when they are creative in their use of design/narrative to build distinctive, memorable experiences that are free from distraction by other, competing, brands. In addition, we can see from the above examples that it is also important to connect the on-site activity to social media that can be viewed and interacted with off-site, and to create integrated marketing campaigns across multiple channels and with multiple elements both within and outside the festival site. Imaginative design ideas can also foster news stories that extend the reach of the campaign, as can working with social media 'mavens' and 'connectors' (Gladwell, 2000). Mavens are respected tastemakers or opinion leaders, while connectors are those individuals with access to disparate groups of people online. This is why Diesel used bloggers in its campaign, and why many brands seek celebrity endorsements of one kind or another. This can be seen strongly in the VIP areas of festivals, where gift-giving is one of the many sponsorship benefits sought by brands. Virgin Media's Louder Lounge is particularly interesting in this respect because, whilst ostensibly a branded area of the type discussed by Carù & Cova (2007a), it actually incorporates many other brands within its village fête theme. In 2013 this included MAC (cosmetics), Vita Liberata (tanning), Batiste (shampoo), Pioneer (DJ equipment), Sony (with its Xperia Access stage) and the Virgin Atlantic Clubhouse. The Louder Lounge was available to festivalgoers who had bought VIP tickets, but also to celebrity guests, journalists and others invited by the V Festival, thus fuelling numerous press stories in, for example, the *Daily Mail*, the *Daily Star*, *OK Magazine*, *Clash*, *Metro*, and *Tatler*, about the brands and the celebrities in this backstage area.

Media rights and broadcast rights

Media rights are agreements made between a music festival and various forms of media to provide access to, or coverage of, an event. Cash sponsorships may be provided to the festival organisers, but benefits in kind are also very important, since there are clear promotional opportunities available to the festival in having positive media coverage. For instance, online and print magazines often publish festival guides and previews, plus post-event reviews, interviews and photo-shoots with festival performers, while local radio stations may actively sponsor and promote events happening in the geographical catchments they serve. These activities are important for creating a buzz of anticipation about a festival, and for creating or reinforcing a media image of the event for people who have not previously attended. The type of print and online media covering festivals has altered in recent years, and now encompasses not only specialist music magazines and broadsheet and tabloid newspapers but also titles dedicated to fashion, lifestyle and celebrity gossip. This shift both reflects and drives changes in public perceptions about festivals and has helped to broaden the sector's appeal to a wider demographic than that seen prior to the millennium. This is also the case for broadcast partnerships made with radio and television companies that transmit live from an event or record performances for later broadcast. Media rights and broadcast rights may not always be discussed as sponsorships, yet they do meet the definitions of sponsorship provided earlier. The publications and broadcasters involved gain a rich mix of exclusive content that meets the needs and expectations of their own audiences while transferring the excitement, positivity and goodwill of the festival onto themselves. In return, a festival can achieve significant exposure to a much broader range of potential attendees than its own marketing budgets might allow and can use the media tie-in to help position itself for its target audience. Indeed, for festivals with significant broadcast and media deals, the audience on television and on the internet is considerably greater than the audience on-site, and this enhanced marketing reach can help to attract further sponsorship deals.

One of the earliest media sponsorships of an outdoor rock and pop festival in Britain was at the Reading Festival, where *Melody Maker* magazine was described as a 'supporter' on posters of the 1989 event. The magazine became a stage sponsor in 1991 and produced its first pull-out 'festival guide' in 1993. By 1994, the event organiser, Mean Fiddler, had arranged sponsorship deals with BBC Radio 1 and MTV, and had added two more branded performance venues: the 'Melody Maker Stage' and the 'Loaded Comedy Stage' (*Loaded* being a then-recently-launched men's lifestyle magazine owned by *Melody Maker's* parent company, IPC Media). Glastonbury Festival was first televised in the same year, with Channel 4 (UK) broadcasting footage of main stage performances in that year and in 1995. The BBC became the event's main media sponsor in 1997 and has broadcast from the festival ever since. Its coverage has grown considerably over the years; for example, in 1999 there were performances and highlights on BBC2, BBC Choice (a digital television channel which closed in 2003) and BBC Radio 1, but by 2014 there were over 250 hours of festival programming across all of the BBC's national radio, television and digital channels, including on-demand availability through BBC iPlayer online and through the 'red button' interactive service on digital television. Coverage was also available to global audiences through the BBC's commercial arm, BBC Worldwide, through which it supplements its license fee income. The relationship has been highly beneficial for both the festival and the BBC. For instance, the festival nearly doubled its audience capacity between 1994 and 2004 (from 80,000 to 150,000 per day) and by nearly a quarter more in 2015 (capacity 198,000 per day). In the process, the BBC has placed itself at the heart of the British summertime festival season, and its brand has become intrinsically linked to the Glastonbury Festival without it needing to have title sponsor status. However, while this level of coverage has been welcomed by many music fans, especially the many who are unable to attend the festival itself, the BBC's expenditure on the event has been regularly criticised in newspapers such as the *Daily Mail* and brought into question by the House of Commons Culture Select Committee. It has been argued that the festival is treated as a press junket, with far more people on-site than are necessary to do the job. When these criticisms were first raised, the National Audit Office (NAO) conducted an investigation into the BBC's coverage of a number of high-profile events. It reported that, in 2008, the total cost of the BBC's Glastonbury Festival coverage was £1,737 million, though this figure was dwarfed by its spending on Euro 2008 (£8,682 million) and the Beijing Olympics (£15,565 million). The NAO found that the corporation had met most of its budget targets but criticised it for failing to have 'a clear view' of total expenditure, due to different platforms (radio, television, and so on) being budgeted separately (BBC, 2010). Staffing levels have reduced slightly since the NAO reported in 2010, though negative news reports continue. For instance, in 2014 the *Daily Mail* reported that the BBC sent 300 staff to cover the Glastonbury Festival, which was more than it sent to Brazil to cover the FIFA World Cup (Brady & Cox, 2014). BBC Head of Music, Bob Shennan, responded to criticisms by arguing that every member of staff was required to produce the coverage and that each had 'a clear and accountable role' (Spence, 2014).

Pseudo-sponsorship

Pseudo-sponsorship is found whenever a brand manages to associate itself with a festival but does not actually enter into a formal sponsorship agreement with that festival. In effect, this is a form of ambush marketing in which a company seeks to deflect attention from a legitimate sponsor's activities and towards its own products or services (Meenaghan, 1998: 306). The competitive nature of this parasitic relationship detracts from the legitimate sponsor's effectiveness, thereby devaluing the economic worth of official sponsorship agreements for both sponsors and festivals. This is particularly the case where the ambushing company is a direct competitor to the legitimate sponsor (McKelvey, 1994: 20). A number of pseudo-sponsorship strategies have been attempted over the years, such as sponsoring media coverage of an event (rather than the event itself) and engaging in advertising campaigns that indirectly link in some way to the name and brand of an event (Meenaghan, 1998: 310–12). However, such activities are not always carried out by direct competitors, and companies may instead 'piggyback' on the success and media attention of a festival, arguably without detracting from other campaigns. In the process these ambush strategies may extend the marketing reach of the event, and so add to the media exposure that the festival has gained from its official sponsorships. A good example of this is Hunter's #beaheadliner campaign from 2013, which was managed by the Frukt Agency. The campaign had a variety of elements, but the main thrust was to 'seed' a distinctive and exclusive bright orange version of Hunter's 'Original Headliner Boot' design to celebrities and festivalgoers attending the Glastonbury Festival. The intention was to get publicity from an event which typically downplays the sponsorships that it has on-site. One strategy for doing this was to set up 'welly exchanges' a few miles from the festival on the A39. Festivalgoers could swap their existing wellington boots for a pair of the limited edition boots, with old boots donated to the Red Cross. They were also encouraged to photograph themselves in their new boots and to share their photographs to the twitter hashtag #beaheadliner in order to build awareness of the campaign and brand online (Frukt 2013a). In addition, celebrities were gifted with boots and encouraged to wear them on the festival site so that they could be photographed. A range of fashion and celebrity magazines, including *Cosmopolitan*, *Elle*, and *Grazia*, then published the pictures and included stories about the campaign, while festival footage showed performers such as Rizzle Kicks wearing the boots onstage. A month after the event, Hunter created another limited edition run of the boots for online sales through its website, priced at £89.99 per pair. The campaign effectively 'ambushed' the brand of Glastonbury Festival for its own purposes, but also offered further promotion of the event through the publicity it received. A less successful campaign was that launched by the smartphone brand Blackberry in 2012. Blackberry sponsored a television show called *Summer Daze with Blackberry*, which aired during the summer of that year on Channel 4. The programme followed a cast of festivalgoers and workers across eight episodes and eight festivals, including Wakestock, Latitude, Global Gathering, V Festival and Boomtown Fair. It was a 'constructed reality' show, rather than a documentary, and made by the television production company Monkey which had previously produced the popular *Made in Chelsea* series. *Summer Daze* met with poor reviews which criticised the lack of a music soundtrack and the stilted dialogue of 'characters' deemed to be too upper class (Tinkler, 2012), and therefore contrary to the egalitarian imagery of rock festivals.

Music festival sponsorship strategies

British music festivals have adopted various strategies for engaging, negotiating or avoiding sponsorship of their events, with three key imperatives driving their decisions. The first, as noted earlier, is instrumental and relates to notions of 'brand fit'. For instance, if the demographic and psychographic audience profile of a festival matches that of a proposed brand sponsor or, perhaps, matches the aspirational audience demographic sought by a festival organiser, then a sponsorship deal is more likely to be considered. The second imperative is ideological and refers both to how festival organisers understand the psychographic needs of their audiences, and to the personal or organisational beliefs of the organisers themselves. For instance, psychographic profiling of an audience may indicate strong non-conformist or anti-corporate traits, or an interest in environmental sustainability, craft production and thinking 'local'. These latter traits may link directly to the beliefs of organisers who want to communicate their own ideologies or ethical stance through the organisational ethos of their events or seek to reflect the cultural and historical understandings and meanings of the term 'music festival' within British society. Hence, some festivals will refuse to accept corporate sponsorship because it conflicts with their ideological or ethical stance, or due to a broader belief that festivals should offer utopian freedom (Anderton, 2011). The third imperative relates to the 'value' that the sponsorship brings to a festival, whether in terms of funding, exposure, kudos and media coverage, or in terms of the 'added value' activities and opportunities that a sponsor may offer to an event, such as on-site brand activations. Festival organisers will also need to consider the range of sponsor categories that they make available, and how the various sponsor brands may work alongside each other to support the overall ethos and image of their event. These imperatives underlie three main strategies that may be identified in festivals' approach to sponsorship: affirmation, acceptance and avoidance (Anderton 2015). It is important to note that this delineation should be seen as a heuristic device, as the decision-making process is more complex than these three positions might suggest, and there are crossovers between them.

Affirmation

Festival organisers who adopt an affirmative strategy with regard to sponsorship will consider a range of sponsorship deals, and make commercial decisions based on the demographic and psychographic 'fit' of those sponsors to their event. Major promoters such as Live Nation and Festival Republic could be described as taking this view of sponsorship. For example, Live

Nation promotes both the Reading and Leeds festivals and the Latitude festival, with each event having sponsors that are appropriate to their specific audience profiles. Reading and Leeds have sponsor/media partnerships with BBC Radio 1, *NME* and Relentless (amongst others) which are relevant to a youthful rock music audience, while Latitude has deals with the *Independent*, the *New Statesman* and *DIY* magazine, which links to the event's 'boutique' image and older, middle class demographic. Similarly, the Green Man Festival lists three music magazines (*Mojo*, *The 405* and *Crack*) as 'Friends of Green Man', thus drawing attention to its image as a quirky, independent festival focused on curating a musical programme of quality acts. There will be some overlap between the affirmation strategy and the 'acceptance' strategy discussed below, since sponsorship decisions are made by individuals and teams who have their own particular understandings of what will 'fit' their event best. The marketing and management literature gives advice about how to profile audiences, prepare sponsorship proposals, and evaluate the offers that sponsors put before festival organisers (e.g. Skinner & Rukavina, 2003; Allen et al., 2011). However, research into decision-making within organisations or by specific festival organisers and staff is largely absent, though this may reflect the commercial sensitivity of the decisions being made. This is also true of the following strategy of 'acceptance'.

Acceptance

Sponsorship of one kind or another is commonplace within the British music festival sector and reflects the fact that festival organisers often need sponsorship to reduce the risk profiles of their events, or to produce events of the quality expected by festivalgoers (Anderton, 2008; Goldblatt, 2011). However, in contrast to the strategy of affirmation where commercial considerations are paramount, the 'acceptance' strategy sees festival organisers negotiating offers in terms of their publicly stated ideological and ethical stances. In other words, a fundamental aspect of the sponsorship decision is based on the 'fit' of the sponsor with the ethical principles which guide the festival organisers, and the right choice of sponsor will help to communicate and reinforce those overarching principles both to returning and potential festivalgoers. For instance, Sunrise Celebration states on its website that it is Britain's 'leading Sustainable Education, Arts and Music Festival' (Sunrise Celebration, 2015). The event organisers were initially inspired by the Transition Town movement which, through the Transition Network, links together an array of community-led projects focused on reducing energy consumption and the environmental impacts of our everyday lives (Smith, 2011). As a result, Sunrise Celebration only accepts sponsors (or 'partners' at it prefers to term them) on the basis of 'their values and suitability to our core aims as a festival and nation. We believe that innovative partnerships add value to Sunrise and help us in our quest for sustainability on all levels' (Sunrise Celebration, 2015). The acceptance strategy is often found at events that highlight environmental ideals, and their sponsorship deals may well favour local businesses (in order to reduce carbon emissions and support local communities), or those which espouse a similar pro-environmental stance.

A variation of the acceptance strategy is that used by Glastonbury Festival, which does not offer overt publicity for its sponsors on its website yet does have sponsor-style arrangements with a number of companies. For instance, EE (formerly Orange) has been providing mobile phone recharging services at Glastonbury Festival since the late 1990s, yet one of the few mentions of the company on the festival's official website in 2015 was a single news item about the portable phone charging equipment that EE were using on-site. The Glastonbury Festival is protective of its brand name and operates a 'proactive ethical policy which means that we will always be concerned what companies or organisations seek to link themselves to the festival, even if indirectly' (Glastonbury, 2015). The words 'Glastonbury' and 'Glastonbury Festival', as well the logos associated with its brand, are all registered trademarks which require written permission from the festival organisers before use. This gives the festival considerable control over how it is represented in the media and, as a result, in the broader public consciousness. The festival thereby maintains a public image consonant with its countercultural heritage and obscures the various sponsor relationships in which it engages.

Avoidance

Some festivals choose to operate without commercial sponsorship, and while various motivations may be given by the organisers, there is an underlying logic derived from the countercultural carnivalesque view of festivals: that the presence of corporate branding and sponsorship detracts from the 'real' or 'true' experience of a festival. For example, the Beat-Herder Festival, which began in 2006, is a resolutely independent event which is rooted in the alternative and underground dance music scene, with some regarding it as carrying on the style and feel of early 1990s UK free parties. The festival makes use of local businesses as stall-holders, works with local sound systems and creatives, and features stages and tents that have been hand-crafted rather than hired in. One of the organisers, Nick Chambers, has said that: 'All we've ever really wanted to do is to put on a weekend of pure fun where people can escape the likes of advertising and branding and really let their hair down and have a good time' (cited in Dimond, 2013). The Shambala Festival, which was sub-titled 'Adventures in Utopia' in 2015, makes the links to the countercultural carnivalesque even clearer on its website, where its 'guiding principles' state that festivals 'should be an alternative vision of society.... This means being free of any external agendas or demands, excessive advertising and branding and mindless consumerism' (Shambala Festival, 2015). The festival promotes sustainability and innovative ways of living and argues that its independence allows it to 'concentrate on making unbiased decisions that will benefit our community and, hopefully, society as a whole' (ibid.).

The Hop Farm Festival also claimed to be a 'no frills, back-to-basics event', and operated without branding or VIP areas so that 'everyone is treated equally' (Vince Power, cited in Masson, 2008). According to the official website, the decision to become sponsor-free was taken after an audience survey found that festivalgoers felt they were 'the lowest on the pecking order' (Hop Farm, 2012). In avoiding commercial headline sponsors, the festival traded on the notion of non-corporate egalitarianism, though it still operated as a profit-motivated business. It was organised by Vince Power, a live music veteran who founded the Mean Fiddler Group in 1982. In 2005, he sold Mean Fiddler to a consortium of MCD Promotions and Clear Channel Entertainment; as part of the sale agreement, a non-competitive clause precluded him from staging music festivals in the UK for at least three years. As a consequence, he moved to the international market and acquired a stake in the International Festival of Benicassim, held in Spain. Hop Farm marked his return to the British market in 2008, and was initially successful, relying on headline artists such as Neil Young, Bob Dylan and Prince to drive ticket sales and cover costs. In June 2011, Power formed Music Festivals PLC, which was valued on its launch at over £9.5 million. However, 2012 proved a difficult year for the company's portfolio of events, which included Hop Farm, Benicassim, and a newly launched heavy metal and hard rock event, Costa de Fuego. A profit-warning issued by the company in August 2012 led to the suspension of its share-trading, and administrators were appointed the following month. The rights to the Hop Farm Festival were held by a related company, Kent Festival Ltd, but on the liquidation of that company, Vince Power regained control of the Hop Farm Festival name via a new company, called All Music Live. He intended to stage a scaled-down version of Hop Farm again in 2013, with My Bloody Valentine and Rodriguez as headliners, but poor advance sales led to its cancellation. This demonstrates that even the most seasoned promoters may find it difficult to operate a large-scale festival without the support of brand sponsorship, and that the economic climate for outdoor music festivals remains challenging.

Festival audiences and critiques of branding and sponsorship

As we have seen, the rapid growth of the British outdoor music festival sector since the early 2000s has been mirrored by rapid growth in commercial sponsorship and brand activity. This has led to challenges and critiques by those festivalgoers and commentators who are influenced by the sector's countercultural heritage and believe that music festivals should be utopian spaces. Yet, contemporary audience surveys have found that festivalgoers are not necessarily averse to these developments: that, as with festival organisers, there is a continuum of responses to sponsorship ranging from acceptance through to mistrust. As several of these studies have shown, audiences not only accept the need for sponsorship activity in order to make a festival financially viable but may actually welcome brand involvement at festivals as an enhancement of their overall festival experience. For instance, Havas (2012) found that 65 per cent of festivalgoers surveyed at European festivals thought that 'brands improve the festival experience' and that 85 per cent liked the 'brand activations they visited'. However, the only British festival included in the survey was the V Festival, which has a reputation as a brand-heavy event, and whose attendees have been accepting of sponsorship and branding activity since the mid-2000s (Anderton, 2008: 44). The UK Festival Awards Market Report 2013 found that 23.1 per cent agreed with the statement 'I think it [sponsorship] can make the overall experience more enjoyable for fans' (up from 15 per cent in 2012), while 6.3 per cent said that it put them off (Drury, 2013: 25), which marks a fall from 10 per cent in 2010 (Brennan & Webster, 2010: 36). These findings suggest that while there is still a significant minority of festivalgoers who are actively opposed to branding and sponsorship, the majority either embrace it or at least accept the need for it.

Festivalgoers' apparent acceptance of branding and sponsorship may reflect wider shifts in consumer society and in the positioning of music festivals within it. For instance, Rojek defines commercial music festivals and events as part of the global tourism and leisure industries (2013), as do various music industry reports which stress the tourist revenues generated by the British music and festival industries (UK Music, 2011, 2013, 2016). When viewed through the tourist-economic lens, the countercultural or carnivalesque elements of festival history recede in importance and are merely part of the staging which distinguishes music festivals from other forms of event within the marketplace. On this understanding, music festivals are primarily leisure spectacles, thus the utopian potentialities that other authors have ascribed to them are downplayed. In this sense commercial music festivals are little different from the commodified and themed environments of theme parks, casinos and shopping malls discussed by Ritzer (1999) and Bryman (2004). Hence, in the British context, contemporary commercial music festivals may be regarded as hyperreal settings in which the imagery and ideas of the countercultural carnivalesque (whether related to the received mythologies of the hippie counterculture of the 1960s, 1970s and 1980s, or to the raves and free parties of the 1990s) are used playfully and stripped of their deeper ideological meanings.

Firat and Venkatesh define hyperreality as an 'inclination or willingness among members of the culture to realize, construct, and live the simulation'; they argue that people understand that the simulation is not 'real', yet treat it as if it were (1995: 252). By participating in a festival or in a brand activation, festivalgoers become willing accomplices in the creation of the festival as a brand, and of specific on-site brand activations. Through this, festivalgoers come to offer both immaterial labour and affective labour to the process of brand building and communication. 'Immaterial labour' refers to the 'informational and cultural content of the commodity' (Lazzarato, 1996: 133) which is created through interactions with the brand and through the photos and other media uploaded by festivalgoers and brand representatives to social media sites as a consequence of their brand activity. This online content becomes part of the broader mediation and marketing of the event and helps not only to show others what they have missed, but to inform readers about the relationship of the brand with the festival and its target audience. Related to this is the 'affective labour' (Hardt & Negri, 2000) of festivalgoers in interacting with each other to create the atmosphere of the activity on-site, and to communicate that activity and atmosphere to others through social media discussion. Successful brand activations will see festivalgoers co-creating their experiences, integrating the brand into their lives and lifestyles, and mediating their experiences through their online profiles. However, Carah warns that while consumers are being encouraged to think of themselves as empowered through active involvement with a brand, they are actually 'performing actions within an instrumental space that produces surplus value for corporations' (2010: 12). Similarly, Carù and Cova have suggested that brand activations are only able to offer shallow and manipulative forms of experience and that there is little space for truly participatory activity within them (2007b). This is because brand activities and settings are staged for the benefit of sponsors and are closely controlled by them for their own benefit. These activations may, therefore, offer a rather more passive than active experience due to the directorial efforts of the brands.

These critiques mirror Adorno and Horkheimer's classic argument that within the culture industries 'consumers feel compelled to buy and use ... products even though they see through them' (1997: 167). This leads Carah to juxtapose two competing ways of understanding brand engagement: as 'liberal empowerment' (associated with marketing theory and practice), and as the exploitative reproduction of capital (2010: 19). This neo-Marxist view of brand engagement as exploitative can also be related to the criticism of festivals as lacking a countercultural or carnivalesque character. A good example is the following quote from the *Independent* newspaper:

> For a while, there has been an increasing feeling that festivals have shifted too far from their original hippie-spirited ethos. The point was to offer an alternative reality. Now, it's a slick industry. The television rights have been sold, and with that have come price rises, mass audiences and corporate domination – the antithesis of everything they stood for.
>
> (Corner, 2012)

This short paragraph neatly sums up objections to the presence of corporate sponsorship and commercialism at British music festivals and is echoed by a number of academics. For instance, Klein argues that 'when any space is bought, even if only temporarily, it changes to fit its sponsors' (2000: 51), while McAllister notes that '[the event] becomes subordinate to promotion because, in the sponsor's mind and in the symbolism of the event, they [the event] exist to promote' (1996: 221). Mistrust regarding the motivations of corporate sponsors can turn to criticisms about their presence. For instance, a review of the 2004 V Festival stated that 'the relentless adverts, plastered over every surface and played on big screens between every band ... [made] festivalgoers feel less like music fans and more like rats in a giant marketing experiment' (Smyth, 2004).

However, as noted above, it would appear that festivalgoers' attitudes toward sponsorship and branding is more supportive or accepting than these views might suggest. This reflects broader shifts in how branding, marketing and advertising activity in general has become integrated into contemporary consumer society and media. For instance, in the 1990s, commercial satellite and cable television significantly expanded the range of channels available to the public in the UK, and thereby also the amount of commercial advertising that viewers could be exposed to. Since then, brand opportunities have extended to include the sponsorship of individual programmes or sets of programmes and, since February 2011, paid-for product placements have been allowed on British television. This permits companies to pay for their products to be seen or mentioned within programmes, which helps to integrate brands into storylines and contexts in a manner that traditional advertising could not. In addition, sponsorship and advertising have now become ubiquitous on popular internet and social media sites that offer free services on the basis of an indirect cross-subsidy model of funding (Anderson, 2009). Here, brands help to fund the running of the online platform by paying for advertising banners and links that appear on the site; in return, consumers receive the platform's services for free. This encourages consumers to use the services, while providing the platform with income and the potential for up-selling to a premium, paid-for version of the service. The brands aim to profit from the relationship by gaining online exposure (much cheaper than traditional advertising) which they hope will be converted into attention, interest and subsequent sales opportunities when visitors click on the adverts and are directed to external brand websites.

Another shift in consumer society is the emergence of the so-called 'millennial generation', which has also been termed Generation Y, the Net Generation, the Experience Generation and the Me Generation. These terms all refer to people born at some point between the late 1970s and early 2000s – in other words the typical target demographic for commercial rock and pop festivals in the second decade of the twenty-first century. The millennial generation is said to have followed Generation X (born between the mid-1960s and the late 1970s), which in turn followed on from the Baby Boom generation (born between 1946 and the mid-1960s) (Howe & Strauss, 2000). Each generation is posited as having recognisable psychographic characteristics, with the millennial generation described as the first to grow up with the Internet (Lammiman & Syrett, 2004: 6). As a consequence, some rather broad claims have been made for it. For instance, Tapscott argues that the millennial generation (or 'net generation' as he terms it) is technologically savvy and likes to customise products and services (2009: 34). This links with Miles' argument that consumerism is 'part and parcel of the very fabric of everyday life' (1998: 1), and that people work with commodities to help define and communicate a sense of identity. Tapscott goes on to argue that this generation seeks entertainment and play in all areas of life, and that they are more likely to be influenced by friends and social networks than to respond to traditional advertising. Furthermore, they like innovative ideas and rapid information flows, and seek corporate integrity and transparency. These theories are readily criticised, since there are geographic and economic biases implicit in the ideas put forward by Tapscott and others. For instance, while the claims might be relevant to parts of the affluent suburban consumer culture of the developed world, it is difficult to apply the same characteristics to the developing world, or to the entire millennial demographic of the developed world. Similarly, the mechanisms by which a particular generation (however defined) may come to share attitudinal and behavioural characteristics are unclear, which suggests that such ideas are subject to a high degree of generalisation.

Nevertheless, the notion of a millennial generation is more important than its actuality, and it has gained much support within the music, lifestyle and marketing sectors, where the discourse of 'liberal empowerment' noted by Carah (2010) is at play. An example is the MusicTank report *Meet the Millennials*, which used the term to help explain the decline of traditional models of the music business and the changing online economy of music and music fandom. It also suggests and justifies some solutions to profitably communicating with music fans online, and thus the potential for reasserting some level of control by the music industry (McBride & Muhle, 2008). Another example is the marketing agency Frukt's 2013 *Field Work* report on festivals and branding, which characterised the millennial generation as 'the most hyper connected, technologically savvy, and socially adept generation the world has ever known' (Frukt, 2013b: 10). The discourse of the millennial generation helps festival sponsors justify their brand activations as meeting the perceived needs of their target markets through brand activations that favour novelty, sensation, interaction and collaboration, as well as through integration with social media applications. As noted earlier, the latter offers a platform for user-generated content and conversation which acts as word-of-mouth marketing, while also allowing connections to be made to broader marketing campaigns beyond the weekend of a festival. Statistical information can also be collected which can help to quantify and justify the success of a campaign, and in so doing, offer the appearance of control within a rapidly changing context of online communication and marketing. However, a neo-Marxist view of these developments would argue that marketers are continuing to find new ways to draw consumers into offering their immaterial and affective labour to the benefit of profit-seeking companies.

Conclusion

This chapter has charted and discussed the developing relationships between music festivals, sponsors and brands. It has been argued that the countercultural carnivalesque underpins objections to the rise of sponsorship and branding activity, whilst changes in consumer society and the commercialisation of the music festival sector as a whole mean that these objections are not shared by all. There are significant financial pressures associated with promoting festivals; hence sponsorship of one form or another has become a useful and often necessary way for festival organisers to reduce the risks involved. As festivals have become more professional, more numerous, and more varied in their audience profiles, so sponsors have sought to align their values with those of relevant festivals in order to transfer the positive associations and goodwill of the events onto their own brands. The growth and diversification of the festival sector over the past twenty years means that many festivals have had to become more brand-focused in order to stay competitive, while brands themselves have turned increasingly to experiential activities in order to capture the imagination, creativity and interactivity of festivalgoers. There has been a shift towards campaigns that lead more directly to sales rather than awareness, and an increased focus on social media and interactive digital technologies – an area that will continue to see growth and innovation in the coming years. However, there is also space within the market for other forms of festival, which hark back to the countercultural carnivalesque and offer a more ethical and participatory experience. These may avoid branding and sponsorship altogether, or only work with those companies and organisations that match their ethical stance. This can become a significant part of their festival 'brand', and there is a strong tendency for such events to promote the discussion of social justice and environmental sustainability concerns. The importance of the environment to the festival experience is highlighted in the following chapter, which examines festivals' relationships with their host locations and with broader cultural understandings of the British countryside.

4 Always the same, yet always different

Music festivals as cyclic places

Outdoor popular music festivals are typically held on a cyclical basis (most often annually, but occasionally biannually or biennially), and they may become closely associated with the locations in which they are held, or with the broader place-based social and historical contexts of their localities. A well-known example of such close place association is the Glastonbury Festival of Contemporary Performing Arts which, as discussed in Chapter 1, is held on farmland several miles from the town of Glastonbury, yet draws upon that town's mythological associations and broader cultural positioning with respect to alternative lifestyles and belief systems. Another is Festival No 6, based in the tourist village of Portmeirion in North Wales. The village was designed by architect Clough Williams-Ellis in the style of the Italian Riviera and became the principal filming location for the late 1960s cult television series *The Prisoner*. The festival draws upon the aesthetics of that series in both its design and name (the lead character of *The Prisoner* was called Number Six) and makes use of the village's iconic buildings and gardens to create multiple performance stages.

Festivals of all sizes form important social gatherings, whether constituted at the level of a local community, or formed from a wider elective grouping of people sharing similar beliefs and interests. As a result, they encompass a wide array of forms, meanings and mediations, yet all are rooted in, or influenced by, the physical and human landscape of the locations in which they are held, even where organisers choose to use a site as a blank canvas to construct a themed setting. Choices made regarding location, layout, staging, design and genre will influence the overall construction (and annual reconstruction) of a music festival 'place', which may develop a recognisable character and identity over time. Furthermore, the creation of an identifiable festival 'place' may be crucial for the longevity of an event, since it can provide a sense of continuity, familiarity and belonging for repeat attendees. These arguments are central to my examination of space and place in relation to British music festivals and stand in contrast to previous theories of music festivals as ephemeral or liminal spaces: theories which are discussed and critiqued in the first section of this chapter. As the festival sector has, since the mid-1990s, become increasingly commercialised and ever more integrated into the mainstream leisure market, so new ideas of festival space and place are required. The second section addresses this by drawing on the spatial theories of Doreen Massey (1994; 2005) and Henri Lefebvre (1991), prior to examining two music festivals in detail – the Cambridge Folk Festival and the V Festival. The concept of 'cyclic place' is then introduced and explored: a new way to conceptualise the annual (re)construction of outdoor music festivals in specific locations. In the final section of the chapter, the focus is on broader spatial narratives affecting the music festival market in Britain and the cultural positioning of festivals within changing notions of Britishness and rurality is analysed.

Liminality and the outdoor music festival

In Chapter 1, Bakhtin's (1984) characterisation of the medieval carnival as a licensed period of letting loose was explored: a time during which everyday social structures and norms were overturned and authority mocked. Bakhtin extended his theory to include not merely the regularly-held religious festivals of the medieval era, but also the social life of the marketplace, and certain kinds of theatre and literature. His ideas regarding carnivalesque behaviours and attitudes are, therefore, not specifically spatial in nature, though such behaviours were associated with the markets and fairs that he discussed and could be found throughout entire villages or towns during festival times. Instead, his theory of the carnivalesque is principally a temporal one, with physical spaces simply providing public sites in which socially transgressive behaviours could be enacted for a limited time. This may be contrasted with a similar theory of festivity proposed and elaborated by Turner (1969; 1982; 1987), who not only demarcated a specific time for such behaviours, but also suggested that there were geographical settings (which he termed 'liminal' spaces) set aside for them. Turner's concept of liminality has since been applied to both pop music festivals and electronic dance music raves by authors such as Hetherington (1998a), St John (2001; 2008; 2010) and Jaimangal-Jones et al. (2010). Turner's ideas will be discussed and critiqued in the following section, before turning to Bey's (1991) concept of the Temporary Autonomous Zone, and St John's (2001) depiction of 'alternative cultural heterotopias' which he develops from the work of Foucault (1986).

Liminality

The concept of liminality was originally introduced by van Gennep (1960) to denote the middle or transitional phase in a societal rite of passage that begins with the separation of individuals or groups of people from the established rules of everyday society, and ends with their reincorporation to the broader society, often with a new status or rank. The transitional phase is described using the Latin term, *limen*, meaning threshold, and is accompanied by social rituals and observances which occur in separation from everyday social life.

The rites of passage discussed by van Gennep include childbirth, puberty, marriage and death, and he argues that societies adopt specific rituals for dealing with these changes. Turner (1969) built on van Gennep's ideas to propose the concept of anti-structure: a concept that has similarities to Bakhtin's notion of the carnivalesque but was formulated after research into early agricultural and tribal cultures in Africa. In Turner's formulation, the anti-structure consists of two key elements. The first, liminality, refers to the transitional or socially marginal nature of anti-structural activities and experiences: 'Liminal entities are neither here nor there; they are betwixt and between the positions assigned and arranged by law, custom, convention, and ceremonial' (Turner, 1969: 95). Liminality involves the separation and designation of a specific space and time during which normative social structures are flattened, and where social behaviours may be transcended or reversed. For Turner, the inverted behaviours and meanings of this liminal phase emerge from 'collective representations': they are the creation of society as a whole rather than of specific individuals. The second element of anti-structure, *communitas*, refers to a state of spontaneous, communal and spiritual intimacy and togetherness that participants are said to experience during a liminal time and space. We will return to this aspect of anti-structure in Chapter 5, when the meaning and experience of festivals to those who attend them will be examined.

Turner describes the anti-structure as a shared, ritualistic and obligatory action central to the maintenance of social life in the tribal societies he studied. During liminal periods, such as harvest festivals, participants collectively engaged in the free and playful manipulation of social norms and symbols (Turner, 1987: 76), prior to a phase of reaggregation and reintegration. As in van Gennep's work, various rituals and rites are employed to signal the preliminal, liminal and postliminal stages (1960: 21) and, as also seen in Bakhtin's (1984) work, the liminal phase is a temporary phenomenon that supports the maintenance of existing social systems: it is part of the ongoing work of the society as a whole, rather than a truly subversive disjunction (Turner, 1982: 54). In his later works, Turner started to translate his theories to post-industrial Western societies, arguing that the separation of work and leisure time had led to two distinctive forms of anti-structure: the liminal and the liminoid (ibid.: 35). In his view, the liminal persists from earlier times in the form of churches, religious sects and fraternities, for which membership, loyalty and ritual are all important; by contrast, the liminoid is depicted as a new form of social interaction based on choice rather than obligation, and typically sold as a leisure commodity: for example, participation in a variety of artistic and sporting pastimes (ibid.: 55). As with the liminal, the liminoid is characterised by intense feelings, the dismantling of social hierarchies, and by playful or transgressive social behaviours and rituals. Rather than being collectively created, the symbolism of the liminoid is formed (in books, films, artworks and so on) by specific individuals or cliques (though they may have broader collective effects) and will often develop on the economic or political margins of a society. Liminoid activities can expose political injustices and the ineffectuality of mainstream culture in a playful manner, and they are typically experienced on a continual rather than a cyclical basis: therefore, liminoid phenomena may potentially be found in clubs, bars, galleries, and so on throughout the year, rather than at fixed moments on an annual calendar (ibid.: 54–5). For Turner, this liminoid form of anti-structure offers not only a 'freedom from' social norms, but also a 'freedom to' generate new ones and transform society: a potentially more radical, subversive and utopian prospect than the liminal form (ibid.: 36). Rojek (2000: 148) argues that participants in 'modern leisure settings [such as festivals] ... engage in role playing which enables them to stand outside the structures of ordinary society and subject these structures to critical reflection.' This role-playing might include the 'weekend hippies' that Clarke (1982) referred to as making up a considerable part of the outdoor music festival market in the 1970s, and a form of this may still be found today. The weekend hippie does not live a countercultural lifestyle but takes on carnivalesque and countercultural behaviours and styles during the temporary liberation afforded by the festival, perhaps by dressing-up, drinking to excess, openly smoking cannabis or using other drugs, forgoing the usual routines of work and cleanliness, or using the site of the festival in other ways to implicitly critique social norms and moralities through conspicuous consumption practices.

The concept of the liminoid is relevant to those music festivals and events characterised by an anti-mainstream attitude: for instance, anti-war protests and illegal raves are both constructed as oppositional and involve intense or communal feelings and goals – whether politically motivated, or in the form of drug-fuelled hedonism. The liminoid might also be suitable for examining commercial events such as Secret Garden Party or Boomtown Fair, since they incorporate a high degree of participation and theatricality from festivalgoers amid a playful, 'no spectators' mode of engagement which draws on notions of social and personal experimentation (Robinson, 2015a; 2015b). However, it has been argued that the playful nature of liminoid phenomena constitutes a rather shallow form of resistance that is unlikely to challenge societal norms in the subversive and utopian ways suggested by Turner (Weber, 1995: 532). Furthermore, in overstating the radical potential of the liminoid, Turner downplays the affirmative element implied by the phase of reaggregation (Grimes, 1990: 145), and gives little sense of what exactly the mainstream 'structure' is, against which, or outside of which, the liminoid anti-structure supposedly acts (Flanigan, 1990: 52). Turner argues that liminoid phenomena develop on the social or political margins of society, yet it is relatively unusual to find contemporary music festival organisers who seek to occupy such a position; instead, they target their events at specific and commercially viable market niches based on demography, geography, lifestyle and genre. Turner's descriptions of the liminoid tend to draw on the language of ritual and religion, with the implication that liminoid phenomena have a sacred role to play within secular society (Deflem, 1991). There is a degree of support for this today, as a small number of events exist to celebrate the Christian faith, such as the long-running Greenbelt Festival (est. 1974), and others to celebrate pagan beliefs, such as Pagan Pride (first held with a music programme in 2010). Some events also have ritualistic elements. Green Man Festival in Wales, for example, features the burning of a Green Man structure which is accompanied by fireworks, but while this might be viewed as a pagan ritual cleansing to mark the end of the festival it can also be seen simply as an exciting finale spectacle. Overall, the contemporary commercial music festival sector is better characterised as part of the leisure, tourism and music industries – as catering primarily to social and entertainment needs rather than to spiritual ones. A final point to consider is that the social production and bodily performances of liminoid sites and events are largely overlooked by Turner in favour of an analysis that focuses on their symbolic construction (Weber, 1995: 531). We will return to this in the following chapter, in a discussion of the crucial role of festivalgoers in creating and performatively reproducing the meaning and atmosphere of events.

Turner's ideas are useful because they acknowledge the importance of physical space to the experience of a festival, and a number of authors have subsequently developed his concepts of liminality and the liminoid in explicitly spatial terms. For instance, Shields draws on Turner's work to describe 'towns and regions which have been "left behind" in the modern race for progress' and which have, in his terms, gained marginal (or liminal) status due to their 'out-of-the-way' geographical locations or because they have become the sites 'of illicit or disdained social activities' (1991: 3). This form of liminality has been applied to outdoor music festivals by Hetherington (1998a; 1998b), who studied the free festivals of the 1970s and 1980s: events which, as noted in Chapter 1, became strongly associated with the New Age Travellers. He characterises the sites of free festivals as 'not generally integrated within the rituals of modern societies; they are out of the ordinary, out of place' (1998b: 18). Rural locations such as the Rhayader Valley in Wales and Deeply Vale in northwest England, as well as prehistoric sites such as Stonehenge, Avebury, and Cissbury Ring, were particularly favoured by the free festivals, though events in the 1980s could also be found at sites of political contestation such as Greenham Common (supporting the Women's Peace Camp's protests against nuclear arms) and at Waterlooville (the Torpedo Town Festival), where a camp was established to protest the manufacture of the Stingray anti-submarine missile. Thus, location was an important aspect of the symbolic construction of these festivals, since these locations 'fit' the beliefs and understandings of the Travellers and others, and enabled them to physically enact their beliefs and lifestyles in what might be termed liminal spaces.

In contrast, contemporary commercial festivals might, in Turner's terms, be considered as liminoid phenomena, since they fit many of his characteristics: they are primarily organised, marketed and sold as leisure commodities; attendance is voluntary rather than obligatory; they are often considered egalitarian in their social relations; they offer a weakening of social norms and expectations; and organisers, marketers and media represent them as offering an experience beyond that of the everyday. However, as with liminal phenomena, outdoor music festivals are typically held on a cyclical rather than continual basis, and they may become sites of pilgrimage and celebration for groups of friends or families who regularly attend the same event (thus reinforcing 'traditional' or 'tribal' relationships). The modern festival sector may, then, occupy a middle position between the liminal and the liminoid, though the sites on which they are held are rarely liminal in the manner discussed by Shields (1991) or Hetherington (1998a; 1998b). For instance, festivals are now held in a great many locations, with larger events often held in publicly-owned parks, such as Hyde Park in London (British Summer Time Festival) and Hylands Park in Chelmsford (the southern leg of the V Festival), or in the grounds of privately-owned stately homes, such as Bramham Park (Leeds Festival) and Donington Park (Download Festival). Smaller events are also held in public parks, private estates and on farmland, and such sites are often well-integrated with their host localities and may even be tourist attractions or amenities in their own right. For instance, the northern leg of the V Festival is held in the grounds of the historic country house of Weston Park, which regularly plays host to horse-riding competitions and other non-music shows and was used as a weekend retreat for representatives of a G8 conference in 1998. Such a site is neither 'left-behind' nor 'out-of-the-way' geographically (since it boasts excellent transport links) and it is certainly not the locus for socially marginal activities. Events held on farmland and in other rural locations might be regarded as being 'out-of-the-way', yet, as will be discussed later in the chapter, the British countryside has a central role to play in both mainstream and countercultural notions of Britishness and Englishness.

Temporary Autonomous Zones (TAZ)

Another concept which has been adopted for the study of outdoor music festivals and raves is Bey's notion of the Temporary Autonomous Zone (TAZ), which draws on ideas of the Roman Saturnalia and 'festal culture' to argue for a body-centric, non-hierarchical, non-commodified and non-mediated sociality based on direct and immediate experience (1991: 105). This differs from the perspectives of Bakhtin (1984) and Turner (1969; 1982) in two important ways. First, the site of transgression is considered to be ephemeral, mobile and potentially revolutionary: the TAZ is 'a guerrilla operation which liberates an area (of land, of time, of imagination) ... [then] dissolves itself to reform elsewhere/elsewhen, before the State can crush it' (Bey, 1991: 101). Hence, the TAZ constantly shifts location, which is often liminal in the sense used by Shields (1991) and, due to its anarchistic, revolutionary and autonomous rhetoric, is regarded negatively by the authorities. This contrasts with Bakhtin's carnivalesque spaces, and with Turner's liminal/liminoid phenomena, for those are seen as sanctioned, to varying extents, by the authorities that they critique: to be a transitional stage between societal disjunction and its inevitable reaggregation. Second, Bey draws on a neo-Marxist understanding of the music and cultural industries (see Adorno & Horkheimer, 1997) to privilege the unmediated nature of social experience within the TAZ: its form and experience should not emerge from the false needs of commodification and media (which keep people politically passive and unquestioning of authority and the status quo), but from direct, spontaneous and mutual relations between attendees: a manifestation of radical struggle which is deliberately open and anarchic. While the TAZ bears similarities to Turner's antistructure and Bakhtin's carnivalesque (in that all promise some form of utopian freedom), Bey's focus is on the relationship between capitalism and the festival, with the TAZ only able to offer the possibility of meaningful social critique where it emerges from the people and is uncontaminated by commercialism and media attention.

The TAZ has been used to examine Acid House raves and warehouse parties in both Britain (Ingham et al., 1999) and Australia (Gibson, 1999): events which were characterised by the temporary and illegal appropriation of privately owned, though often abandoned or unused, buildings and rural sites. Here, the site of transgression was not only ephemeral in its existence, but also highly mobile; it was predicated on a 'hit and run' strategy that brooked no repetition or solidity. This contrasts with the vast majority of contemporary British music festivals and events which are held at the same location and on the same weekend each year. These latter events may be 'temporary' in terms of their material existence, but the continuity provided by their annual re-construction gives them a cyclic form which is absent from the concept of the TAZ. They are also commercially and legally managed, and accompanied by a range of physical and online marketing materials, as well as by media coverage in newspapers, magazines, websites, radio and television. They must also hold a local authority licence and meet the increasingly stringent requirements of a range of health and safety laws, standards and regulations. As a result, the TAZ is only applicable in a relatively limited set of circumstances, such as the remnants of the free party scene discussed at the end of Chapter 2. Nevertheless, as Connell and Gibson note, the success of illegal raves and festivals may be based not simply on the ability of the organisers to provide unlicensed music events, 'but also [on] the specific sites chosen as venues, and the transformation of these sites into imaginative landscapes' (2003: 204). This points once again to the significance of both the physical characteristics of a site and the use of design aesthetics in general for the success of events – not only of illegal raves but of commercially motivated festivals operating within a crowded marketplace.

Heterotopia

The theories proposed by Turner (1969; 1982) and Bey (1991) have been criticised for homogenising the beliefs and behaviours found within festivals, since they each imply that participants have a shared understanding of the meaning of 'festival', and are all working towards the same goals (St John, 2001: 49). One way to overcome this is to draw upon Foucault's ideas regarding heterotopia, which he described as an 'effectively enacted utopia' (1986: 24). For Foucault, utopia refers to an idealised and imaginative space in which human societies can exist in 'perfected form', rather than a space which is grounded in the real world; hence, 'utopias are fundamentally unreal spaces' (ibid.: 24). A classic example, from which the term is derived, is Thomas More's satirical book *Utopia*. Originally published in 1516, it describes a fictional island society which offered, amongst other things, religious tolerance, a welfare state and communal ownership of property (Logan & Adams, 2002). In contrast to such fictions, heterotopias are described by Foucault as *real* places that can be found in all societies and may be categorised as based either on 'crisis' or 'deviance' (1986: 24–5). 'Crisis heterotopias' are 'privileged or sacred or forbidden places' which deal with important life changes, such as adolescence and pregnancy. Crisis heterotopias are, therefore, similar to the liminal rites of passage discussed by van Gennep (1960) and Turner (1969). Foucault argues that crisis heterotopias are now rare in modern societies, since 'heterotopias of deviance' have become more common. This latter form of heterotopia refers to places where individuals who are 'deviant in relation to the required mean or norm are placed', such as psychiatric hospitals or prisons. To relate this to contemporary music festivals, we could argue that deviance is made possible at these events by a loosening of social restrictions and norms. Festivals may, therefore, become useful sites for people and groups who follow alternative lifestyles, such as the New Age Travellers of the 1970s and the ravers of the 1990s, to create their own heterotopic spaces and to celebrate their 'deviance' from mainstream capitalist society. St John follows this logic to introduce the term 'alternative cultural heterotopias' which he develops using the example of ConFest in Australia: 'a significant pilgrimage centre for the vast number of constituents of Australia's alternative lifestyle movement' (2001: 47–8). These alternative cultural heterotopias are described as 'communities of resistance' exiled from mainstream culture, and as places 'where hedonistic consumption practices are licensed' (ibid.: 51). However, in the twenty-first century few British festivals are strongly rooted in alternative lifestyles; instead, they cater to demographic and psychographic niches based on leisure-centric attitudes, behaviours, interests and pastimes. Festivals may, therefore, encompass multiple voices and understandings, not simply the transgressive or the deviant (Wilks & Quinn, 2016).

Foucault argues that heterotopias change meaning over time and that their societal function is contingent upon the specific contexts of any given era. In addition, they encompass multiple understandings of place simultaneously: they are 'capable of juxtaposing in a single real place several places, several sites that are in themselves incompatible' (1986: 25). St John identifies this in his study of ConFest, arguing that the same festival site was used by multiple groupings with both conflicting and complementary interpretations

(2001: 52). This can also be seen at British music festivals of all kinds, where different groups may use a festival site and occasion for different purposes or understand the festival in different ways. Similarly, festival sites and meanings may interact with the histories of their host locations, such that the changing nature of those host locations must be taken into account when attempting to understand the shifting dynamics of an event (Anderton 2007). Foucault also coined the term heterochronies, which he described as a 'sort of absolute break with ... traditional time' (1986: 26). With regard to festivals he specifically stated that these were places where time may be experienced 'in its most fleeting, transitory, precarious aspect': as places in which people's sense of time is orientated to the temporal and immediate, rather than the eternal (ibid.). During the time of the festival, the 'real' world of work is temporarily forgotten and life proceeds with other imperatives. Such descriptions are consonant with those of Bakhtin (1984), Turner (1969; 1982) and Bey (1991), though the 'real' world of work, and of life outside of festival, is increasingly encroaching on the festival experience, through the use of digital media technologies such as mobile phones, internet cafés and radio-frequency identification (RFID) wristbands linked to social media accounts.

Foucault suggests that access to heterotopias is predicated on 'a system of opening and closing that both isolates them and makes them penetrable' (1986: 26). Access may be compulsory (such as entry to a prison or an army barracks) or subject to 'rites and purifications' (ibid.). This translates poorly to the case of the contemporary festival where the event may be offered for free, or access may be secured through the relatively simple purchase of a ticket. But Foucault's work is useful in that it draws attention to exclusionary forces: some people may be unable to afford the price of a ticketed event, lack the freedom or ability to travel to it, or feel socially excluded from participation: they do not 'fit in' with the social expectations of an event. It is noticeable, for example, that many outdoor rock, pop and folk music festivals in the UK have audiences that are predominantly White European, which suggests a form of self-regulation based on the mediated image and history of these events. At another level, the trend towards niche market events means that the potential audience for specific events becomes significantly narrowed, as does the ability of people to 'fit in' with those events. Foucault concluded his discussions with the metaphor of a boat: 'a floating piece of space, a place without a place, that exists by itself, that is closed in on itself and at the same time is given over to the infinity of the sea' (1986: 26–7). This metaphor is somewhat applicable to outdoor greenfield festivals, since they appear to create temporary towns or cities with their own infrastructure, policing, boundaries and so on. By contrast, city-centre events need not exist in separation from the host cities in which they are staged: they are not closed in on themselves, but temporarily interact with and transform their host locations.

As noted earlier, there are shortcomings to using Foucault's heterotopia as a way to describe contemporary festival places, yet certain elements point towards an alternative way of conceptualising and describing the sites on which festivals are held. Festivals change over time and are created in part from the interactions of people with place, and between the event organisation and its host location. They contain the potential for multiple interpretations, even conflicting ones, regarding the nature and experience of a festival place. Festivals are, in this sense, a palimpsest consisting of different layers of meaning, with new layers added as time passes and as different combinations of people experience, discuss, remember, work and market the event on an annual basis. The foregoing theories of liminal and heterotopic space inform my development of the concept of 'cyclic place', where festivals are regarded as part of a broader leisure economy which may include the potential for transgressive, carnivalesque or anti-structural behaviours, but does not need to be defined by them.

Cyclic place

Outdoor music festivals are ephemeral in nature: they are constructed over a period of days or weeks prior to opening to the public and exist in physical form for only as long as the entertainments and attendees are present on-site. When the festivalgoers leave and the event is over, there is a short period of cleaning up before the site returns to its everyday use or is repurposed for some other use. Despite this temporary existence, some festivals – especially those that have returned to the same site for a number of years – may cultivate a recognisable 'sense of place', defined in humanistic geography as the 'persistent sameness and unity which allows [one place] to be differentiated from others' (Relph, 1976: 45). For a few days each year, a festival will take on a material form that is perceived by festivalgoers to be a 'real' place, with its own history, rules, culture and meanings; its own emergency services, accommodation and police force; its own entertainments and shops; and its own catering, water and sanitation provisions. The imaginative construction of a festival 'place' is fostered further by its representation in media and memory, and by its cyclic nature, since it is annually reconstructed in its own image. Outdoor festivals require the deliberate construction and superimposition of a festival place within a pre-existing host location, thus the sense of place of each – the host and the festival – may become intimately interlinked. The characteristics of a cyclic place will be outlined later, but first it is useful to explore the particular conceptions of space and place which underlie the notion of cyclic place, and to discuss some specific examples of festivals.

Space and place

There are many definitions of space and place, as well as conflicting views regarding the relationship between them. For the purposes of this book, a relational understanding of space is adopted and adapted – one which is consistent with the processual understanding of festivals seen in the work of

Bakhtin (1984), Turner (1982) and Bey (1991). This understanding of space draws on Massey's suggestion that spaces are 'constructed out of the multiplicity of social relations', rather than constituted as bounded areas with intrinsic, fixed or singular identities (1994: 4). Furthermore, since 'spaces' are always in the process of construction, 'places' should be characterised as 'spatio-temporal events' formed of multiple narratives – stories, beliefs and understandings – that are centred on particular geographical locations, and are subject to change over time (Massey, 2005: 130). It is, for Massey, the accumulation of narratives that helps build a history for a particular place, yet she tends to overemphasise the processual and relational nature of space, which she also terms the 'event of place' (ibid.: 139–40), rather than consider the potential of those narratives to construct relatively stable place-images. Outdoor music festivals are an interesting case in point, since they encompass the deliberate construction and reconstruction of an 'event of place' yet, as the title of this chapter suggests, each cyclical return of a festival is characterised as being 'always the same, yet always different': the festival 'brand' and place remains recognisable to regular attendees and commentators, yet the overall experience of the event will differ from year to year in terms of its entertainment, audience, weather and so on. Festivals can, therefore, be said to construct an ephemeral and shifting form of 'place identity' that is communicated through media, memory and performance.

One way to investigate the space and place of festival sites is to draw on Lefebvre's (1991) suggestion that space is produced perceptually and conceptually through the body: it is the practices of the body (the social) that produce meanings for spaces and places. He proposed three interconnected and simultaneously operative 'moments' within this productive work (Schmid, 2008: 43), which are historically and geographically contingent: spatial practices, spaces of representation and representations of space. First, spatial practice refers to the everyday activities and routines of people in relation to space and how those people perceive the world around them (Lefebvre, 1991: 38): certain forms of behaviour are deemed appropriate (even expected) of people in particular places, and these behaviours are enacted and repeated in an ongoing cycle of re-affirmation that serves to confirm their appropriateness (Shields, 1991). At festivals, this can be seen in activities such as all-day drinking, late-night partying, dressing up in outlandish or amusing costumes, spending an evening in the crush of people in front of the main stage, and the acceptance of mud and dirt as a necessary consequence of the event. Second, Lefebvre defines 'spaces of representation' as discursive spaces invested with symbolism and meaning (Lefebvre, 1991: 39): in other words, people give meaning to the world around them, and this can refer just as well to specific topographical features and the broader rural landscape as it can to the urban environment of buildings, towns and cities. There are parallels with Foucault's notion of heterotopia (1986), since the same site or location can be invested with different meanings by different people and organisations. The ancient monument of Stonehenge in the south of England is a good example of a space of representation: the Druids view it as a site of religious importance; UNESCO classifies it as a World Heritage Site; archaeologists regard it as a Prehistoric riddle to be questioned in social, cultural or mystical terms; and the New Age Travellers of the 1970s and 1980s saw it as having such great social significance that the summer Solstice was celebrated there with a music festival (NCCL, 1986; Hetherington, 1992; Worthington, 2004). Finally, Lefebvre refers to 'representations of space', which are ideological in nature: for example, plans, maps, architecture and urban planning (1991: 38–9). These 'conceived' spaces (as he also refers to them) are typically associated with formal institutions that have the ability to produce and distribute them to others. They are therefore powerful in creating spatial imaginations and symbolism (ibid: 42) and may have a direct impact upon both spatial practices and spaces of representation. With regard to festivals we could include the site diagrams and management plans of organisers, or the licensing documentation and requirements of local authorities, all of which an impact on the physical layout, flow, organisation and aesthetics of a festival site. The official programme and website of a festival will include information derived from those plans, in addition to marketing messages aimed at communicating particular representations of the event to the intended audience. Beyond these official sources of mediation, there are increasing quantities of informal media created by festivalgoers themselves, which can be found through Internet message boards and social media applications such as Facebook, Twitter and Instagram. These sites may memorialise past events through reviews and photography, or provide a resource for festival newcomers to gain a better understanding of a festival and its sense of identity and place. These more informal representations of space are closely connected to the discursive practices of festivalgoers (spaces of representation), hence the differences between Lefebvre's categories are somewhat blurred.

Lefebvre's tripartite distinction is useful because it demonstrates that the spatial cannot be conceived as a passive or abstract arena for human actions to take place but must instead be regarded as actively created through event plans, mediations and audience behaviours and understandings. Shields draws on this for his notion of social spatialisation, which he defines as: 'the ongoing social construction of the spatial at the level of the social imaginary (collective mythologies, presuppositions) as well as interventions in the landscape (for example, the built environment)' (1991: 31). For Shields, the heterogeneous reality of place is obscured through over-simplification (concentrating on a single trait, or a few specific traits), stereotyping (intensification of those traits), and labelling (the symbolic association of those traits with a specific place) (1991: 47). Where simplified narratives and place-images of a festival become widely disseminated, they may impact upon festivalgoers' beliefs about that event; in turn, this may have consequences for the range of activities and behaviours that festivalgoers believe to be acceptable at the event. This may occur whether or not the 'real' nature of the site (its experience in situ) actually matches the narratives and expectations that have previously been created. There is therefore a need to interrogate the multiple ways in which music festival places are mediated by organisers, the media and festivalgoers themselves, and to study the differing ways in which attendees experience, discuss and perform festival culture.

Festival sites may, then, be conceived as embodying the intersection of multiple meanings that have been provided through the symbolic work and material practices and behaviours of (amongst others) event organisers, artists, traders, security personnel, licensing authorities, media, and festivalgoers (Duffy, 2000; Chalcraft & Magaudda, 2013). Outdoor music festivals may only be physically present at host locations for a limited time each year, yet their annual reconstruction in material form remains aligned with the narratives and discourses of official documentation, media, and memory. This causes a relatively stable sense of identity and place to emerge and develop over time, yet also allows for changes from year to year, and for festivals to remain relevant to both regular and new attendees. Festivalgoers may also develop strong affective bonds with particular events, which may be likened to Relph's notion of 'insideness' (1976: 51–5): a personal identification with a place (and the festival sited there) which may lead to feelings of attachment and belonging. As Waterman notes, festivals are given meaning through their 'active incorporation into people's lives': they are 'not simply bought and "consumed"' (1998: 56). This sense of insideness or incorporation can not only be applied to individuals and their attachments to, and feelings for, particular places, but may also be discussed in terms of how temporary events such as festivals may connect with their broader host locations.

In order to explore the development of festival place image, and the relationship between festivals and their locations, two contrasting examples are discussed using a mix of field research and secondary sources: the Cambridge Folk Festival and the V Festival. Both are long-lived camping events which benefit from media coverage by the BBC yet are quite different in terms of their organisation and size. The Cambridge Folk Festival, established in 1965, is a four-day event with a daily attendance capacity of 10,000 people, and is currently organised by Cambridge Live Trust (a charitable company created in 2014 by former organisers, Cambridge City Council). The V Festival was first held in 1996 and is owned by a consortium of national and international event promotion companies. It is held at twin sites – Hylands Park in Essex and Weston Park in Staffordshire – each of which has a capacity of 90,000 people. The festival was the first in Britain to hold events at two locations on the same weekend, with the Saturday and Sunday night headlining acts rotating between the two sites.

Cambridge Folk Festival at Cherry Hinton Hall

The Cambridge Folk Festival was launched by Cambridge City Council with the aim of focusing 'attention on what was going on in the city and ... [to attract] greater support from tourists and residents alike' (Adams, 1986: 75).

In event tourism terms, the event was both an attraction (for tourists and locals) and an 'animator': a themed event which draws in new audiences, creates positive publicity, and encourages repeat visits and spending in the wider locality (Getz & Page, 2016: 191). Ken Woollard, a local fireman and folk music enthusiast, was appointed to run the first event in 1965, and managed the event until his death in 1993. Woollard's working class background and socialist beliefs were consonant with those of the British folk music tradition, which was experiencing the boom of the second folk revival at the time. In 1966, Woollard became president of the Cambridge Folk Club, where he met Mike Meeropol – an American student who introduced him to many up-and-coming American folk artists and influenced his booking policy for the Cambridge Folk Festival (Stoodley & Grainger, 2001). Another important influence was the film *Jazz on a Summer's Day* (1960), which documented the 1958 US Newport Jazz Festival and showed how such an event could encompass many different genres of music, including Dixieland, bebop, jazz, blues, gospel and rock and roll. Woollard adopted a similarly broad approach which brought together the traditional folk music of the British Isles, alongside American blues, country and bluegrass performers, contemporary singer-songwriters such as Paul Simon, and crossover artists like (The) Pentangle and Steeleye Span, who were adding jazz and rock elements to their music. The event's genre eclecticism has continued since Woollard's death, allowing his successors to book relatively mainstream rock, pop, blues, reggae and world music artists over the years, such as The Zutons, The Divine Comedy, The Robert Cray Band, Jimmy Cliff and Ladysmith Black Mambazo.

Drawing on his socialist roots, Woollard instigated a non-hierarchical approach to artist programming. This can be seen in the festival's advertising posters, which use standardised font sizes to list artist names (rather than having the headliners in larger text), and in the format of the event itself. For instance, artists often play more than once on different stages/days, and the highest profile performers do not necessarily appear as the final act of an evening. As the marketing manager Neil Jones stated in 2004,

> we feel that no one act is more important than just the actual ethos of the festival itself ... just because you're the biggest name, it doesn't mean you're actually going to technically close the show because what we like to do is put those acts on that have more of a party feel.
> (Cited in Anderton, 2007: 132)

In addition, it is one of the few festivals of its size that has maintained a 'club tent' where enthusiastic amateurs have the opportunity to perform short sets during the day in a style most often seen on the folk club circuit. This was extended in the 2000s by the addition of The Hub (a space for teenagers to congregate and play music) and other areas such as The Den and The People's Front Room, all of which allow amateurs to perform, and which are situated in quieter areas away from the main arena.

Like Michael Eavis of the Glastonbury Festival, Ken Woollard became the public face and guiding force behind the structure and character of the Cambridge Folk Festival. When he lost his post as Festival Director in 1974 (due to a reorganisation of the Council), folk music fans successfully petitioned the Council to reinstate him (Laing & Newman, 1994: 16–18). He envisioned the event as a family-friendly, inclusive and participatory space requiring a limited police presence, and his principles continue to guide the festival in the twenty-first century. For instance, there are discounted ticket prices for children under 17, and under-5s can attend for free. Concessionary tickets are also offered to Cambridge residents, with further concessions available to those in receipt of certain state benefits. In addition to the main stages, the festival offers a range of participatory activities, including ceilidhs, singarounds, storytelling, circus skills, music and dance workshops, and a children's procession, plus quiet camping areas for families. The market area not only includes the standard festival fare of hand-made, ethnic and New Age goods, jewellery, pendants and necklaces set with 'healing crystals', bright tie-dye t-shirts, Mexican ponchos and brightly painted Doc Marten boots, but also a selection of children's clothes and toys such as hand puppets and juggling apparatus. There is a stall selling the performers' music, and a musical instrument tent where traditional acoustic instruments suitable for both children and adults may be bought. The site boasts toilet trailers fitted with flushing toilets and running water, which may be used at no extra cost. This is in stark contrast to many other outdoor music festivals where rows of portaloos and open-air urinals are typically found alongside commercial operations such as Comfy Crappers, Seat of Luxury and When Nature Calls.

Woollard chose to stage the festival at Cherry Hinton Hall, an Elizabethan-style mansion and grounds owned by Cambridge City Council, that had been used by the local fire brigade when Woollard had worked there as a fireman in the 1960s (Watts, 1986). The grounds encompass 36 acres of woodland and fields in a suburban area about one-and-a-half miles to the southeast of Cambridge city centre and, outside of festival times, the park is freely open to the public as a leisure amenity. During the festival, attendees may stay entirely within the site, or make excursions to the centre of Cambridge to visit the tourist and leisure attractions of the city. Woollard's choice of Cherry Hinton Hall, surrounded as it is by suburban residential property, may seem somewhat incongruous, for it is rare to find an outdoor festival with camping in such a small, almost city centre, location. However, several aspects make it ideal. It is a walled park (which aids security) and the site is already owned by the council, hence there is no rent payable. It is in a relatively central location, thus simplifying access and management, and there are broad grassed areas for the arena and campsite. Shady woodland areas offer protection from the sun, and a small nature reserve can be found at the rear of the site: it is, in effect, a piece of the countryside in an otherwise urban landscape. When the festival's attendance figures grew during the

1970s, concerns were raised by the Council regarding the site's size and suitability. Discussions were held in 1977 (and subsequent years) to consider alternative sites, but the organisers felt that the character of the event would be unduly affected by moving it away from the site Woollard had chosen (Laing & Newman, 1994: 18). A motion was passed to restrict attendance to 10,000 people, with other measures introduced over the following years, such as using the nearby school playing fields as a car park and adding dedicated family-friendly camping at another site a mile away. In the mid-2000s, the rapid pace of ticket sales led to speculation that the organisers would relocate and expand the event to take advantage of the increased demand (since the festival regularly sells out), but they were keen to deny that such a move would take place. For instance, Nigel Cutting, Head of Cambridge City Council Arts & Entertainments said in 2004 that 'this site is very special and part of what makes the festival the success that it is. We would be taking a very big risk if we were to move it somewhere else' (cited in *Cambridge News*, 2004).

The festival's official website and photo galleries represent it as a leafy, green, outdoor event, with many photographs showing the woods, the nature reserve, the campsites, and festivalgoers involved in yoga and tai chi. The suburban location is downplayed in favour of a natural, countryside image, further enhanced by photographs of traditionally dressed Morris dancers, amateur musicians playing acoustic instruments in the park, and children playing with simple toys or paddling in the stream. There are photographs of the professional musicians and stages, as well as gaudily dressed festivalgoers and the street entertainers hired to enliven the festival arena. The focus on the physical environment of the festival is also given preference in television coverage of the event, where interviews with performers are conducted in the nature reserve at the rear of the site. This alludes to an imagined history of folk music as simple, rural, close to nature, non-commercial and authentic, even though the genre has been reliant on commercial exploitation and mediation for its success since the 1950s (Brocken, 2003). These idyllic media representations show a festival that is turned in on itself, thus akin to Foucault's (1986) description of a heterotopia. Yet, at Cambridge Folk Festival we do not find a heterotopia of crisis or of deviance, but one which is based on leisure, and strongly rooted in its location.

The festival has grown organically within the confines of Cherry Hinton Hall and within the context of Woollard's particular vision of the event – a vision that has been translated into a set of stabilising tenets that guide how the organisers manage the event today: small-scale, non-hierarchical, musically eclectic, family-friendly and participatory. These tenets have become rooted in a specific location: the festival is seen as belonging to the park, which is complicit in its success and emblematic of its non-commercial, socialist and folk music roots. This constrains the potential for future growth of the event, since a move to an alternative site would be an explicit statement of commercial intent, yet there are still possibilities for innovation within the confines of the site. Each year, the organisers make incremental changes to its structure and management in order to counter the problems of the site's small size and suburban location, and to vary its entertainment offering. Yet the basic layout of the stages and amenities has remained the same, fostering a sense of a familiarity: regular attendees know where everything will be before they arrive, and they treat the festival site as a home-from-home. Their knowledge of the layout, ethos, history and atmosphere of the site allows them to feel comfortable within it, and they act as behavioural models for those who are new to the event. These repeat attendees value the intimacy that a small site brings to the event, and many seek out the same parts of the camping grounds each year in order to stake out their own areas:

> the group I go with always camp in the same place. It means we always know where to find each other.... It's behind the club tent so we can always hear the club tent and main stage one. It's close to two festival site entrances and the toilets. Also the food stands are pretty close too. The whole group camps in the same place. It's normally a huge area and most years the number of people camping with our group gets bigger.
> (Interview with Emma at Cambridge Folk Festival 2004)

The same is true within the festival arena, where festivalgoers domesticate an area of the main stage field to use as a base for the day:

> There's about twelve of us and about fifty percent of us go and watch the bands while the rest just stay here and drink beer ... it's great to sit here and if it sounds good I just go down there and check it out.
> (Interview with Catherine at Cambridge Folk Festival 2003).

Nearly three-quarters of attendees in 2003 were aged 36 years or older, with around 2,000 children's tickets sold (Cambridge City Council Arts & Entertainments, 2004). This creates a family-friendly and largely trouble-free event in which behaviours are self-regulated. As one festivalgoer stated:

> It's quite laid back. I mean, considering there were so many people drinking last night there wasn't any aggravation or any violence or anything – not even anyone swearing at each other.
> (Interview with Serena at Cambridge Folk Festival 2004).

There is a collectively-held view of the festival as a secure and trouble-free environment, one where you can leave your belongings in your tent with no fear of them being stolen, and where trouble is unlikely and police action rare. There is a positive will amongst festivalgoers to maintain this view, since they take ownership of the event and are protective of its reputation and image in much the same manner as fans of a favourite artist. Their personal biographies have become intertwined with the history and ethos of the event they attend and, as a result, there is a largely subconscious (or at least unspoken) determination to make the event match the image they hold of it: to act in a manner appropriate to that image, and to downplay or discount the impact of anything that unsettles it. For instance, one festivalgoer reported that:

> The only anti-social behaviour I saw was teenage males being noisy and rude. I think they may have been throwing things too. I think the boys had drunk a little bit and were just being obnoxious. I don't think it was behaviour with a particularly malicious intent but just disruptive.
> (Email from Laura about Cambridge Folk Festival 2004).

Similarly, a blind eye is turned to the smoking of cannabis in the campsite so long as it does not disrupt others' enjoyment, showing that liminal behaviours can occur even at such a family-friendly, suburban event; however, such behaviours are neither overt nor celebrated by festivalgoers, and are absent from media representations of the event. In this way, festivalgoers, organisers and media may annually reconstruct the event in a pre-existing and utopian image: one strengthened by the presence of many repeat attendees. This contrasts with the valorisation of such behaviours found, for example, in the recollections and commentaries of attendees and artists quoted in books about Reading Festival (Carroll, 2007) and Glastonbury Festival (Aubrey & Shearlaw, 2004). Cambridge Folk Festival's family-friendly atmosphere and compact layout is, instead, akin to a traditional village fête, and to some degree modern music festivals such as this may be said to take the place of the traditional, community-centred, fête. In this way, they follow in the footsteps of the revivalist fairs discussed in Chapter 1, in that they offer an alternative and elective version of traditional festivities that can attract visitors from far outside the immediate locality and community.

V Festival at Weston Park

As noted in Chapter 3, the V Festival was initially planned as a showcase for the British band Pulp in 1996, although its remit soon extended beyond Pulp and other Britpop groups of the time to encompass a mix of British and American chart acts in a range of rock, pop, dance, soul and hip hop genres. It was the first festival in Britain to adopt a twin site format, with a 'southern' event at Hylands Park in Chelmsford, and a 'northern' event at Victoria Park in Warrington. The latter event was shifted to Temple Newsam in Leeds in 1997 as Victoria Park was no longer big enough, and then to its current home of Weston Park in Staffordshire in 1999, after rival concert promoter Mean Fiddler took on the Temple Newsam site to create a northern leg of the Carling Weekend. The V Festival was launched and managed by a consortium of concert promoters consisting of SJM Concerts (based in Manchester), Metropolis Music (based in London), DF Concerts (based in Glasgow) and MCD Productions (based in Dublin). In the mid-1990s, these companies were looking to expand into the festival market, because as Bob Angus of Metropolis Music has stated:

> We spent the whole year working on artistes and then sat around in the summer twiddling our thumbs and carrying the overheads while they played the festivals.... [Concert] Promoters just weren't part of the festival scene.
>
> (cited in Palmley, 2002: 8).

Each member of the consortium had extensive experience of live concert promotion and of working with the emergent Britpop bands of the 1990s, and this experience gave artists, sponsors and contractors the confidence to work with the consortium on launching a large-scale event of over 65,000 audience capacity for the first time (Masson, 2004). Fortuitously for the promoters, the Glastonbury Festival was absent from the festival calendar in 1996, having been cancelled following crowd trouble the year before. This created space for a major new festival to be launched, and the V Festival's approach to festival production soon proved popular with its audience and also with festival insiders, who named it European Festival of the Year for seven years in a row at the annual Live! Magazine awards. Since December 2013, the V Festival has been majority-owned (50.1 per cent) by LN-Gaiety Holdings: a joint venture between the US-based Live Nation Entertainment and the Ireland-based Gaiety Investments (which owns MCD Productions). Substantial minority stakes in the holding company which owns V Festival (Maztecrose Holdings) are owned by Simon Moran (SJM Concerts) and Customblock Ltd (Metropolis Music) (Mintel, 2014).

The commercial background of the promoters informs the ethos and management of the event, which has attracted considerable brand sponsorship since it began in the mid-1990s. The sponsorship deals were originally brokered to offset the financial risk of an untested festival brand staging large outdoor shows, while the increasingly sophisticated and expensive technical specifications of the performers led to further deals being made (Holden, 2001: 9). Once the Virgin Group had agreed to become the principal title sponsor in 1996 (in order to cross-promote its Virgin Trains, Virgin Radio and Virgin Cola brands), there were moves to christen the event the 'Virgin Cola Festival'; however, as noted in Chapter 3, Pulp are reported to have blocked this decision on the basis that it did not fit with the band's public image and beliefs. This is the first sign that the overt commerciality of the V Festival and its organisers was in conflict with the countercultural and anti-establishment heritage of rock music and music festivals in the British context (Anderton, 2008: 44). This heritage was still relatively current at the time, as shown by the street protests held in London against the 1994

Criminal Justice and Public Order Act (see Chapter 2). Nevertheless, the festival has continued to court sponsorship deals and a mass-market audience of popular music fans who are attracted by its mainstream and often chart-friendly musical programming, and less concerned with countercultural ideals or politics.

The V Festival main stage is branded by Virgin, while the second stage is sponsored by a media partner, such as Channel 4, NME, MTV or BBC Radio 1. There is also a dance tent within the arena and a variety of smaller stages and brand activations which offer live music or DJ sets. The number and variety of stages changes each year, though the main and second stages are consistently sited in the same parts of the arena each year, which lends a sense of familiarity to the regular contractors who build and manage the site, and to those festivalgoers who have visited the event in the past. The main arena is a large field which has a number of small copses within it. These copses need to be fenced off for health and safety reasons, so the smaller stages and concessions are sited around these landscape features (which have the added advantage of providing natural barriers to the transmission of sound between different areas of the site). Over the years, numerous stage sponsorships have been seen, including clothing brands such as Puma and JJB Sports, drinks companies such as Strongbow, Bacardi and Volvic, the deodorant brand Sure, and the car manufacturer Nissan (promoting its newly-launched Juke model in 2010). The ever-changing mix of stage sponsorships and brand activations (from the likes of Duracell, Red Bull, Nintendo, X-Box, Braun, Very and many others) are part of what keeps the festival fresh each year, and those attending the event do not seem to be put off by the presence of so many commercial sponsorships. The following quotes collected from festivalgoers in the mid-2000s are indicative:

> It doesn't really bother me to be honest. I think it adds a certain vibe to the festival but not a bad one.
> (Interview with Rachel at V Festival 2004)

> I think people accept this stuff without question these days. It's just wallpaper.
> (Email from Michael about V Festival 2004)

V Festival does attract repeat attendance from some festivalgoers, but with a site capacity of 90,000 people, the organisers cannot rely on this to ensure the sell-out attendances required to make the event financially viable. Instead, it needs to attract new attendees each year, which in part explains the high level of sponsor activity that it engages in, since this greatly increases the event's marketing reach. The target market for the event is 16–34-year-olds: a mix of those attending their first music festival, and older professionals who may have grown up with rock music, but now seek a festival with a varied musical bill and a higher level of service provision than was available in the past (Holden, 2001: 8). Speaking in 2004, Andy Redhead of SJM Concerts suggested that:

> We place ourselves in the middle ground as far as festivals go. We are not a 'hippy' or 'rock' festival, rather a festival for people who want to have a great weekend and see and hear good music in a safe environment.
> (Email cited in Anderton, 2007: 235).

The aim is to create a festival that moves beyond the 'prison-camp conditions' which the organisers saw as characteristic of the festival market in the 1980s (Rob Ballantine of SJM Concerts, cited in Lambert, 2000: 22). Promotional literature in the 2000s boasted that the V Festival had more toilets than any other event of comparable size, and the organisers have brought in numerous added-value brand activations over the years, such as the Wella Hair Rescue Centre, the Kotex Powder Rooms (regularly-cleaned flushing toilets with mirrors and washbasins), and the Very Fashionable Tent, in order to counter the perception of festivals and festivalgoers as dirty or unhygienic. In addition, the festival has shower facilities, cash machines, a 24-hour newsagent and pharmacy, Wi-Fi availability, and a wide range of non-music attractions such as a fairground, comedy tent, sports competitions and areas for trying out new mobile phones and computer games. Some aspects of the festival experience have been further commercialised at the event, such as premium camping and pay-per-visit luxury toilets, while in the 2000s the market area not only sold the typical festival goods of tie-dye clothing, jewellery, crystals, and so on, but also 'legal highs' and unprepared and unpackaged liberty cap mushrooms – so-called 'magic mushrooms' or 'shrooms' (Anderton, 2008: 45). These latter activities were technically legal at the time and tapped into the legacy of festivals as relatively safe havens for the public use of drugs. They have since been removed from the event as laws have tightened and attitudes toward drug use at festivals have changed (as discussed in Chapter 2). There are now strong security checks at the main entrance to the site, where police pull over cars to search for drugs; nevertheless, a walk around the campsites at night soon shows that drug usage continues, albeit in areas where surveillance by the police and security staff is fairly limited.

The northern leg of the festival has been held at Weston Park since 1999 and is described by Rob Ballantine of SJM Concerts as its 'spiritual home' (cited in Lambert, 2000: 22). The site's central UK location, and its proximity to two motorways, means that it is easily accessible for audiences from major population centres such as Liverpool, Manchester and the Midlands, as well as for contractors, concessions and touring artists. There is ample car-parking and camping space, and disruption to the surrounding area is kept to a minimum by the bounded nature of the estate and the valley setting of the main arena; this effectively precludes festivalgoers from leaving the site once they have pitched camp and reduces noise overspill that might otherwise adversely affect local villages. Weston Park is a privately-owned 1,000-acre estate with landscaped gardens and has a long and illustrious history: the present house was constructed within a medieval deer park in 1671 and is today a Grade II listed building which has regularly played host to royalty and heads of state. The house and grounds are managed by the Weston Park Foundation with the principal aims of conserving Weston 'for the public benefit and to develop its role as an educational charity' (Weston Park, 2016). To these ends, the estate is open to the public from mid-April to the beginning of September, and in addition to its core activities of conservation, fine dining, wedding receptions, residential conferences and educational tours, the Trustees have also sanctioned an annual season of special events, including the Spring Horse Trials, the Midland Game Fair, the Last Night of the Proms, and a Festival of Transport. The estate and local area are therefore quite used to dealing with large numbers of visitors and sporadic traffic congestion, and a good infrastructure has been developed within the grounds, including roadways, water supplies, and a specialist management team who deal solely with parkland events. This has been a boon to the V Festival organising team, as it reduces the time and costs required to construct and then clear the festival. The landscaped grounds are also seen as beneficial: 'Weston Park is such a beautiful site that it helps to attract a broad age range of audience' (Andy Redhead of SJM Concerts, cited in Holden, 2001: 9).

The official Instagram page of the V Festival (www.instagram.com/vfestival/) does not especially focus on the site itself, though there are some photographs of Weston Park House and its grounds in its pre-festival phase, including shots of the lake and of deer in the parkland. Instead, the majority of the photographs focus on showcasing the spectacular stage sets and light shows of its artists, and on providing close-ups of those artists on stage. In this sense, the festival uses and transforms the site in a heterotopic fashion in that it constructs festival space within the pre-existing site of Weston Park's extensive grounds. In addition, the festival is largely closed in upon itself, and for its duration there is no need for festivalgoers to venture beyond its boundaries or otherwise interact with the local area. Using Instagram, festival organisers construct an image of the festival as mainstream, popular and fun: there are numerous photographs of well-known television celebrities and artists posing in the backstage areas, plus panoramic views of packed audiences in the main arena, and some of festivalgoers in fancy dress costumes. There are images of pre-erected tents, teepees and podpads in the luxury camping zones and of the fairground Ferris wheel lit up at night. The mainstream image of the festival has been reinforced by its broader mediation in magazines and blogs which lampoon its commerciality and criticise its focus on chart-friendly performers. For instance, a review of V Festival 2015 for the *Guardian* [online] begins: 'Commercial radio is all very well in background bursts, but would you want to live inside one for a weekend?' (Beaumont, 2015). The webzine *Drowned in Sound* was more magnanimous in its review, noting first that the festival is often criticised 'for being overly commercial – like that isn't something you can aim at every top tier music festival', before suggesting that the pop-orientated line-up actually helps it to stand out from its competitors (Beardsworth, 2015). This latter point is important, since V Festival was one of the first outdoor camping festivals to understand the potential of the mainstream pop market, and to target that market through its musical programming, sponsorship choices and a focus on improving customer service. As Andy Redhead states, 'our first priority [at V Festival] is to make our customers' stay as pleasant as possible and to this end we work to ensure that on-site facilities are the best they can possibly be' (email cited in Anderton, 2007: 247).

Nevertheless, accusations of bland, commercial line-ups, and of experiences which lack the carnivalesque atmosphere associated with rock music festivals, are relatively common with respect to V Festival. These criticisms are reminiscent of those made by humanistic geographers about airports and shopping malls: locations that seem to lack an essential infusion of 'human meaning' (Tuan, 1977: 35). This lack of individual character or distinctiveness has been termed 'placelessness', and such sites are deemed to be relatively anonymous and interchangeable with each other (Relph, 1976: 143). V Festival's wholehearted acceptance of media and brand partnerships, and of on-site 'added value' brand activations, enables detractors to criticise the event in similar ways, since branding is ubiquitous and many of the activations, food and drink concessions, luxury camping companies and so on found at V Festival are also to be found at other large-scale festivals. However, it is the event's brand-heavy, mainstream and chart-friendly image which gives it its distinctiveness within the marketplace, while its focus on customer service has proved attractive to festivalgoers:

> People criticise it for its corporate image but we feel that this means it is clean, safe and has a huge variety of music performed by the best in the business. And what that means for us, is the difference between attending a festival or not, as we have three teenaged sons and I wouldn't feel happy about taking them to another venue'.
> (Email from Rob about V Festival 2004)

The event attracts relatively few long-term repeat attendees, so the sense of place which was seen at Cambridge Folk Festival does not develop. Nevertheless, V Festival is a leisure resource which is regularly occurring and heavily mediated through print, broadcast and online media; consequently, it has developed a consistent place-image. Critiques of the festival help to reinforce that place-image and identity, and festivalgoers (and non-festivalgoers) are aware of the ethos and style of the event: it is not, therefore, entirely placeless, since 'human meaning' has been given to it, and festivalgoers can be seen to have incorporated it into their lives, even if only for a few years of attendance. For them, Weston Park becomes V Festival for the festival weekend and, as will be seen in Chapter 5, is treated as a real place which can create real and meaningful memories.

Defining 'cyclic place'

The examples of Cambridge Folk Festival and V Festival demonstrate the importance of place to music festivals, and how music festival places may be constructed symbolically and materially on an annual basis to form a relatively stable sense of place. In the process, these events have managed to service a particular musical and audience niche and achieve longevity within the festival market. It is clear that they are co-constructed through the actions, interactions and beliefs of organisers, mediators and attendees, and thus are defined not simply by their functionality, marketing or service offering, but by the communal and personal images, meanings and experiences that have become attached to them. This network of people, place, meaning and image is strong enough to provide a cohesive sense of place, yet loose enough to allow changes to occur over time: these festivals are always recognisably the same, yet always different each time a festivalgoer returns. In addition, these examples demonstrate that there is no need for outdoor popular music festivals to have a poor, strained or antagonistic relationship with their host locations. Hence, McKay's suggestion that 'local opposition, police distrust, and even the odd rural riot' (2000: ix) are key elements of British festival culture would seem to be rather overstated, or at least to relate to events of the past more than to those of the present. Theories of festival spaces which rely on notions of liminality are inadequate for exploring the meanings and forms of the majority of mainstream popular music festivals; yet carnivalesque or liminal behaviours, such as drug use, do still occur at these festivals: hence, festival places retain the potential for such behaviour even if they are not, as a whole, defined by them. Instead, we should interpret contemporary festivals as 'cyclic places' – spaces which are used in an ephemeral yet recurring manner, and which exhibit the narrativisation and social performances of festival culture, thereby allowing a cohesive sense of place to develop over time.

Cyclic places may be conceptualised through the application of four interrelated aspects (see Figure 4.1), which will be discussed in turn. First, a cyclic

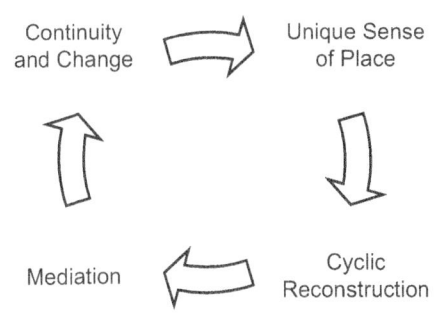

Figure 4.1 Diagrammatic representation of 'cyclic place'
(Source: author)

place is characterised by a unique and consistent sense of place that may be intimately connected to the pre-existing meanings of a host location: the host location is not neutral in this relationship, but part of what makes a festival the place it is. For the mainstream and/or commercial events that make up the majority of outdoor music festivals in the UK, the relationship between the festival and its host location is rarely antagonistic to any great degree. Indeed, local people and authorities may actively support events due to the economic, social and cultural benefits they provide. For instance, festivals may enhance the image of a host location, provide paid work and enterprise opportunities to local people, foster tourist spending and venue profits, or help combat social problems and enhance community integration (Aldskogius, 1993; Derrett, 2003). In accordance with Massey (2005: 9), a festival's sense of place is always 'under construction', yet it also takes on a semblance of stability due to the creation of narratives by organisers, media and audiences: narratives which invest the festival site with meaning. As will be seen in Chapter 5, there may be multiple individual narratives about a festival which intertwine or even conflict with each other, yet, like Foucault's heterotopia, cyclic places are able to encompass many different meanings in one location and time, even though a relatively stable and recognisable place image has been constructed.

The second aspect of a cyclic place is that it does not simply represent a temporary appropriation of *space*, but the annual reconstruction of festival *place*: a place which persists in memory, media and other 'representations of space' (Lefebvre, 1991) throughout the remainder of the year. In material terms, a site is transformed into a festival place on an annual basis through the provision of on-site services, facilities, entertainments, accommodation and design aesthetics: a self-contained village or town emerges in which we find continuity from year to year in terms of layout, contractors, imagery and organisation. This promotes feelings of familiarity for both festival workers and audiences; hence, while a festival may be physically ephemeral, for those few days of its annual existence it is every bit as 'real' as any other place a person might visit on an occasional basis. The cyclic nature of festivals is such that they are reconstructed in their own image by those involved in running and attending them: they are consciously created and recreated in a process which takes note of previous events and of the wider social image and history of festivals. Festivals develop their own histories, behaviours, landmarks, rules and policing that are shaped not only through the production practices of the organisers, but through mediations of the event and through the social performances and communications of audiences both on-site and off-site.

The third element follows on from the above: cyclic places are necessarily mediated in formal and informal ways. With regard to festivals, this includes: official marketing messages, advertising and interactive media such as Instagram, Twitter, Facebook and Youtube; print, online and broadcast media which cover the event as sponsors or reviewers; and internet message boards, blogs, photo galleries and so on created and used by festivalgoers themselves. It is these various forms of mediation which help to broadcast, promote and reinforce the narratives and meanings that allow a relatively stable place image to be constructed, and to be envisioned throughout the rest of the year when an event is not physically present in the landscape. Mediations can also be used to build a sense of excitement and exclusivity prior to an event, to attract new festivalgoers, and to reassure local people, potential attendees and the local authorities about safety, security and service quality. The increase in broadcast, print and online coverage of festivals in the UK not only provides a promotional shop-window for festivals and their performers, but also helps to endorse music festivals as a mainstream leisure activity that can be enjoyed by everyone. Festivals are no longer the preserve of youthful hippies and fans of rock, folk and dance music, but are designed and promoted to meet a much wider range of demographic and psychographic target markets than those seen in the 1970s and 1980s. The mediation of individual festivals also helps to construct stereotypes and expectations that reinforce the unique sense of place of those events and, as will be discussed further in the following chapter, this also serves to influence the attitudes and behaviours of festivalgoers and others towards them.

Finally, cyclic places are characterised not by fixity, but by a combination of continuity and change, since they are constructed from so many different social interactions, mediations and performances. For festivals, this encompasses not only organisers, attendees, musicians, staff and media, but the ongoing influence of local authorities, music industries and music festival histories. As the case studies have suggested above, the annual reconstruction of music festivals is coherent yet fluid, allowing each festival to be recognisably the same each year, yet also different. This helps them to avoid stagnation and to be reactive to changes in legislation and regulation, and to developments in the composition and taste of their audiences. Festival organisers may also be proactive in guiding those changes: for example, by adding new stages, promoting up-and-coming new artists, extending the styles of music they offer, or by improving the overall quality and range of facilities and entertainments provided. The aim is to maintain a sense of familiarity and belonging, while also adding a frisson of difference by providing exciting and novel experiences that have not been offered before.

This depiction of festivals as cyclic places builds on Lefebvre's understanding of place as produced by people (1991: 38–9), and on Massey's notion of the 'event of place' (2005: 139–40). Narratives and understandings of place are constructed over a period of time, so new festivals lack the accumulated histories, stories and meanings which become attached to longer-lived events. They have yet to be incorporated into festivalgoers' lives, and the organisers of new events will need to work much harder to design and market their events in such a way as to create a sense of place that will attract repeat attendance.

Music festivals, Britishness and the rural

The final section of this chapter turns to broader aspects of place in relation to music festivals, and in particular to the cultural politics of sound and music in the context of Britishness and rurality. This is important to consider, since so many festivals are staged in countryside locations, and, as noted earlier, the meanings associated with cyclic places are intimately connected with the host locations in which they develop. Furthermore, earlier chapters have shown how outdoor popular music festivals in rural areas have, in the past, been subject to moral panics regarding the behaviours associated with them and may still be denied a license should nearby residents make objections. The underlying reasons for these objections are explored, as are changing ideas and beliefs about the countryside, to show how both festivals and rural areas have shifted their cultural positioning over the past hundred years.

Leyshon et al. (1995: 424) argue that concerns regarding music, sound and the rural first emerged in the UK in the 1920s and 1930s, when Vaughan Cornish and others attempted to develop an aural aesthetic for town and country planning that categorised sounds as 'in place' or 'out of place': for example, the sound of a radio as acceptable in a city street but intrusive in a country lane. Underlying this was the construction of a moral geography of landscape, nation and citizen, which portrayed 'an idealised rural life' through the use of the pastoral: 'a key set of aesthetic criteria by which certain kinds of sound are judged' (Revill, 2000: 601). Debates over the appropriateness of music (and of popular music in particular) in rural environments have continued, with particular emphasis on outdoor popular music festivals and raves (Sibley, 1994; Worthington, 2004). At their heart, these debates relate to a politics of control. What counts as music and what counts as noise is dependent on power relations that are historically, socially and geographically situated. Definitions of music, sound and noise are, therefore, a locus for power struggles over, for example, ethnicity, nationalism and economic funding. In the context of this book, the power struggles relate to the perceived appropriateness, or otherwise, of particular sounds, musical activities and people within the British countryside and its associated conception of the rural idyll. Four historical moments are important in this regard: the views of the planner-preservationists and others of the early twentieth century; the portrayal of rural England fostered by the BBC during the Second World War; the emergence of countercultural appropriations and understandings in the late 1960s and 1970s; and the development of a post-productivist countryside in the 1990s. These will be discussed in turn.

Planner-preservationists in the early twentieth century

During the early twentieth century, town planners such as Patrick Abercrombie, and preservationists such as the geographer Vaughan Cornish, constructed a picturesque myth of an idealised southern landscape of the

UK (Matless, 1993; 1998). It was a landscape of rolling hills, agricultural land and simple rural lifestyles, characterised by a sense of orderliness, such that urban-associated sounds such as 'the honk of the motor-car, the sound of the gramophone ... do not enter into the chord' (Abercrombie, quoted by Matless, 1998: 69). Such conceptions influenced the development of rural planning, which came to be based on a 'countryside aesthetic' wherein the countryside should be enjoyed 'through solitary and quiet pursuits' (Harrison, 1991: 2). A sharp contrast between rural and urban life can also be seen in a statement made by Cyril Joad of the Council for the Preservation of Rural England in 1937, who stated that: 'the townsman let loose upon the country is from the point of view of utility a liability, and from that of amenity a blight' (cited in Mandler, 1997: 172). This reflects a longer history of conceiving and representing rural and urban life as dichotomous, as qualitatively different (Tönnies, 2001). Such views can be found in local press responses to urban visitors celebrating the summer solstice at the prehistoric monument of Stonehenge in the 1920s and 1930s. Here, the sound of gramophones broadcasting jazz music (the popular music of its time) from the backs of cars and vans came under considerable criticism for 'spoiling' the solstice celebrations (Stout, 2003): an attitude seen again during the 1970s and 1980s when the New Age Travellers and others staged free festivals at or near Stonehenge, and at other rural locations (Hetherington, 2001; Worthington, 2004).

It would seem that, for much of the twentieth century, popular music, and latterly popular music festivals, were deemed inappropriate for rural areas, due in part to the style of the music and in part to the urban masses associated with it. For the planner-preservationists and others who sought to protect the countryside, Britain's rural areas were instead represented by two main spheres of music: the pastoral (for example the orchestral compositions of Vaughan Williams), and traditional folk music (based around the song collections of Cecil Sharp, Francis Child and others). Revill describes the pastoral as setting moral judgements in sound by employing an 'iconology of environmental symbolism' and 'logical aesthetic structures' that mirrored the notion of an ordered landscape (2000: 598). Similarly, folk music was, as discussed in Chapter 1, imbued with notions of preservationism (a kind of ordering) and of moral uplift. Hughes and Stradling (2001) argue that these two spheres, the pastoral and the folk, were promoted as national musics, and as representing Englishness or Britishness – terms which are often conflated (Cloonan, 1997). This sense of Englishness or Britishness is closely associated with the notion of the 'rural idyll', a rather ambiguous and contested concept which has been mobilised in varying ways (Short, 2006: 133). For example, it has been described 'a bucolic vision of an ordered, comforting, peaceful and, above all, deferential past' (Thrift, 1989: 26), and positively associated with adjectives such as uncomplicated, genuine, traditional, and real (Little & Austin, 1996). Furthermore, Bunce (1994; 2003) has argued that an 'armchair countryside' of mass media advertising, television and literature communicates and reinforces such imagery and stereotypes in mainstream British culture. There are also, however, countercultural versions of the rural idyll that are in conflict with the rather conservative and historically normative conceptions noted here, and these will be discussed shortly.

Portrayals of rural England during the Second World War

The views of the early twentieth century planners and preservationists were not widely accepted by the public of the time, or even by many rural landowners (Mandler, 1997); however, as Boyes (1993) has suggested, idyllic imagery and nationalist ideas came to great prominence during the Second World War, as a patriotic mythology of the 'Southcountry' grew. Boyes describes this imaginary vision of southern England's rural landscape as a key symbolic resource for the government and media, and one which was symbolic of the whole of Britain:

> its rolling hills and village greens [reflected] priorities set by nature rather than current events, [and] offered a timeless and indestructible conceptual retreat to those whose uncertain present was bombing raids, the rubble of destroyed cities, factory production lines and foreign battlefields.
> (Boyes, 1993: 181)

Such ideas not only resonated with the views of the preservationists, but also conflated Englishness and Britishness within a broader idealisation of country life: this was a way of life that the armed forces were protecting by going to war with Germany and its allies. Radio programmes such as the BBC's Country Magazine promoted folk music as the sound of this idyllic countryside but, unlike Cecil Sharp and his followers, presented it as a living and breathing culture, rather than a fast-vanishing remnant in need of preservation (Boyes, 1993; Brocken, 2003). The association of folk music with rural England was, therefore, given a considerable boost at a time when the countryside became a key resource in mobilising national identity. This national identity established images and discourses of Englishness which placed rural England at its symbolic heart and were underpinned by notions of stability: of 'unchanging values and practices connecting back to a simpler, purer age', of 'belonging to land and locality', and of 'appreciation and respect of property' (Woods, 2006: 590). It is unsurprising, then, that alternative conceptions of the rural should be seen as a threat to that stability, and lead to conflict over the appropriate use and symbolic value of the countryside, especially as the countercultural youth culture of the late 1960s, which drew in part on the music of the second folk revival, turned toward that countryside in the 1970s.

Countercultural understandings of the rural idyll

Rob Young's *Electric Eden* (2010) charts the development of a 'Romantic yearning for an intense communion with nature' which emerged amongst the youthful counterculture, artists and musicians of the late 1960s and early 1970s. He discusses how bands such as Traffic, Fairport Convention, Incredible String Band, Donovan, Led Zeppelin and many others worked in, or moved to, the countryside to get 'back to the garden' (2010: 7) and incorporated acoustic instruments and stylings into their records. British folk-rock artists in particular sought to 'reconnect with ... [an] imagined vision of pastoral, pre-industrialised Britain', and had 'a desire to return to a mythic past' (Wiseman-Trowse, 2008: 107, 114). This new pastoralism became encoded with mythic, Arcadian and fantastic symbolism, and is epitomised by Marc Bolan's song 'Trelawny Lawn' which appeared on the *Prophets, Seers & Sages, the Angels of the Ages* album of 1968, that included 'references to unicorns, prophets, scribes and messianic lions' (Wiseman-Trowse, 2008: 115). This turn to pre-industrial mythology and pastoralism was also seen in Chapter 1, where the 1971 Glastonbury Fayre was shown to tap into Arthurian legends and alternative New Age belief systems associated with the nearby town of Glastonbury, as well as with the broader landscape of prehistoric monuments in south west England. More broadly, a back-to-the-land movement arose in the early 1970s that saw many people (not just musicians) dropping out of mainstream capitalist society and living what they considered to be a more natural, authentic or self-sufficient life – sometimes communally – in the countryside (Halfacree, 2006; 2009). For these people, the rural was a symbolic and physical resource for envisioning alternative futures and ways of living. As noted in Chapter 1, the free festivals and revivalist fairs of the 1970s and 1980s – and the attitudes and lifestyles that grew around them – were initially the most visible manifestation of this shift to the rural, and their environmental and ecological beliefs have since diffused into mainstream culture and commerce. For instance, it is now common to see organic and wholefood produce in shops, for householders and companies to recycle their waste, and for the environmental sustainability agenda in general to be taken seriously by national governments. However, for much of the 1970s and 1980s, the countercultural conception of the rural was in conflict with the more conservative image of the countryside discussed earlier and gave rise to objections from those who regarded outdoor music festivals as representing unwelcome noise (literally and metaphorically) in an ordered landscape (Cresswell, 1996). The loud music, colourful clothing, muddy fields, drugs, alcohol, sexual freedom and so on offered an alternative vision of the countryside, and one which had popular music (especially rock music) as its primary soundtrack. Moral fears regarding drugs, sex, dirt and disorder were frequently cited in press reports in the 1970s and 1980s (Clarke, 1982), and continued to be mobilised into the 1990s, where they were attributed to outdoor raves and free parties. Unlicensed free parties are still held in rural areas in the twenty-first century, though police and local authorities continue to employ a variety of measures to prevent them or take action against those running them. However, since the mid-1990s, attitudes have changed towards music festivals in rural areas, reflecting changes in the rural economy, conceptions of the rural idyll, and developments in both festival production and the target markets of contemporary events.

Music festivals in a post-productivist countryside

Outdoor music festivals are held in a wide variety of locations, from publicly-owned parklands and recreation grounds to privately-owned racecourses, sportsgrounds, farms and country estates. As the festival sector began to gain popularity in the first decade of the twenty-first century, so the need for new host locations grew. In a parallel development, a new paradigm of post-productivism had been emerging in the countryside which would favour the hosting of music festivals as a way to bolster falling incomes and make alternative use of rural landscapes. Woods (2011) describes productivism as 'a discourse of agricultural organization in which the function of farming was singularly conceived as the production of food and fibre' (2011: 67). In contrast, post-productivism refers to a discourse of diversification driven by, amongst other factors, increased competition, a reduction or withdrawal of state subsidies, and an increase in environmental regulation (Ilbery & Bowler, 1998). For music festival organisers, this new paradigm was welcome, since farmers and other rural land owners were increasingly open to the potential of hosting events, especially as the festival sector has become more mainstream and professional in its management and planning, and more fashionable as a tourist and leisure attraction. Related to this is a change in how the rural idyll is conceived, with Bell (2006: 150) suggesting that it now encompasses three main types: farmscapes (agricultural and pastoral), wildscapes (natural wonders, closeness to nature) and adventurescapes (sports and leisure activities). Music festivals can be characterised as adventurescapes alongside a range of other modern leisure pursuits such as off-road motor sports, paintballing, laser tagging, zorb balling, paragliding and so on. These consumption-based uses of the rural differ markedly from the quiet contemplation and solitary pursuits deemed appropriate by the planner-preservationists of the early twentieth century but have become an important new income stream for rural locations and land owners.

Music festivals are now an important cultural attraction within the British summertime leisure landscape, with a variety of events catering to a multitude of demographic and psychographic markets. Debates regarding the appropriateness of festivals in rural locations will no doubt continue, since the disruption and noise brought by festivals contrasts with classic conceptions of the rural idyll and can be unwelcome for residents living near to festival sites. Yet, as Bell (2006) has noted, and the above sections have suggested, the rural idyll itself has shifted in meaning over time. The stereotypes associated with this changing rural idyll affect how local populations and licensing authorities think about events being held in their locales, and how festival organisers, in turn, must adjust and manage the material organisation and aesthetic design of their events to meet the terms of their licensing agreements. For a festival to build a sense of 'insideness' (Relph, 1976) with its host location, organisers must take account of both the specific needs and meanings of that location, and of the wider landscape in which it is situated.

Conclusion

In this chapter it has been argued that place plays a crucial role in the construction of the social and cultural meanings of music festivals, and that existing theories of festivals as liminal need to be updated in order to take account of the mainstreaming of festival culture in the twenty-first century. Taking inspiration from the spatial conceptions of Lefebvre (1991) and Massey (2005), the notion of 'cyclic place' was introduced, which also draws on insights from humanistic geography and Foucault's concept of heterotopia (1986). Cyclic places are characterised not as the ephemeral use of otherwise neutral space, but as capable of building a sense of belonging and uniqueness, of feeling real for the duration of their existence, and of having a virtual existence in media and memory throughout the remainder of the year. The case studies of Cambridge Folk Festival and V Festival demonstrate how festival sites become the locus for numerous flows of people, ideas and mediations, and how, despite their temporary material existence, festivals can construct relatively consistent place-images that nevertheless embrace developmental change from year to year. This allows returning festivalgoers to build a sense of familiarity, belonging and ownership that aids loyalty, drives repeat attendance, and can help a festival to survive within an increasingly crowded marketplace. The cyclic place of a music festival is influenced by the host location in which it is staged and, in the British context, by the broader landscape, imagery and meaning of the rural idyll – a conceptualisation of the British countryside that has developed over time. Where outdoor music festivals and their attendees were once regarded as a rural irritant transgressing conservative norms and expectations, they are now, in the main, regarded as part of a post-industrial mixed economy, or adventurescape. The commercialisation, professionalisation, regulation and mainstreaming of the festival sector, as discussed in Chapter 2, have served to change how land owners and local populations view the presence of events in their locales, though resistance can still be found towards unlicensed music events, and at times with regard to such issues as noise pollution, traffic congestion and waste. A recurring theme throughout the chapter has been the pivotal role played by attendees, organisers and the media in the development of festivals as cyclic places. The following chapter examines their contributions to the meaning of festival culture, and to the place-image and brand of specific events, with a particular focus on the socialities, behaviours, performances and understandings of festivalgoers, and the ways in which organisers seek to influence them.

5 The social life of music festivals

Audiences and atmosphere

This final chapter addresses the social life of music festivals, and festivalgoers' contribution to the atmosphere, image and cyclic place of outdoor events. It does so from three main perspectives: their motivations, their social interactions and groupings, and their role in creating the festive atmosphere that is characteristic of such events. We also examine how event producers seek to influence festivalgoers through aesthetic and site design, as well as through their creative choices regarding musical programming and other attractions. The first section of the chapter draws on a range of academic literature and fieldwork interviews to examine the motivations of festivalgoers. The discussion is organised around four key themes – freedom, authenticity, belonging and transcendence – which demonstrate how the social interactions, beliefs and behaviours of festivalgoers have transformed in the twenty-first century, while still retaining aspects of the sector's countercultural carnivalesque heritage. The second section discusses and critiques neo-tribal portrayals of social life at festivals, prior to introducing a new concept of 'meta-sociality', which refers to the shared meanings that come to be attributed to cyclically-held events such as music festivals. This meta-sociality is performatively produced (Butler, 1990; 1993) during the course of an event, yet also mediated and sustained beyond the event through traditional and online media. Furthermore, the construction of a relatively stable meta-sociality can aid the longevity of an event by creating a recognisable, sought-after and anticipated atmosphere that will be re-produced and re-performed by attendees each year. In this sense, meta-sociality is a crucial component of a cyclic place as well as an important contributory factor in the ongoing development and perpetuation of social and cultural understandings of music festivals. The final section considers the construction and character of a festival's 'atmosphere' – a somewhat nebulous term that is often referred to by festivalgoers, and which may be influenced by both festival organisers and attendees. This section concludes with a discussion of what has been termed the 'specialness' of music festivals (Getz, 1991; Jago & Shaw, 1998;1999). In essence, this is an extension of the festival 'atmosphere' and implies that music festivals can offer more than simply a leisure experience: that they can represent and embody important emotional meanings and attachments for those who attend them.

Motivations

A number of event management and tourism studies have explored the motivations of attendees at music and arts events, with Getz and Page (2016: 297) suggesting that both generic and event-specific factors are at play. Generic factors include socialising, family togetherness, group identity, entertainment and hedonism, while event-specific factors include the programme, the uniqueness of the event, and the potential for co-creation of the event by attendees. According to Li and Petrick (2006), most studies support the 'seeking – escaping' view of tourist motivation developed by Iso-Ahola (1980; 1983). Here, motivation is regarded as a combination of the need to escape from the everyday environment of life and work, and the need to experience an activity or situation that is personally rewarding in some way or meets social needs such as belonging and interpersonal contact. Pegg and Patterson found that the 'atmosphere [of an event] was repeatedly mentioned' by attendees, but that their motivations were otherwise heterogeneous and influenced by a wide range of factors including 'gender, extent of prior attendance, and level of income' (2010: 96–7). This heterogeneity is echoed by both Nicholson & Pearce (2011) and Perez Falconi (2011), with the latter arguing that it is impossible for an event to be 'articulated or experienced in the same way by any two people or groups' (2011: 5). Nevertheless, it is useful to identify some broad themes, as these can help us to understand the influences acting on festivalgoers, and how motivations change over time.

Drawing on both earlier studies and the author's field research, four such themes are identified: freedom from everyday life; the search for authentic experience; socialisation and its associated sense of belonging; and transcendence of the self. Underpinning all of these is the ongoing effect of the countercultural carnivalesque on popular culture and the mediation of music festivals. This provides a cultural backdrop to contemporary understandings of festivals within both official and unofficial media: a set of stereotypes and images such as notions of liberation and escape, of self-expression, transgression and hedonism, of carnivalesque inversions and of spiritual awakening (Flinn & Frew, 2013). These stereotypes, and others, are demonstrated in the classic festival films discussed in Chapter 1 and through the marketing and promotion of events by organisers and sponsors today. Festival mediations, whether officially produced or created by audiences, play an important part not only in sustaining and transforming the images and ideas that are associated with particular festivals, but also in generating anticipation of, and loyalty to, those events. In tourism studies this is referred to as an event's 'destination image' (Kotler et al., 1993): the subjective beliefs and emotions that come to be associated with an event.

Gunn (1972) introduced a three-step model of destination image, which can be modified to fit contemporary festivals (see also Florek & Insch, 2013). First, there is an organic image created through non-promotional sources such as word-of-mouth conversation and news reports. In the twenty-first century, we can add social media and other online sources to this organic image, though it can sometimes be difficult to tell whether a report, site or commentary is truly independent of the organisers, marketers, broadcasters and sponsors involved in an event. Second, there is an induced image, which Gunn describes as being shaped by officially-sanctioned promotional routes such as advertising campaigns. Finally, there is a modified-induced image which equates to how personal experience of an event may shape our beliefs and understandings of it: in other words, how well the image that is portrayed and built up through the first two steps matches the reality on the ground. We may now add a fourth step to the model, in which attendees upload their experiences of an event to social media; this enhances and modifies the organic image, and yet is filtered through the other steps. This model helps to show how anticipation can be built ahead of an event, and how images, beliefs and understandings created prior to an event can potentially influence those felt while attending. If positive associations are created and experienced, the final two steps can help to reinforce loyalty to an event and to drive repeat attendance. Related to this is Campbell's argument regarding the contemporary consumption of products and services as a form of 'imaginative pleasure-seeking': people want to 'experience in reality the pleasurable dream which they have already enjoyed in imagination' (1987: 89). It is to these pleasurable dreams that the following sections now turn.

Freedom from everyday life

The academic literature on outdoor music festivals and, indeed, on festivals in general (see Falassi, 1987; Ehrenreich, 2006), suggests that they offer a temporary escape from the everyday lives and concerns of their attendees. As discussed in previous chapters, this is often presented as a carnivalesque or anti-structural inversion or transcendence of social norms. For example, Ravenscroft and Gilchrist argue that festivals 'offer a liminality in which people can engage in 'deviant' practices without transgressing their wider social life' (2009: 36). Participation in a festival can, therefore, be cast as an inherently political activity where alternative social ideas and ways of being can be enacted, and perhaps even come to threaten the societal status quo. However, as discussed in the first two chapters, contemporary festivals are typically licensed activities which occur within a commercial framework and, like the carnivals and events discussed by Bakhtin (1984) and Turner (1969; 1982), actually serve to reinforce the dominant social order even as they offer opportunities to critique it. A similar conception is proposed by Caillois who, like Turner, considers festivals and festival-like events to be common to all societies and characterised by a time of 'effervescence and fluidity in which everything that symbolises order in the universe is temporarily abolished so that it can later re-emerge' (Caillois, 2001: 87). His descriptions of the fairground are particularly reminiscent of contemporary music festivals, for they are:

> separated in space by porticoes, hedges, ramps, luminous signs, posts, flags, and all kinds of decorations that are visible from a distance and which demarcate the boundaries of a consecrated universe.
> (Caillois, 2001: 133)

Access to this consecrated universe begins with the separation of attendees from their normal lives through the simple logic of physical distance (Jaimangal-Jones et al., 2010: 256–7), while the fairground (or festival) itself offers what Caillois refers to as the seeds of 'vertigo'. For Caillois 'vertigo' refers to sensations of disorientation or dizziness produced by, for example, the spinning of a fairground ride, but more generally as a temporary disruption to our usual way of understanding and perceiving the world (2001: 133). Analogies can be made to the overturning of social conventions seen in Bakhtin's descriptions of the carnivalesque, and with the overwhelming sensations of sight and sound to be found within a festival site. However, the contemporary music festival market does not necessarily conform to these more extreme forms of sensation. Field research suggests that while some events do indeed offer experiences that at times match these ideas (and these will be discussed in the later section on transcendence of the self), the general feeling is that festivals are an exciting leisure pursuit and lifestyle choice: that they offer a relaxation of the social conventions of the everyday world, but that these conventions are not necessarily inverted. For instance, events allow attendees to forge, experience or renew friendships among like-minded people and family groups/social circles, to express in a public forum their musical preferences and fandom, or simply to enjoy the spectacle and excitement of live performances (all of which are discussed in later sections). Festivals continue to offer an escape from the concerns of the everyday world, but this escape is less political and more social; less an inversion and more a heightening or excess of specific experiences. This focus on personal experience has also been noted in city-based dance music scenes (Thornton, 1995; Malbon, 1999). Ehrenreich has coined the term 'post-festive' to describe these events and scenes, since their radical potential is rather limited in scope (2006: 181). The following quotes illustrate some of these more mundane or post-festive motivations for festival attendance:

> It's a great weekend where you get the chance to see loads of bands, lie about in the sun (hopefully), drink lots, relax and not have to give a monkeys about anything all weekend really.
> (Email from Kate about V Festival 2004)

> Just getting away from work, to relax, just a break away from everything. I had friends who came in the past, so I came along.

It's an excuse for loads of drinking and laying about and not doing anything.
(Interview with Ian about Cambridge Folk Festival 2003)

Turner describes liminoid phenemona, such as music festivals, as offering both 'freedom from' social norms and 'freedom to' generate new ones (1982: 36), but field research typically shows this as relating to forms of excessive consumption. Activities that might be frowned upon in the attendees' everyday world are accepted for the duration of the event: daytime or excessive drinking of alcohol, the relatively open use of illegal substances, dressing up in fancy dress or body paint, or late-night amateur music-making sessions in the campsite. Of course, there are other social occasions when such activities are considered acceptable by their participants, so the binary opposition drawn between everyday life and festival life is somewhat artificial. Yet, festivals remain spatially and temporally demarcated, and are commonly mediated and marketed as special occasions where the normal rules of social life and everyday experience are expected to loosen. However, this utopian dream of festival life will differ from event to event, with some attracting and facilitating greater levels of carnivalesque or liminoid behaviour than others. For instance, there are considerable differences between the hedonistic experience of the Boomtown Fair or the Secret Garden Party (Robinson, 2005a) and the family-friendly experience of Camp Bestival or the Cambridge Folk Festival, even though these events all offer participatory activities and/or spectacular and themed aesthetic design.

The search for authentic experience

The second motivational theme to be considered here is festivalgoers' desire to achieve an authentic experience. In field research conducted during the 2000s by the author it was found that the notion of 'authentic experience' was related, in part, to the stereotypes and concerns of the countercultural rock and folk festivals held in Britain since the late 1960s, and particularly from the mid-1970s to the mid-1990s, when free festivals, green fairs and free parties were regularly staged. These events, discussed in Chapter 1, espoused non-commercial values, concerns for the environment, and the adoption of alternative lifestyles and other non-hegemonic ways of experiencing social and cultural life. Media representations of the New Age Travellers, and of outdoor music festivals more generally, as a hangover from the countercultural sixties were commonplace in the 1980s and 1990s, though increasingly under challenge as commercial promoters such as Mean Fiddler became involved in the sector. During the 1990s, events such as V Festival and Tribal Gathering were deemed 'inauthentic' because of their commercial ownership and use of sponsors. Such views were especially clear in the writings of alternative media magazines like *Squall*, *Red Pepper* and *Urban75*, as well as in academic accounts of the Glastonbury Festivals

(McKay, 2000) and the Stonehenge Free Festival (Worthington, 2004). The lack of authenticity ascribed to such events extended beyond their economic organisation and ownership to encompass their on-site management and social atmosphere: authentic events were deemed to be necessarily anarchic, to involve the minimum of commercial or state intervention, and to be utopian sites of carnivalesque freedom. In comparison, commercial events were regarded in negative terms as professionalised, controlled and surveilled: as commodified forms of experience that failed to offer the transcendence and autonomy of 'true' festival. As discussed in Chapter 2, outdoor music festivals have, since the mid-1990s, been licensed by local authorities and subject to a high degree of state regulation in many areas. Licensing applications require the active participation and support of local emergency services and, whether commercial or charitable, contemporary festivals are often reliant on the financial support of sponsors and the media to garner publicity and encourage economic success. In this, they are indebted to the pioneering events of the eighteenth and nineteenth centuries, which were managed by volunteers, municipal authorities and entrepreneurs in much the same way. Nevertheless, the meanings and expectations associated with the countercultural carnivalesque history of British music festivals remain important to the stereotyping of contemporary events and are frequently taken into account by festival organisers when establishing, managing and marketing their events (Anderton, 2008; 2011). This helps festival organisers to promote a sense of authenticity through historical continuity and allusion to a collective and mediatised memory of a 'golden age' of hippie festivals and outdoor raves.

In Chapter 3 it was argued that the expansion, commercialisation and market differentiation of music festivals had largely led to the acceptance of commercial brand sponsorships by both organisers and festivalgoers in the post-millennial era. This argument may be extended further to suggest that many festivalgoers now expect outdoor commercial events to be professionally managed, safe and secure environments. Our understanding of authenticity needs to reflect the changes in the market, and three often interrelated forms have been identified. The first concerns the authenticity and excitement of seeing musicians performing live; the second to various notions of independence; and the third to 'hedonic consumption' (Hirschman & Holbrook, 1982). The following quotes illustrate the importance of live performance to festivalgoers:

> I found the alternative music in here [a 'new bands' tent] really great and it's brill to see a band up close in this environment. We saw quite a few bands we'd never heard of, and who we are now dedicated followers of. The Saturday night I crammed in 9 bands, spending no more than 20 minutes at each. I ran from one side of the site to the other. There were too many bands and not enough time.
> (Email from Hayley about V Festival 2004).

> What I like about this festival is there's lots of people that I want to see on that I don't actually have most of the music being played. It gets me into different things by being here. I've bought a few albums already by people I haven't got anything by at all.
> (Interview with Terry at Cambridge Folk Festival 2003)

> I'm open to a lot of music, but there's one particular genre of American music I really like and two of the artists that I like are appearing in Britain for the first time this weekend.... I have to say that I'm act driven rather than festival driven ... it really does depend on who's playing.
> (Interview with Mike at Cambridge Folk Festival 2003)

Festivals offer attendees a highly cost-effective way to see many bands in a short space of time: a form of excessive consumption which differs from event to event. For instance, Gelder and Robinson's survey of festivalgoers found that 49.2 per cent of responses about the V Festival mentioned the artists performing at the event, while responses about Glastonbury Festival saw a much lower score of 12.9 per cent (2009: 189). This points to the differing ways that events seek to position themselves in the marketplace and is echoed in the words of author and DJ Andrew Collins, who said of the Reading Festival: 'it lacks [the] ley-lines and healing fields and men on stilts [of Glastonbury Festival], but that merely concentrates the mind. It's all about the music. It has to be. It doesn't have anything else to offer' (cited in Carroll, 2007: 102). This is perhaps a rather extreme view, as the social interactions of festivalgoers and the overall atmosphere of a site are also important to attendance (see later sections); nevertheless, the quotes above show how physical proximity to artists performing live is often valued by festivalgoers, as is the opportunity to see and hear music that is new to them (Faulkner et al., 1999; Bowen & Daniels, 2005; Henderson & Wood, 2009). A sense of novelty is important to the continued success of festivals, as the composition of the programme from year to year is one of the key elements in the formation of a cyclic place: while the site may remain largely the same in its layout from year to year, the musical programme offers a sense of freshness and difference. The intangibility of live performance is also important to a feeling of authenticity: of being there while a unique performance takes place. Laing has suggested that at festivals 'the key thing is to be present at the event ... not necessarily to see or experience a particular act. The latter is the motivation to attend a concert' (2004: 7). However, the expansion of one-day and non-camping events over the past twenty years indicates a shift towards concert-style festival experiences and, as the quotes above suggested, festivalgoers who attend camping events may also be primarily 'act driven'. Furthermore, niche genre events allow a mix of the two motivations, since groups of fans can congregate to see and hear their favourite artists and celebrate their fandom and music taste among like-minded others. The staging of individual performances has also developed markedly since the 1970s, with festival headliners at major festivals now using spectacular stage shows that are comparable with their arena tours: the hard rock band AC/DC even brought a bespoke stage to the Download Festival in 2010, which was erected alongside the event's usual main stage. These stage shows create a 'must see' motivation and enhance feelings of uniqueness.

A second source of authenticity is the notion of independence, which can be explored in relation to the organisational base of an event and should be distinguished from 'indie' as a musical genre (Hesmondhalgh, 1999; Cummings, 2008). According to the Association of Independent Festivals, a festival may be classed as independent if its operating company does not account for more than 5 per cent of the global turnover of the live music industry, and the festival is not more than 50 per cent owned by such a company (Webster, 2014). As seen in Chapter 3, festivals which embrace an affirmative approach to corporate brand sponsorship are often operated by or related to major national and international companies. They may be regarded as inauthentic since they contradict the anti-establishment and utopian community ideals that have previously been ascribed to outdoor rock, pop and dance music festivals in Britain, or are deemed to be overly profit-centred, as shown in the following quote from a Cambridge Folk Festival attendee:

> I'm way beyond Reading, V, T in the Park, anything that Mean Fiddler Org [now Festival Republic] has its grubby hands on ... where the whole mentality is to pack as many people into a field, feed them burgers and chips (at a price!), sell them crap lager, and make as much money as possible.
> (Email from Paul about Cambridge Folk Festival 2004)

In contrast, independent events which adopt policies of sponsorship avoidance or acceptance, rather than affirmation, may be seen as more authentic because they either eschew the overtly commercial approach altogether, or make sponsorship and other choices that are congruent with the beliefs of their target audiences. For instance, they can ensure that the food, drink and retail concessions they work with are ethically sound or locally sourced, and they can find various ways for the local population to become involved in the management and operations of their events. An example of the former is the Shambala Festival which promotes environmental causes and sustainable living, and of the latter is the Cropredy Festival where local residents run 'fringe' live events in the local pubs, and organise car boot sales, pop-up breakfast concessions and other activities in and around the village (Anderton, 2016). As one festivalgoer stated:

> The village is lovely and they [the villagers] help make the festival. They get in on the act with breakfast and there's something magical about that. I remember from the first time that you felt welcome, that the festival was

not imposing on them. The festival is enhanced by the village, it's one of the key things in making it what it is.

(Email from Alex about Cropredy Festival 2004)

This interaction creates a feeling of symbiosis: in some sense the festival becomes the village and vice versa during the festival weekend each year. Small boutique festivals may also involve festivalgoers in the co-creation of participatory spaces within their grounds and will often commission artworks to enliven their sites (Robinson, 2015a; 2015b). Such activities help to bring the event, location and audience together, and to provide the festival with a sense of uniqueness in the minds of festivalgoers. This uniqueness, and the active involvement of local people and audiences in the running of an event, helps to reinforce a sense of authenticity that may aid repeat attendance and the overall longevity of the event.

The types of authenticity discussed above differ markedly from the final form to be considered here: hedonic consumption. This term refers to 'those facets of consumer behaviour that relate to the multi-sensory, fantasy and emotive aspects of one's experience with products' (Hirschman & Holbrook, 1982: 92): in other words, consumers seek absorbing experiences that arouse the emotions, trigger memories and stimulate physical reactions (Santoro & Troilo, 2007: 110). Hedonic consumption is primarily 'pleasurable, or expected to be', which drives attention away from utilitarian motivations and concerns, such as value for money, and towards a range of other factors from which people derive pleasure (Alba & Williams, 2013: 4). Examples include aesthetics and design, the interaction between attendees, festival staff and other festivalgoers, the experience of 'flow' states (see the next section), and the creation of memories that can be savoured and revisited later (ibid.). Campbell's concept of 'imaginative hedonism' (1987: 203) is similar in that it places importance on anticipation and expectation, though he also argues that the reality of the experience is never likely to match up with the anticipation: gratification will inevitably lead to disillusionment and a search for new ways to satisfy longing and desire (ibid.). This logic underpins Ritzer's description of 'cathedrals of consumption' (1999): spectacularly themed settings such as Disneyland, Las Vegas casinos, and Canada's West Edmonton Mall or, at a smaller scale, the scripted customer service encounters and décor of themed restaurants such as the Hard Rock Café. Ritzer argues, after Baudrillard (1983), that these spectacular sites are 'simulated settings' in which the distinction between the real and the imaginary has eroded to such an extent that the sites' authenticity or fakeness has become irrelevant (Ritzer, 1999: 144). Furthermore, he suggests that people are perhaps more comfortable with the simulation than they are with the real.

Applying these ideas to outdoor music festivals, we can regard the contemporary commercial sector as a site of spectacular consumption, where festivalgoers consume the sensory pleasure of the music and light shows, the aesthetic design of the stages and on-site art installations, the food, drink and retail opportunities of the markets, and the social interactions with, and spectacle of, other festivalgoers. The presence of these elements, and the pleasures involved in experiencing them, can be viewed as a postmodern form of authenticity, because this is what festivalgoers are expecting from their commercially-managed festival experience. Commercial sponsors have understood this too, so larger events now feature 'branded retail environments' (Carah, 2010: 8) provided by companies that are well-known to those attending: a form of event marketing which engages festivalgoers not only on-site but through advertising campaigns and social media both before and after an event. This serves to embed these brands organically within a peer network of festivalgoers: to become part of their mediated social lives online (ibid.: 58). In recent years, this has been extended by the introduction of radio-frequency identification (RFID) wristbands that can be synchronised with social media applications: when festivalgoers enter different parts of a festival arena, their online profiles are automatically updated with 'check-in' messages that can be viewed by their followers.

Ehrenreich argues that the spectacular environment of the contemporary festival does not demand creativity from festivalgoers, that it offers an 'inherently more limited experience than a participatory event' (2006: 206), yet social media, wireless connectivity and brand activations now play an important role in creating and enhancing new forms of participation. For instance, festivalgoers can now live stream their experiences while on-site and interact with organisers and brands through bespoke applications available on smartphones and tablets. These activities are carried out using commercial products and services, and are ultimately aimed at supporting corporate aims and objectives, so 'traditional' festivalgoers may regard them less as a form of authentic and democratised participation, and more as the further commercialisation and commodification of the festival experience. Nevertheless, for those festivalgoers who engage in hedonic consumption, the 'real' or authentic experience of a festival derives from its ability to live up to their expectations: expectations that have been created through various forms of media and marketing, as well as through word-of-mouth accounts from friends or internet message boards and blogs. They are motivated by a desire to experience the spectacular designs and shows, to be emotionally and/or bodily moved by the music, to see novel or unusual people and artworks, and to do so within an exciting, festive atmosphere. If a festival meets their expectations, it can be perceived as authentic, even though it is provided and guided by commercial profit-seeking organisations.

Socialising and a sense of belonging

Outdoor music festivals offer festivalgoers the opportunity to attend with, or meet up with, both family members and friends in a largely relaxed, yet out-of-the-ordinary, atmosphere: it is a time to renew and reaffirm the strength and importance of social relationships, and studies have consistently found that family togetherness and peer group socialising are significant motivations for attendance (Wilks, 2011; Tjora, 2016). This is further supported by the following:

> You always end up making friends with people you camp next to or just chatting to people you meet. Most people seem to be really friendly.
> (Email from Sophie about V Festival 2004)

> I first went when I was only eleven years old but I met the people I went with this year at sixth form college and have known them for four years but hadn't seen or spoken to most for at least two years. I heard from one of them that he was going and knew that the others may be going so I texted a few people and we agreed to meet up. I enjoy meeting up with them but during the day I go and do what I want and see whoever I want. It's nice to be able to socialise with a large group once the music has finished.
> (Email from Emma about Cambridge Folk Festival 2004)

> Although I go primarily for the music and would still go if there was nobody there I knew, the social side has been a great added extra that has grown over the years. We have a loose band of friends that come most years ... there are loads I see only at the fest.
> (Email from Eddie about Cropredy Festival 2004)

Music festivals may also foster a strong sense of belonging amongst attendees, which relies not simply on the co-presence of festivalgoers and their socialisations, but on inculcating feelings of safety, security and homeliness: on festivalgoers adopting the site and event as 'theirs'. This characterisation fits Relph's definition of an 'authentic sense of place', wherein a person has a feeling of 'being inside and belonging to *your* place both as an individual and as a member of a community', and of feeling this without the need to reflect on it (1976: 65). This sense of socialisation, place and belonging is characteristic of events which attract regular attendees. For instance, as noted in Chapter 4, regular visitors to the Cambridge Folk Festival often have 'their' part of the campsite, or arrange to camp with the same groups of friends and families each year. Similarly, at the Cropredy Festival:

> A lot of people who go have been going for a number of years from an early age and have grown up there. They in turn have started bringing their kids along and so are used to looking after children and so look out for others as well.
> (Email from Thomas about Cropredy Festival 2004)

This generational sense of belonging can be found at many family-friendly festivals (such as Blissfields, Larmer Tree Festival or Camp Bestival), with children being introduced to festival culture from an early age and later attending either the same event or similar events on their own or with their own groups of friends. Over time, some festivals may become so intensely associated with a family or group of friends that attendance becomes an annual pilgrimage and, in a sense, the event and site come to 'belong' to them. This sense of belonging is harder to find at festivals like V Festival, since events of this kind attract relatively few long-term repeat attendees; nevertheless, the social experience of being around like-minded others is a strong driver for creating a temporary sense of belonging and sociality during a festival weekend.

A strong sense of belonging may also develop at events which attract specific audience demographics such as genre enthusiasts (Dowd et al., 2004; Bennett, 2013). For instance, individuals and groups may attend an event in order to celebrate their fandom – to publicly affirm their fan identity or genre interests in the supportive atmosphere and presence of like-minded others; they may otherwise be unable to do so publicly, as music fandom is often regarded in somewhat negative terms (Jensen, 1992). Public affirmation may simply entail their presence at the event, or it may involve a more overt display: chatting to others about the object of their fandom; wearing festival or artist merchandise; or singing and dancing to their favourite songs. Festivals are also a good opportunity for fan clubs, which might have members scattered across the globe, to meet in person. An example is the TalkAwhile discussion group, which offers an online meeting-place for Fairport Convention and Cropredy Festival fans, and which, in the mid-2000s, had a dress code (a fez for men, and a tiara for women) to allow otherwise anonymous members to meet each other on-site (Anderton, 2007: 219). Fairport Convention, who also organise the event, have even been known to contribute to the group's message board, and past and current members can often be found mingling with festivalgoers at the festival bar: in these ways the event promotes the spatial expression of a pre-existing but virtual sense of belonging, and associates that belonging with the festival site and the band:

> We never set ourselves apart from the punters, never ignored what the fans say. When we walk around the field at Cropredy, we see so many people we recognise. Those we don't know by name, you know by sight. And it's great to see them bringing their friends and families too.
> (Simon Nicol, singer and guitarist of Fairport Convention, cited in Schofield, 2002: 3)

> I've got cousins in Canada, don't know their names, don't know what they look like, but if my Gran said they can stay at mine when they're in Edinburgh, they'd be welcome, I think I'm that to Fairport. They don't know me, but I'm welcome [at the Cropredy Festival]. I'm part of the family. They just haven't met me.
> (Email from Alex about Cropredy Festival 2004)

Transcendence of the self

A final motivation identified through my field research relates to Turner's (1982) concept of *communitas*, which he depicts as an intense feeling of spiritual intimacy and comradeship. Drawing on Csikszentmihalyi (1974; 1975), Turner argues that *communitas* involves the integration of awareness and action into a 'flow' state, where individual consciousness is narrowed and intensified into a limited bodily and sensory sphere: a complete immersion of the self into a group with no goal other than the experience of *communitas* itself (1982: 56–8). There are parallels here with Maslow's notion of 'peak experience', which involves the 'free, uninhibited, uncontrolled, trusting, unpremeditated expression of the self' (1999: 218). For Maslow, these moments of peak experience are 'self-validating' and 'self-justifying' and may change a person's view of themselves or of others (ibid.: 104). Furthermore, 'the person is more apt to feel that life in general is worthwhile, even if it is usually drab, pedestrian, painful or ungratifying... that is, life itself is validated' (ibid.: 110). Nakamura & Csikszentmihalyi concur, arguing that people can find meaning through immersive involvement, or 'vital engagement' with an activity (2003). However, these peak experiences, vital engagements or flow experiences are not felt continually through a festival event, and their intensity may vary. Such experiences are influenced by the actions of the performers on stage and by their ability to engage an audience (Jennings, 2010), as well as by the rhythm of the festival day and the activities available to, or created by, festivalgoers themselves:

> My best mate and I wanted to go and see the final band of the weekend in the JJB/Puma stage, but it was packed and they wouldn't let us in. So we decided not to be miserable like all the people around us just because we didn't get in so we went up the side of the tent where we could hear it best and danced the night away with our whistles and glow sticks. In the end we must have managed to get about another 50 people to do the same! Magic!
>
> (Email from Sophie about V Festival 2004)

Peak experiences are perhaps most likely to be found during the evening sets of a festival, when the arena in front of the stages becomes increasingly crowded with attendees, and the senses become more highly focused on the sights and sounds of the performances. Feelings of togetherness and *communitas* may be engendered at these times, though there is no guarantee of this, nor that each attendee will achieve a peak experience as a result. Nevertheless, the potential exists for festivalgoers to transcend the self through peak experience or feelings of *communitas*, and festivals are organised in such a way that transcendence of the self may be achieved in other ways too. For instance, attendees may become involved in participatory activities or feel free to perform alternative identities that might not otherwise be open to them: to be carnivalesque or anti-structural in their behaviours and dress, or to gain pleasure from watching the carnivalesque spectacle of others (Jaimangal-Jones et al., 2015; Robinson, 2015a). Several festivals, such as Bestival, publicise fancy dress themes for their events, or host fancy dress stalls on their sites. This might be seen as an opportunity for festivalgoers to participate and be creative, or as a further commercialisation of what might otherwise be regarded as a carnivalesque activity. It also feeds into carnivalesque representations of these events through photographs published in both print and online media.

The likelihood of a truly festival-wide or constant experience of *communitas* would seem rather limited, though it may be sporadically felt by different people, or groups of people, at various times. The experiences and behaviours of contemporary festivalgoers are highly heterogeneous: unlike Turner's tribal societies (1969), music festivals are characterised by a wide range of activities, diversions and spectacles which are available at various times and in different parts of a festival site. In addition, an audience's responses to the musical programme and other attractions cannot be reduced to a singular and homogeneous experience, since tastes and preferences are highly subjective: one person may find a performance exhilarating, while another might find the same performance banal or simply uninteresting (Tjora, 2016: 76); some listen attentively, while others are easily distracted; some spend all their time wandering between the stages and other attractions, while others establish a semi-permanent camp of chairs and belongings in the arena fields; and some spend the majority of their time propping up the festival bar, while others head for the stage barriers to dance, to mosh and to get closer to the performers.

An alternative way to understand the festival experience is provided by Barthes' distinction between *plaisir* and *jouissance*. He sets out these dichotomous forms of reception and enjoyment in relation to literature and music (1975, 1977), but his ideas can be extended to the music festival experience. His depiction of *jouissance* is reminiscent of the flow states and peak experiences described by Csikszentmihalyi (1975) and Maslow (1999), for he writes of *jouissance* as a non-rational and almost uncontrollable joy or ecstasy accomplished through the body; an experience that lies beyond the ability of language to express adequately. It involves the intensification or heightening of experience most often seen amongst music fans listening to their favourite artists and songs; yet it might also characterise the feelings of those people who love to be part of the crowd, or like to actively and unreflexively participate in singing, dancing or moshing alongside others (Cummings & Herborn, 2015). Barthes contrasts *jouissance* with *plaisir*, which he regards as the pleasure of mental stimulation in cultural pursuits; as gratification and enjoyment that may be felt and described without a loss of self. This is probably the more common experience at greenfield music festivals, as listening practices are often inattentive, distracted or secondary to the social activities of the audience (Gillespie, 1987). In such instances, the musical performances are simply a backdrop, rather than something that is actively engaged with. Furthermore, even for the most committed of fans, a state of *jouissance* cannot realistically be maintained for the duration of an event (even with the assistance of legal or illegal substances). Yet, when it does occur, the festival is felt to 'take off', to become special and memorable to the festivalgoers concerned, and the anticipation and fulfilment of this feeling of *jouissance* may be an important driver for attendance.

Sociality

The previous section discussed how outdoor music festivals attract a range of people with multiple motivations and multiple overlaps in terms of their social relations. Some of the latter are relatively stable, such as families, pre-existing friendship groups and fan-based collectives; others are more cyclical in nature: for example, where festivalgoers meet up with particular people on-site each year but have little or no contact with them through the remainder of the year; still more are ephemeral: making the acquaintance of neighbouring campers and people in queues, or simply the chance encounters and co-presences of the arena crowds. The sheer scale and diversity of on-site interactions and activities makes generalisations about the social life of festivals difficult, though it may be possible to characterise some events using scene theory or the concept of the neo-tribe. Scenes may be described as 'situations where performers, support facilities, and fans come together to collectively create music for their own enjoyment' (Peterson & Bennett, 2004: 3). The concept is similar to that of subcultural theory, but there is no presumption of deviance from a hegemonic norm, nor any assumption that participants of a scene will share and enact the same beliefs, dress codes and behaviours in all aspects of their lives. Instead, they can 'put on and take off' the scene identity at will (ibid.). If we are to view outdoor music festivals in terms of scene theory, there must be a pre-existing and relatively coherent fan base for a band or musical style that can make use of a festival site to celebrate their fandom. Where this happens, festivals may be described as focal points for translocal scenes to congregate 'with little concern for the expectations of others' (ibid.: 10). Examples of such genre-specific events include Download and Bloodstock (heavy metal), Maverick (Americana), and ArcTanGent (math-rock and post-rock). There are also artist-curated events such as those staged by Fairport Convention (Cropredy Festival) and The Levellers (Beautiful Days), which attract devoted fans of those bands, as well as numerous hybrid events organised around specific pastimes or hobbies, such as the Bug Jam, an event dedicated to vintage Volkswagen car enthusiasts, but which also features several live music stages. However, there are many music festivals which are not genre-specific or hobby-led, and which attract a much broader range of music enthusiasts and attendees. One way to conceptualise this is to think of festivals as gathering places for different groups of people: to see them as a gathering of the tribes, as is claimed of the Glastonbury Festival and the many psy-trance events held globally each year (McKay, 2000; St John, 2009). We will review and critique the notion of neo-tribal sociality in the following section, prior to introducing the new concept of 'meta-sociality' which is a better fit for understanding the sociality of contemporary music festival audiences.

Neo-tribal sociality

Maffesoli argues that previously stable social categories such as class, locality and gender have been replaced by numerous neo-tribal groups characterised by fluidity, temporality and instability: 'it is less a question of belonging to a gang, a family or a community than of switching from one group to another' (1996: 76). He discusses these neo-tribal groups in relation to sports clubs, hobby groups, lobbyists and a range of other lifestyle and leisure activities that cater to a human need for social solidarity: a sense of belonging that has been lost in an ever more fragmented post-modern social world. Individuals may be members of several groups at once and may join or leave with impunity, for membership of these groups is elective rather than a social obligation. In addition, people will perform different roles and identities in different neo-tribal settings, since each grouping will have its own accepted ways of behaving and dressing, and its own sets of values and ideals. These neo-tribes may have a charismatic leader or guru at their heart or exist without any form of centrality: a network of social relations which is 'no longer structured around a single pole' (ibid.: 84–5). Hetherington's description of the 'bund' (1994; 1998b), which draws on the work of the sociologist Schmalenbach (1977), is very similar to Maffesoli's characterisation of the neo-tribe. The bund involves the socio-cultural identification of individuals with like-minded others, a conscious choice to participate (referred to as 'elective affinity'), and a search for emotional solidarity which is expressed 'through their elective and affectual commitment to the people and core values of the group' (Hetherington, 1998b: 93). Like Maffesoli, Hetherington argues that there is no need for a charismatic leader, or any other form of religious or transcendental loyalty, to hold a group together. Instead, the emotional solidarity of the group is forged and maintained by the active and reflexive monitoring of social behaviours by members of the group itself (ibid.: 93).

These neo-tribal, or affinity group, concepts may be useful for our understanding of contemporary music festivals; indeed, Hetherington has previously described the New Age Travellers and their festivals in these terms (1998a; 1998b; 2001). He has also stressed the importance of spatial practices to the construction of neo-tribes, arguing that specific sites 'can take on a symbolic significance around which identities are constituted and performed' (1998b: 106). His focus on the transgressive identities of the Travellers leads him to characterise festival sites as liminal, yet, as discussed in Chapter 4, contemporary commercial events are often staged in locations that are well integrated with mainstream society. Hetherington's analysis can be extended to argue that expressive identities and socialities do not require liminal sites; that they can gain identification from any space or place with which they have developed a sense of familiarity and belonging. This is not only the case for elective neo-tribal groupings, but also for more traditional family and friendship groups. Hence, while contemporary festival sites may be reminiscent of Maffesoli's description of neo-tribes 'as a "multitude of villages" which intersect, oppose each other, help each other, all the while remaining themselves' (1996: 139), they are more often comprised of small collectives of friends and families, rather than broader neo-tribal groupings. This is particularly the case for larger festivals, where numerous groups of people have proximity to, and interaction with, each other, but it may also be true of smaller, genre-specific and artist-specific events. Furthermore, outdoor music festivals are characterised by the creation of new friendships and temporary acquaintances rather than simply the renewal of pre-existing ones, which makes the nature of the social relations found within a festival site rather fluid and variable. Nevertheless, festivalgoers tend to share broad beliefs about the nature of the events that they are attending, which brings us to the concept of meta-sociality.

Meta-sociality

Chapter 4 used Lefebvre's (1991) ideas about the production of space to describe outdoor music festivals as cyclic places. Crucial to this productive work is the way that festivalgoers behave (spatial practices) and think (spaces of representation) about a festival, and how mental images of the event as a whole (representations of space) help to guide their on-site behaviours. Taken together, these construct not only a sense of place, but also a feeling of 'meta-sociality': an overarching and loosely-shared sense of togetherness that is related to the festival's event image but may not be characterised as either neo-tribal or bund-like in form. This all-encompassing meta-sociality is co-created by festival organisers and attendees and will be influenced by their actions and interactions while on- and off-site, and by the mediation of festivals through traditional and online media.

An event's meta-sociality is a key part of its unique social atmosphere (the subject of the section which follows), since it helps to communicate its symbolic meanings and behavioural norms through, for instance, the use of language and bodily performances such as listening, dancing, watching, socialising, shopping, conflict resolution and accepted standards of dress and conduct. Some of these may be performances in the sense suggested by Goffman (1956; 1963; 1967): intentional and conscious acts made by individuals performing the 'role' of festivalgoer. One example is the purchase of a merchandising product such as a festival t-shirt to demonstrate commitment to an event, or the wearing of a previous year's t-shirt in order to express repeat attendance: a kind of social distinction. Similarly, some festivalgoers might dress in unusual or eccentric clothing, engage in illicit activities such as drug use, or spend the majority of their time at the stage barriers in order to play out a particular conception of festival culture or to demonstrate their enthusiasm and fandom. This dramaturgical conception of performance suggests not only that active social agents enact 'masks' or 'roles', but that personal identity must exist prior to performance (Gregson & Rose, 2000: 433). An alternative view is that of Butler (1990; 1993), who argues that identity does not pre-exist performance but is produced through it: identity is not who people are, but what they do. Central to Butler's view of performativity is citation and repetition, with identity being produced through the unconscious enactment (citation) of existing discourses and norms of behavior. This embodied knowledge may be performatively enacted without festivalgoers being able to explicitly justify or articulate why they are doing it (O'Grady & Kill, 2013). Relevant discourses include the stereotyping of outdoor music festivals as levelling social hierarchies and divisions, of tolerating excessive drinking and recreational drug use, and accepting lowered standards of personal hygiene, all of which are strongly associated with the countercultural carnivalesque. There are also behavioural norms that vary from festival to festival and within different parts of a festival site. For instance, you can find a closely attentive and supportive form of listening within the Club Tent of the Cambridge Folk Festival (related to the typical atmosphere and behavior of a folk club), but can also find sporadic outbreaks of dancing, cheering and shouting at the Main Stage (which has a style more akin to a pop or rock concert). Likewise, at rock and heavy metal events a 'mosh pit' may form spontaneously directly in front of a stage, and it is not uncommon for projectiles to be thrown at artists who do not meet the expectations of the audience: behaviours which are not seen at folk music events. Butler argues that the citational practices of performativity are never exactly duplicated, since there is always room for 'slippage' within them and for changes to occur during their reproduction (Gregson & Rose, 2000: 441). Performativity is therefore an ongoing social process that is 'fundamentally specific to the context in which it is sited' (Dewsbury, 2000: 475) and will change over time.

Social norms regarding acceptable behaviour may be subject to developmental change, yet their repetition and citation allows a form of stability to emerge at cyclical events where those norms are restated each year. The social stability that this offers, in particular to longer-running events, means that organisers can allow festivalgoers considerable scope to self-regulate their own behaviours, rather than relying on strong policing or stewarding tactics. Interestingly, new events quickly develop their own social rhythms and behavioural norms, based in part on the citation of performative modes brought to an event through broader cultural understandings and expectations of festivals, and by the prior experience of festivalgoers at other events (Tjora, 2016). This is also influenced by event organisers who adopt a variety of strategies to discourage attitudes and behaviours that they deem inappropriate to the success of their event, and to encourage behaviours that they view more positively. For example, organisers work closely with local police and security companies to exclude festivalgoers who might behave in an anti-social way, and larger festivals have a strong police presence at their site entrances to prevent drug-dealers and other potentially disruptive people from entering. Marketing and media communications are used to attract key target markets who will 'fit' the intended ethos of the event, and to reassure potential attendees about the nature of the festival – whether it is, for example, family-friendly, youth-oriented or hedonistic in style. This means that each event tends to attract a like-minded audience: people with similar musical interests and reasons for attendance, and who have similar demographic characteristics. Attendees' cultural frames of reference are therefore alike, and the behavioural norms of the event become closely related to the pre-existing and broadly shared socio-cultural values of the audience. This allows new attendees, or at least those with similar backgrounds, to 'fit in' with the existing social atmosphere of an event and to conform readily to the behavioural norms that have been established in previous years. This is also aided by discursive processes of place- and event-image formation: for instance, festivalgoers may discuss an event with friends and family members, or interact with others via fan clubs, message boards and Internet sites (Hudson et al., 2015; Morey et al., 2014), while broadcast and print media communicate and reinforce marketing messages and broader understandings of an event's cultural positioning.

On the basis of the above discussions, we can see that festivals are comprised of multiple encounters, friendships, family groups and so on, that interlock within a single location. They have a wide variety of motivations and the different groups remain largely anonymous to each other. Yet, because they draw on shared frames of reference and performatively construct the accepted social norms and behaviours of an event, a loose meta-sociality can emerge. In some ways this is analogous to an interpretative community, a concept originally developed in relation to television audiences, which describes 'relatively anonymous groups of people who interpret particular mediated materials with shared enthusiasm or a common viewpoint' (Lull, 2000: 242). In the festival context we see the development of a shared social imaginary which allows an event to be annually reconstructed in its own social image while still allowing for many different groupings to be present within a single site. This meta-sociality gradually becomes more cohesive over time and with repeated citation (whether in situ or through mediations), such that the acceptable range of actions, behaviours and meanings of an event becomes both normalised and associated with particular places. The 'generalised charisma' that Hetherington (1998b: 93) refers to as holding together elective social groups is even more diffuse under this conception of meta-sociality, as it refers to a shared sensibility that is communicated not only through face-to-face interactions, but through broader mediations. It is akin to the 'subtle and nebulous' sense of place that Relph (1976: 48) writes about: a 'spirit' that, together with the physical setting, activities and meanings of a site and event, constructs a unique and identifiable festival place and atmosphere.

Atmosphere

The 'atmosphere' of a music festival is consistently mentioned by festivalgoers as a key ingredient of a successful festival experience, as well as an important driver for attendance (Gelder & Robinson, 2009; Pegg & Patterson, 2010). This atmosphere differs from event to event and is affected by a very wide range of factors: from the natural and built environment to the programme and services on offer, and from the specific demographic make-up of the audience to the symbolism and imagery with which the festival is promoted, mediated or associated (Nelson, 2009). Some festivals foster an atmosphere of carnivalesque excess, while others offer a family-friendly weekend break. Many offer a level of service which far outstrips that available at festivals prior to the turn of the millennium, with pre-erected tents and luxury camping options, high quality toilet facilities and showers, gourmet food and drink, and a huge range of activities and spectacles. In comparison to events of the past, music festivals of the twenty-first century can now be described as gentrified (Davies, 2005): a term that, in urban studies, implies the renewal and replacement of formerly lower-class city centres by affluent middle class newcomers and the businesses that cater to their interests and needs. This was crystallised by Melvin Benn of Festival Republic, who likened the Latitude Festival to a broadsheet Sunday newspaper supplement because it offers music, theatre, comedy, film, dance and literature (Hudson & Hudson, 2013: 215). As Bloustein notes, festivals are 'implicitly classed, aged and gendered' (2004: 135), and this reflects both the interests and demographics of an event's attendees and the cultural positioning of the event by the festival organiser. It is therefore important to consider the construction of a festival's atmosphere through the actions of event producers (event production), and through the activities and behaviours of festivalgoers (event consumption). The following two sections begin the process of addressing these two areas of study, though concerted research into them is still relatively underdeveloped with the events management and festivals literature.

Event production

Event organisers use a variety of strategies to influence the image and atmosphere of their events, and the process begins by understanding the kind of event they are offering, and the demographic and psychographic market they hope to attract. Pre-event marketing is targeted through broadcast, print and online media, with sponsor tie-ins becoming increasingly important (Kerr & May, 2011). The aim is to foster a consistent message across numerous communication channels, thereby attracting the intended market and discouraging those who might not 'fit in' with the event. This has been aided by the rise of twenty-first century social media and smartphone usage, as festivals are now far more visible than at any time in the past, with thousands of pictures and short videos available both from official sources and from previous festivalgoers. These act as a powerful form of word-of-mouth marketing and often focus on the festivalgoer experience rather than the artists performing on the stages. Social media offer a means for festivalgoers to publicise their attendance at an event, and for others to feel they have missed out. In addition, the interactive nature of social media means that festival organisers and sponsors can engage in two-way communications: asking forum users for recommendations, responding to messages and posts on Twitter, Facebook, Instagram and blogs, and encouraging festivalgoers to upload and tag themselves in photographs. This form of Virtual Communities Marketing (Kozinets, 1999) helps to assuage any fears that festivalgoers might have about their ability to fit in with a previously unvisited event and gives knowledge and confidence about what to expect. Numerous online forums also allow festivalgoers to ask each other questions, thus feeding into a sense of community, particularly where the forum is festival-specific, and where festival organisers actively use the forums too (Hudson and Hudson, 2013).

Pine and Gilmore argue that festivals are an example of a 'fourth economic offering': that what is being consumed is an experience rather than simply a service, product or raw material (1999: 1). This experience economy is characterised by the creation of novel, themed or surprising activities which need to engage festivalgoers who seek to be 'stimulated, entertained, and educated, as well as emotionally affected and creatively challenged' (Karsten, 2009: 29). Such ideas have already been discussed in relation to brand-centric sponsor activations in Chapter 3, but here the principles are extended to the festival as a whole. Decisions need to be made about the physical layout and aesthetic design of a site, about the musical programming and other attractions and services, and about the use or otherwise of brand sponsors. There are many site- and event-specific variables that need to be taken into account by organisers as part of their forward planning, so the key area of concern here is how physical design affects social interactions. The influential analyses of Kotler (1973) and Bitner (1992) are based on research into bricks and mortar businesses, but their ideas may also be translated to temporary settings such as outdoor music festivals. Kotler's notion of 'atmospherics' draws attention to the visual, aural, olfactory and tactile aspects of a service experience. At music festivals, the visual and aural aspects are arguably the most dominant in terms of design and will be discussed here. The visual elements include the size, type and design of the stages, and the use of lightshows, lasers, dry ice and pyrotechnics. Some festivals use standardised stages with aesthetic design limited to other parts of the site: for instance, through the placement of large art installations, painted hoardings, and so on. However, events are increasingly creating bespoke themed stages or hiring professional staging companies such as Block 9 or Arcadia to design fantastical and memorable structures. Boutique festivals often put a strong emphasis on the design of their stages and of their sites more generally, since this allows them to create a sense of uniqueness and wonder. One of the most extreme is the Boomtown Fair which creates a 'town centre' of uniquely designed stages and areas, and also permits festivalgoers to design and build their own themed areas within its 'suburbs' (Robinson, 2015a). The aural elements of festival design are two-fold. First, stages need to be sited within the festival arena in such a way that noise 'spill' from one stage to another is limited, and the effects on local residents are minimised. The natural environment of the festival site has a key role to play in what can and cannot be achieved and may lead, for example, to the introduction of tented stages which contain the sound more effectively than open air stages. A contributing factor is an understanding of how people are likely to move between the stages and how the musical programme can be staggered in terms of start and stop times to avoid congestion. Second, volume is also a consideration in terms of how festivalgoers will engage with the music itself. Very loud electronic music within a tented setting will be attractive for some, but not others, and promotes different forms of interaction between festivalgoers than, say, a smaller acoustic stage. Cambridge Folk Festival is a case in point, since it retains the quiet and attentive atmosphere of a folk club in its folk tent, yet also has concert style performances on its main stage, which has a large covered marquee in case of bad weather. There is also a smaller second stage, housed in a marquee to prevent sound overspilling from the main arena, and there are several further stages located within the campsite. Different styles of stage and music foster different modes of listening and engagement in festivalgoers – an area worthy of future study.

Bitner's discussion of customer service encounters within the 'servicescape' (1992) makes explicit reference to the spatial layout and ambient conditions of built environments (including temperature, lighting, noise and so on), and to the signs and symbols that are produced and used within those environments. This emphasis on symbolism is transferable to music festivals, since aesthetic design and programming not only create an interesting spectacle, but also inform or reinforce festivalgoers' understandings about the ethos and expectations of an event. This symbolism includes, for instance, decisions about the musical content, headliners and running order of an event, the availability of creative and interactive opportunities for festivalgoers, and choices regarding facilities, entertainments and marketing, including the use of on-site brand activations and the employment of 'street performers' to enliven a site with unexpected and unusual encounters. The Glastonbury Festival, for example, continues to make use of symbolic imagery which connects the event to its countercultural past, while the Download Festival draws on visual stereotypes related to the heavy metal genre. This is achieved through physical site design, website and marketing design, and the use of social media. Together, these help to condition festivalgoers as to what to expect from a festival, and how they should relate to it and behave at it; in turn, this influences the meta-sociality of an event and festivalgoers' perceptions of its atmosphere.

Event consumption

The daily actions and behaviours of festivalgoers are a key component of a festival's atmosphere, since camping events in particular are not simply about watching bands on stages, but about numerous other activities. The festival site is, in a way, domesticated by festivalgoers across the festival weekend, with attendees setting up camp and working out routines for the duration of their stay. A study of camping-based rock festivals in Norway, Germany and Sweden found several overlapping phases to festival life that are similar across multiple events: early calm (8 to 11am), brunch (10am to 2pm), pre-concert (1 to 9pm), concert (5pm to 1am) and nachspiel (post-concert, from midnight onwards) (Tjora, 2016). These broad phases may also be found at British festivals, especially those rock events that are similarly skewed towards a younger demographic. However, at festivals with an older or family audience, the daily routines can vary somewhat more, with attendees participating in activities such as yoga, tai chi and shopping in the market areas during the mornings and setting up base camps inside the festival arena in the afternoon. In addition, boutique festivals offer all kinds of activities and zones which draw festivalgoers out of their tents far earlier than at rock festivals. These include dance classes, circus skills, book readings, cooking demonstrations, carnival parades, interactive brand experiences and fairground rides. Many of these activities were, arguably, pioneered by the Glastonbury Festival, and while other large-scale festivals have been slow to take on board the boutique spirit, they are now adding such areas and activities to their events. The leader in this field is perhaps Bestival, which has managed to retain a boutique festival feel despite having had an audience capacity of 80,000 since 2013.

Tjora's (2016) study is useful for its discussion of the temporal rhythm of festival life, and its clear delineations of the behavioural separation between the campsite areas and the main performance arenas. However, it says little about the spatial practices of festival life within the festival arena, or about other aspects of an event's atmosphere. The sheer diversity of event types, attendees and activities makes broad generalisations difficult, so the remainder of this section will tackle two elements which can be examined across festivals of all kinds, though with different outcomes in each case. The first is the behavioural zoning of the festival arena, which shows how attendees make use of a site in a variety of ways. The second is the notion of a flattening of hierarchies, a key characteristic identified by many authors writing on festivals and events, yet under pressure due to the increasing commercialisation of festivals and the development of VIP tickets and luxury camping options.

Quinn and Wilks suggest that there are four 'festival landscape zones': the performance zone (the stages) sits in the centre, surrounded concentrically by a congregation zone (camping, food and drink), a locale zone (the immediate host location) and a hinterland zone (the broader landscape) (2013: 5). However, this macro-level zoning obscures the variety of activity found within the performance and congregation zones: there are, for example, backstage areas available only to festival workers and performers, and the main arena may be divided into a number of zones based not only on how an event is produced and planned, but on how festivalgoers make use of the space. For instance, the author's fieldwork identified both 'settled stages' and 'transient stages' at events. Transient stages (open air or tented) see attendees coming and going but rarely staying for long:

> We're really there for the music, so if we have ten minutes to get to the tent to see Human League at the end of the Dashboard Confessional set, then we'll walk as fast as we can. It's unusual for us to see three acts in succession on the same stage.
> (Email from Steve about V Festival 2004)

Visits to such stages are highly dependent on the musical programme on offer, which will typically be filled by lesser-known or unsigned acts. If the venue does not have an integral bar or other décor and activities within it, there will be times of day when the stage has few if any visitors. In contrast, 'settled stages' are those where many people will spend their entire day, putting down rugs and other belongings in order to secure their space. Where the festival permits, they may bring extendable poles and banners to mark their position on the site. This typically occurs at the main stage of an event where higher profile acts will be performing, though it may also be found at smaller stages offering themed experiences beyond the provision of music, or at brand activation areas managed by event sponsors. These latter venues offer convivial, entertaining and interactive experiences and, because they are easily recognisable landmark locations within a site, they make it simple for friends and family to find each other during the course of a day. This is also true for those who stake their place in the main stage area, as there will be familiar landmarks to provide orientation, and ready access to bars, food vendors, shops and toilets. Other festivalgoers settle in quieter areas of the site, perhaps equidistant from the stages they are most interested in.

Contemporary festivals typically feature what might be termed a 'commercial zone' of food, drink and market concessions, plus further zones dedicated to other non-musical activities such as funfairs, internet cafés and so on, though larger events may have such activities and zones scattered throughout their sites so that each stage has its own nearby facilities and attractions. The campsite areas could be said to form a 'domestic zone' with their own toilets and showers and, occasionally, food concessions, while family-friendly events may offer bespoke crèches or children's entertainment areas within the campsite or arena. The campsite is likely to be quite active in the late morning as festivalgoers prepare for the day, and again in the late evening as they come back from the arena stages either to sleep or to carry on the party atmosphere into the early hours:

> The campsite atmosphere is great. Most people are friendly and everyone tends to join in and chat to each other. The night-time shouting and chants are funny, but when you do want to sleep can get a bit annoying!
> (Interview with Kate about V Festival 2004)

Fonarow's (2006) study of indie music gigs points to how a single concert can be experienced in different ways by different people, and how this translates to their spatial use of a venue: those who are most committed to a band and want to demonstrate their fandom will be found immediately in front of the stage, while older or less committed fans will be further back, and industry insiders and regulars will prop up the bar and largely ignore the performance. A variant of this can be found at music festivals, where individual stages also show differing levels and zones of participation. The area between the stage barriers and the front-of-house structure will normally attract the most committed part of an audience, since it offers close proximity to the artists and the highest quality audio experience. Genre is also important to the behavioural norms of this zone: for instance, some genres and performers lead to the formation of a mosh pit directly in front of the stage. As the evening goes on, the zone becomes densely packed with attendees, so the most dedicated fans will try to arrive early to stake a place at the stage barrier with an unobstructed view of the performers. The heat and crush generated within this zone can be overwhelming, leading some to be lifted over the barrier by security guards, yet it also offers the potential for spontaneous *communitas* and flow experience as the crowd responds to the music produced on the stage (Santoro & Troilo, 2007; Tjora, 2016). As Malbon suggests of dance music clubs, the audience of a festival will consume not simply musical performances but also the proximity to, and interaction with, each other, thus creating an 'emotionally charged space' of shared experience (1998: 271). Beyond the front-of-house structure and to the sides of the venue arena will be those who are, perhaps, less committed to an artist, or seek to watch the performance without such a crush of people around them. They may also be keeping their options open by checking out the artist first before either staying to enjoy the show or heading to another stage. During the daytime it is common for the field beyond the front-of-house structure to be 'settled' by groups of friends and families, but if an artist is popular, the field will gradually become 'standing room only' as more and more people join the crowd. As in Fonarow's description of indie gigs, festival regulars may stay at the nearby bars to view from a distance, though VIP and backstage areas should also be added to the model, as some festivals offer special viewing areas to those who have paid for a premium ticket.

The behavioural and commercial zoning of festival sites leads to a discussion of hierarchy, since many authors, including Bakhtin (1984), Falassi (1987) and Ehrenreich (2006), regard a flattening or overturning of the social hierarchies of the everyday world as a defining characteristic of festival times: a negation of class and rank that distinguishes this form of public event from ceremonial occasions such as coronations, royal weddings, and so on. As discussed in Chapter 1, the perception of contemporary music festivals as non-hierarchical derives largely from their adoption by both the second folk revival and the rock counterculture of the 1960s as well as, in the British context, the development of the free festivals, free fairs and free parties from the early 1970s through to the mid-1990s. The latter events in particular based themselves on a rhetoric of participation and openness, with the divide between organisers, performers and audiences dissolving to a fair extent. However, relatively few festivals of this kind are staged today, except on a very small scale, and contemporary commercial events are far from non-hierarchical in nature. For instance, within each festival there are various levels of accreditation pass that allow entry to specific backstage areas that are generally off-limits to ticket holders, and sites are typically surrounded by security fencing and guards to prevent non-ticket holders from gaining access to the event for free. As discussed in Chapter 2, many events also offer VIP tickets that provide entry to dedicated areas and facilities unavailable to regular ticket holders, while festival accommodation has expanded to include premium-priced pre-erected tents and other structures, together with enhanced amenities such as dedicated catering areas, flushing toilets and even 24-hour 'room service' for those willing to pay.

As noted earlier, festival organisers have a target market in mind when creating and marketing their events, so it is common to find demographically similar attendees at any specific event. Events such as Latitude and Cornbury have been branded as 'posh' festivals, indicating a middle- or upper-class attendee profile and a programming strategy that goes well beyond the music. Melvin Benn (organiser of Latitude) was quoted in 2014 as saying that 'I wouldn't be so presumptuous as to say working class people don't do yoga, but yoga absolutely reinforces our middle class credentials and I've no qualms about that at all' (BBC Suffolk, 2014). Interestingly, festivalgoers at events with a folk heritage often insist on their event's inherent classlessness. This may derive from the feelings of togetherness and meta-sociality that emerge at such events, or from the underlying history of folk festivals being associated with left-wing political views; yet it may also relate to the broader mediation and marketing of outdoor music festivals as utopian and countercultural. The following quotes are suggestive of the negotiations made by festivalgoers when thinking about the events they attend:

> You have everything from unreformed hippies from various countries and eras to workers from The City who spend Sunday pondering how to

reconcile their weekend of extraordinary spirit and inebriation with the staid and proper reality awaiting them the next day.
(Email from Adam regarding Cropredy Festival 2004)

I think it's fairly middle class. But not your normal middle class, I'm thinking more like people like myself. People that have achieved in life, in a career sense, but still do not want to conform to the norms of the people that they live amongst and work with.
(Interview with Barry at Cambridge Folk Festival 2004)

I think the majority of the people who go to the folk festival could be classed as middle class. However, I think there are definitely lots of different groups of people represented from the very old to the very young, the flamboyant to the conservative, the punks to the Goths and so many more.
(Email from Laura about Cambridge Folk Festival 2004)

In the first quote, there is an implicit criticism of the City workers' everyday lives, but also a celebration of the event's ability to help them overcome their 'staid and proper reality', whilst the second and third quotes distinguish between different notions of 'middle class'. For instance, the second festivalgoer is quick to offer an alternative version of the middle class which focuses on non-conformism, while the third chooses to highlight the subcultural and neo-tribal variety of the event. At both Cambridge Folk Festival and Cropredy Festival there is an egalitarian mentality and non-judgmental attitude towards others that translates into an easy-going, friendly and cosmopolitan atmosphere. To this extent, these festivals are classless, inasmuch as different neo-tribal groups are welcomed, and there is a positive will to ignore social hierarchies and classifications at the gates of the event, and to treat others as equals.

Festival fashion is another area where notions of hierarchy can be perceived. On one hand, dressing up in unusual, eccentric or comical outfits allows festivalgoers to mask their identities and gives them license to behave in ways that they would not in their ordinary lives (Jaimangal-Jones et al., 2015: 614). This is reminiscent of Bakhtin's (1984) descriptions of the medieval carnival where dressing up allowed peasants and nobles to interact freely with each other, and it may be one of the reasons that attendees experience festivals as classless: the usual markers of social class are often hidden. Yet festival fashion can also provide a key focus for 'people-watching': for looking at others and commenting on what they are doing or wearing (Jaimangal-Jones et al., 2015: 613). As fashion brands have become more involved in the festival market, so trends in clothing have emerged which take inspiration from the hippie fashions of the 1960s, or the raves of the late 1980s and early 1990s. Festival fashions from one year become passé to the fashion-conscious in the next, and wearing the right accessories and clothes (or not) becomes a talking point and a way both to show off and to categorise others. An implicit hierarchy emerges from such activities, which places some festivals as, for instance, fashion-heavy or resolutely middle-class, and thus regarded as less authentic or exciting than others.

The specialness of music festivals

This final section will examine the term 'special', which is often used to describe events such as music festivals, but is difficult to define since it involves the subjective understandings of organisers and festivalgoers. Jago and Shaw's research identifies a number of descriptors for the term 'special' as it relates to events: short duration, relative infrequency, media attention, a large number of attendees, and a sense of being out of the ordinary (1998; 1999). It is notable that, with the exception of the final element, these largely ignore the atmosphere of an event, even though this has been recognised as a central factor in attracting attendance and achieving success. In addition, their research is unable to explain why an event may be deemed special by festivalgoers even when it has little or no media attention or has a small attendance capacity. An alternative is provided by Getz who has argued that events may be regarded as 'special' where there is 'emotional involvement of all those in attendance' (1991: 232), and it is partly in this sense that the following understanding of 'specialness' is developed.

Outdoor music festivals offer festivalgoers an exciting leisure experience for a specific time in a specific place: one that exists in contrast to the everyday world though is not entirely separate from it. These events offer a mix of what Rojek has called 'fast and slow leisure', where 'fast leisure' refers to the casual encounters and interactions of attendees, of people-watching, and of browsing amongst stages, concessions and other activities, and 'slow leisure' refers to social relations existing between attendees who journey to an event together or meet up with old friends and family members (2000: 22). Each event will develop its own social relations, performances and perfomativities: a broadly agreed-upon set of behaviours, norms and meanings (its metasociality), which is influenced by that event's specific heritage, genre, production and mediation, as well as by broader conceptions of music festivals within British culture. Music festivals present the appearance, if not necessarily the reality, of egalitarianism: of everyone sharing the same experience and being on the same level. This allows festivalgoers the freedom to engage in behaviours and actions to excess, to take on alternative identities, or to feel able to display their subcultural or taste interests in a supportive atmosphere. The music provides an emotional charge, moving people to performances such as dancing, singing along, and 'losing themselves' in the crowds: a communal feeling of ecstasy and joy (Turner's *communitas*) or of individual transcendence and bliss (Barthes' *jouissance*). However, the predominant experience of an event is one of having a good time, of enjoying the general ambience of laid-back leisure amongst like-minded others (Barthes' *plaisir*), punctuated by the excitement and pleasure of the musical performances, or of participation in various other activities on-site.

Music festivals also attract feelings of belonging, especially at longer-lived events where regular attendees have made the site and the event their home-from-home: in a sense, it becomes *their* festival. The 'specialness' of music festivals has much in common with the concept of 'cyclic place' discussed in Chapter 4, since it involves the development of a unique, cohesive and recognisable atmosphere, ethos or ambience that is cyclically recreated and experienced, and is difficult to describe in objective terms. For any specific event, this atmosphere is relatively stable from year to year, yet is always open to the possibility of change as the constitution of its audience changes over time and as genre meanings and social expectations also develop. Indeed, such changes are necessary for an event to avoid stagnation and to continue to attract both new and previous attendees. One of the ways that a music festival may be 'special' therefore emerges from the emotional attachment that festivalgoers give to the place and time of an event and how it connects with and becomes part of their personal social lives. This is an alternative and additional form of 'specialness' to that previously identified by Jago and Shaw (1999), and one which helps to account for the success of smaller, less highly mediated events.

Conclusion

This chapter has explored three perspectives on the social life of festivals. The first suggested that festivalgoers demonstrate a wide variety of motivations and that the musical performances themselves are only part of the overall experience and atmosphere that is being consumed. The carnivalesque activities and motivations that have been ascribed to festival attendance in the past are still to be found at contemporary festivals, but there has also been a growth in hedonic consumption (Hirschmann & Holbrook, 1982): the search for immersive, pleasurable experiences related to both participatory activity and the consumption of spectacle. In the second, attention was drawn to two variations on the concept of sociality: Maffesoli's neo-tribes (1996), and Hetherington's elective affinity groups (1998b). These may help to explain the social atmosphere of smaller events, but that a looser concept is needed to account for larger scale ones. The concept of meta-sociality was introduced as a way to understand the development and character of an event's overarching identity and image: one which provides a shared frame of reference for attendees, even though individual festivals are comprised of multiple chance encounters, and the co-location (if not necessarily interaction between) numerous friendship and family groups. It was suggested that the performative behaviours of festivalgoers help to recreate an event in its own social image each year, and that this is supported by the ongoing mediation and discussion of an event during the remainder of the year. The final perspective discussed was the closely related notion of festival 'atmosphere' which results from the actions and interactions of event producers and festivalgoers. Events are designed to cater to the perceived needs of an intended target audience, while festivalgoers first domesticate a site and then develop their own routines and behaviours in response to the layout of the site, the programme of musical and other activities and the various interactions and encounters that they have with each other. Cyclical recreation of these routines can help to reconstruct an event's festive atmosphere on an annual basis, and to foster feelings of belonging, transcendence and specialness.

Conclusion

When I first began to research outdoor popular music festivals in the early 2000s, I met with two common responses from academics, organisers and attendees. One was to ask why I was studying them, and the other was to tell me that 'festivals aren't what they used to be' – the implication being that they were inferior to events of the past because they had lost the alternative or subversive edge with which they were previously characterised. At the time, I justified my decision to study the sector by arguing that the business of music festivals was a surprisingly under-researched area, especially in comparison to the recorded music sector, and that the question of why 'festivals aren't what they used to be' was an important one to examine. What had changed and why? What factors underpinned those changes, and why were countercultural accounts of music festivals as anarchic and utopian sites of political possibility increasingly anachronistic? Furthermore, if this was the case, how are festivals perceived, managed and experienced today? This book has examined such questions through a number of different lenses, and three key themes have emerged: the continued influence of what I have termed the countercultural carnivalesque, the mainstreaming of festival culture as a commercial leisure resource, and the co-creation and annual (re)construction of festival spaces and socialities by organisers, festivalgoers and the media.

In relation to the first of these themes, outdoor music festivals first came to be associated with a countercultural version of the carnivalesque in the late 1950s, and that this view of festivals dominated from the late 1960s until the mid-1990s. The cultural stereotypes most commonly deployed by the media today were developed during this era, and include environmentalism, new age or alternative belief systems, psychedelic imagery and clothing designs, anti-corporate and anti-war ideals, participatory and transformatory experience, the flattening of social hierarchies, and the overturning of social norms regarding drugs, nudity, sexual behaviours and cleanliness. In the first chapter, it was suggested that these emerged, in part, from the oppositional ideology of late 1960s rock music and the mediation of festival films such as *Monterey Pop* (1967), *Woodstock* (1970) and *Glastonbury Fayre* (1972) as well as, in the specific context of Britain, the development of free festivals, medieval fairs, and the mobile lifestyles of the post-hippie

New Age Travellers in the 1970s and 1980s. These stereotypes later became attached to the free party raves of the early 1990s, and they underpin the objections of those festivalgoers, promoters and commentators who feel that the contemporary festival sector has become too mainstream, too safe and too commercial. Moral fears about outdoor festivals led to repressive state action and subsequent legislation in the 1980s and 1990s, and can also be recognised in the rural opposition raised against festivals in the past, though, as noted in Chapter 4, the transformation of festivals into mainstream leisure commodities has allowed them to fit more easily within the contemporary adventurescape of the post-productivist countryside. Similarly, concerns regarding environmental impacts have now become normalised within wider society, and festivals of all sizes reflect this through the adoption of 'green' initiatives. However, opposition can still be found in police action against unlicensed music events, and in the objections of some residents to the disruption and noise of staging festivals in rural locations. The festival mythology, ideology and aesthetic produced through the countercultural carnivalesque is communicated through the media and continues to be mobilised by organisers, brands, sponsors and advertisers: it is part of how festivals are sold as participatory spectacles that transcend everyday life and experience. Some festival organisers and attendees remain resistant to what may be regarded as the co-optation of true or authentic festival culture, hence, as discussed in Chapter 3, a number of festivals have chosen to operate without commercial brand sponsorships in order to promote their social and environmental ideals. Nevertheless, for many festivalgoers, the authenticity or value of a commercial event lies not in its ideological concerns but, as shown in Chapter 5, in its ability to meet their preconceptions about aesthetic, social and hedonic experience. Those preconceptions vary between different demographic and psychographic groups, and this has led to diversification in the sector and the emergence of commercially profitable niche and hybrid events in addition to large-scale pop and rock festivals.

As Chapter 1 demonstrated, both commercial and non-commercial music festivals have been in existence since the seventeenth and eighteenth centuries in the UK, and these precursor events reflected the social mores and concerns of the organisers and attendees of their particular eras and cultural milieux. They were either satisfying a commercial niche or being used by organisers as part of a broader attempt at social education and control of the working classes. There is therefore no need to understand festivals as inherently radical or countercultural; instead, we should consider them as a cultural form that adapts and responds to different historical, geographical, political, social and economic circumstances. Chapters 2 and 3 examined this in relation to the mainstreaming of the music festival market in the post-millennial era – the second key theme of the book. For instance, major national and international companies now dominate the festival market in terms of event production, promotion and sponsorship, with a broad range of business start-ups and lifestyle-orientated businesses seeking to capitalise on the festival experience.

Festivals have also become increasingly mediated, with coverage of many medium- and large-scale festivals now offered by major radio and television networks such as the BBC, ITV, Channel 4 and Sky, with previews and reviews found not only in the traditional music magazines, but in the broadsheet and tabloid press, and in lifestyle, fashion and celebrity titles. This both reflects and helps to promote changes in the demographic profile of outdoor music festivals. In particular there has been growth in family-focused, design-led and hybrid festivals that have responded to changing tastes and interests. Notably, this also includes events which espouse countercultural aims or approaches, and this may be why the backlash against the commercialisation of the festival sector has largely waned since the late 1990s: the continued diversification of the sector allows alternative events to develop alongside the more overtly commercial ones, while changes in legislation, regulation and policing mean that truly anarchic and oppositional events are now much smaller in size and less common than they were in the past. In addition, changing demographics and expectations regarding service quality and professionalisation have led to campaigns and action regarding hygiene, drug usage, and issues of sexual health and harassment. The self-policing and laissez-faire attitudes of the past are hard to sustain in the twenty-first century and it is unlikely that many festivalgoers would seek a return to them.

The era of rapid growth identified in the first decade of the twenty-first century now appears to have stalled, but there are still many people willing to stage events on a volunteer basis, and many entrepreneurial and charity-led festivals are launched each year by enthusiast promoters, as well as by commercial companies. This is because, other than funding, barriers to entry are relatively low for novice organisers, since no specific qualifications are required. In addition, the growing professionalism and maturity of the sector has seen the creation of specialist companies that provide staging, fencing, security, catering, toilets, amplification, lighting, noise monitoring and so on, which greatly aids the organisational aspects of putting on an event. Furthermore, *The Purple Guide to Health, Safety and Welfare at Music and Other Events* (EIF, 2014) gives advice on a range of practical matters that are crucial to an event receiving a license, allaying the fears of local residents, and operating in a safe manner, and this gives enthusiast promoters as well as commercial companies the tools and knowledge required to get started. The main issues facing all promoters seeking to enter or survive in the market are access to a suitable location, funding to pay for contractors prior to the receipt of ticket income, and the ability to book artists and other attractions that will draw the interest of the public. Funding issues are usually tackled with recourse to sponsorship deals and, in some cases, successful applications for Arts Council, National Lottery and PRS Foundation grants – an area of provision which has yet to be researched in much detail within the event management and arts marketing literature. A related area for future study is the potential for popular music festivals to attract direct funding from personal donors in the form of membership schemes, patronage schemes and legacies (leaving funds in a will), as this has become relatively common practice in the high arts sector. Access to suitable artists has become more difficult in recent years, as ownership of the country's major festivals has fallen into the hands of a limited number of national and international companies – a pattern previously seen in the recorded and live concert industries. Furthermore, the fall in revenue from recorded music means that managers and artists have turned to the concert venue and festival circuits to boost their income. At the same time, festival promoters have tended to play safe with their headliner booking policies and to institute exclusivity clauses at all levels of their programming. This drives artist fees even higher through price competition, and leaves many events in a precarious financial situation, with some having to cancel because they have been unable to afford a suitable line-up. Many in the industry consider this situation to be unsustainable, and it is likely that festival organisers will need to take more risks on finding and developing the headliners of the future, and to continue diversifying their entertainment content beyond music.

The growing commercialisation and mainstreaming of festivals has also affected festival sponsors, who have had to adapt to changing demographics and psychographics by creating experiential campaigns that engage festivalgoers both on- and off-site, and are formulated towards sales rather than awareness. This helps to justify and offset the expense involved in creating experiential zones on festival sites but has also led to well-known brands such as Very, Nando's and Wagamama appearing in festival arenas, in addition to the more traditional alcohol sponsors who have also adapted in some cases by creating themed experiential areas rather than simply bars. On the one hand this may be regarded as contributing to the commercialisation, gentrification and placelessness of festival sites, which is furthered by the provision of paid-for toilet facilities, internet cafés and other commercial and branded services. On the other, it can be viewed as an understandable evolution of the festival form in response to the changing needs and demands of audiences. Some commercial festivals might be criticised as simulacra of the 'true' festival experience of the past, yet those who attend them engage with these events on their own merits and revel in the social experience, festivity and spectacle they offer. If contemporary festivals are analogous to Ritzer's 'cathedrals of consumption' (1999), then a key difference is that what is being consumed goes beyond the commercial offering of the event itself, to encompass the personal interactions of those on-site.

This leads to the third theme of the book, which is that audiences and places play a crucial role in constructing the meaning, image and atmosphere of music festivals, and this turns attention to a question raised in the Introduction: can music festivals still be experienced as special and unique when so many of them have the same basic structure, form and content? It was argued in Chapter 4 that specific places may have a significant impact on the meaning and atmosphere of an event, and introduced the concept of cylic place to show how this may be conceptualised. Two case studies were presented as examples, but the idea of cyclic place can be extended to other events, each of which will have its own specific attributes and relationships with its host location, geographical setting, and the accumulated and mediated history of both the event and regular attendees. When this is connected to the role of festivalgoers and media in creating a broad meta-sociality for an event, so it may come to feel special, and to embody a sense of uniqueness and differentiation related to its specific location, image and atmosphere. The demographic and psychographic constitution of the festivalgoers attracted to an event is therefore important to the creation of that event's atmosphere, as are the perceptions, beliefs and personal biographies of its audience. These factors also feed into the 'brand matrix' of music festivals introduced in Chapter 3 – a way to conceive of festivals as branded environments and events whose image and meaning are influenced by the intersections of artists, media and sponsor brands with the place-branding of their host locations and the motivations and ideologies of festival organisers. The festival form may have broad universal meanings in the sense of letting loose and overturning everyday life, and of doing something different, to excess, or with full absorption, but each festival is otherwise a rather varied assemblage of people, place, organisation and entertainment. Where a festival manages to develop a sense of uniqueness – to be perceived as special by festivalgoers – this can lead to repeat custom and a greater likelihood that the event will achieve longevity. This remains an under-researched area of festival studies, but one with the potential to help us understand why some festivals become successful while others fail.

Outdoor popular music festivals represent complex social, cultural and economic phenomena, yet while academic research on the events industry in general has expanded rapidly, festival research remains relatively underdeveloped, particularly in terms of connecting cultural and business perspectives (Getz & Page, 2016). This book has added to a growing field of 'music festival studies' by focusing on the commercial sector – one which is often neglected by scholars interested in more alternative or subversive events or tackled in instrumental ways by the events management literature (Anderton, 2008).

The book has addressed a number of questions, yet there are many more that are yet to receive thorough investigation. For instance, how do organisers perceive their own events? What ideologies underpin their decision-making, and what factors constrain their ability to create the events they want to stage? How do they negotiate the compromises needed to meet the requirements of legislation, funding and sponsors, as well as the expectations of artists and audiences? What are the motivations and experiences of the many volunteers involved in managing festivals? What more can festivals do to minimise volatility and to foster success and longevity? How much further can technology be taken to enhance the festival experience or, in contrast, should internet access be banned from festival sites in order to get people more engaged in the event experience? Spontaneous feelings of euphoria, transcendence and *communitas* are commonly discussed by the media and

Conclusion 169

festivalgoers, but how do these feelings form, what is their impact, and how might organisers foster them? How are attitudes changing towards drugs, alcohol and violence, and what political or radical potential can commercial events offer in an ever more regulated and professionalised sector?

What these various questions share is a sustained focus on music festivals as events that have to be organised, managed and paid for, but also as cultural and social phenomena. This acknowledges that while economic and managerial factors are important considerations, festivals are often experienced as a network of social relationships and are multifaceted celebrations capable of creating feelings of transcendence and specialness – even at the most commercial of events. In many ways, this is the one true constant for outdoor music festivals in the UK and, despite significant changes to the sector over the past sixty years or more, the following quotes, originally published in 1974 and 1947, continue to hold true:

> [The] basic feeling at a typical festival is a good one. They feel good to be at. And, at the best of them the feeling can be more wonderful than this; festivals with their overnight cities of tents and polythene shacks really can seem like a new Jerusalem, erected amid England's green land.
> (Sandford & Reid, 1974: 9)

> [They] have added richness to living, and with the other festivals, greater or lesser, each with a peculiar quality, unique and yet related to those preceding and succeeding, have built up the dance of the year.
> (Whistler, 1947: 19–20)

Bibliography

Adams, R. 1986. *A Book of British Music Festivals*. London: Robert Royce Limited.
Adorno, T.W. & Horkheimer, M. 1997. *Dialectic of Enlightenment*, trans. J. Cumming. London: Verso.
Advance. 1994. 'Enuff's enuff!', *Advance Party Newsletter*, Issue 3, November 1994. [Scans available at: https://freepartypeople.wordpress.com/2011/02/27/advance-party/ (last accessed 5 July 2015)].
AFO [Association of Festival Organisers]. 2004. *A Report into the Impact of Folk Festivals on Cultural Tourism*. Matlock, Derbyshire: AFO.
AIF [Association of Independent Festivals]. 2017. *Sexual Assault at Festivals: AIF Charter of Best Practice*. Available at: http://aiforg.com/wp-content/uploads/Charter-of-Best-Practice-Final.pdf (last accessed 10 July 2017).
Alba, J.W. & Williams, E.F. 2013. 'Pleasure principles: a review of research on hedonic consumption', *Journal of Consumer Psychology*, 23(1): 2–18.
Alcohol Concern. 2013. *Stick to the Facts. Alcohol Advertising Regulation that Balances Commercial and Public Interest*. London: Alcohol Concern.
Aldskogius, H. 1993. 'Festivals and meets: the place of music in "Summer Sweden"', *Geografiska Annaler. Series B, Human Geography*, 75(2): 55–72.
Allen, J., O'Toole, W., Harris, R. & McDonnell, I. 2011. *Festival & Special Event Management*, 5th edition. Milton, Qld: John Wiley & Sons Australia Ltd.
Also. 2015. 'About us', *Also Festival* [website]. Available at: www.also-festival.com/about/ (last accessed 27 July 2015).
Anderson, C. 2009. *Free. The Future of a Radical Price*. London: Random House Business.
Anderton, C. 2007. '(Re)Constructing music festival places', Unpub. dissertation, Swansea University.
Anderton, C. 2008. 'Commercializing the carnivalesque: the V Festival and image/risk management', *Event Management*, 12(1): 39–51.
Anderton, C. 2011. 'Music festival sponsorship: between commerce and Carnival', *Arts Marketing*, 1(2): 145–58.
Anderton, C. 2015. 'Branding, sponsorship and the music festival'. In G. McKay (ed.), *The Pop Festival: History, Music, Media, Culture*, pp. 199–212. New York & London: Bloomsbury Academic.
Anderton, C. 2016. 'Musikfestivals als "zyklische Orte": Fairport's Cropredy Convention'. In J. Springer and T. Dören (eds), *Draußen: Zum neuen Naturbezug in der Popkultur der Gegenwart*, pp. 119–38. Bielefeld: Transcript Verlag.

Arcodia, C. & Reid, S. 2008. 'Professional standards: the current state of event management associations', *Journal of Convention & Event Tourism*, 9(1): 60–80.
Aubrey, C. & Shearlaw, J. 2004. *Glastonbury Festival Tales*. London: Ebury.
Aufheben. 1995. 'Kill or chill – an analysis of the opposition to the Criminal Justice Bill', *Aufheben*, Issue 4 (May 1995). Available at: http://libcom.org/library/kill-chill-aufheben-4 (last accessed 10 June 2016).
Bailie, S. 1993a. 'Up against the law', *NME*, 8 May 1993, pp. 26–9.
Bailie, S. 1993b. 'Puff: the magic drags on', *NME*, 17 July, p. 25.
Bakhtin, M. 1984. *Rabelais and His World*, trans. H. Iswolsky. Bloomington, IN: Indiana University Press.
Bannister, F. 2003. *There Must Be A Better Way: The Story of the Bath and Knebworth Rock Festivals, 1969–1979*. Cambridge: Bath Books.
Barrett, C. 2009. 'Live: field study', *Music Week*, 14 November, p. 14.
Barsham. 1976. *Build Another Barsham: A Guide to Faire Making*. Private press.
Barthes, R. 1975. *The Pleasure of the Text*, trans. R. Miller. New York: Hill & Wang.
Barthes, R. 1977. 'The grain of the voice'. In R. Barthes (ed.), *Image – Music – Text*, trans. S. Heath, pp. 179–89. London: Fontana Paperbacks.
Baudrillard, J. 1983. *Simulations*, trans. P. Foss, P. Patton & P. Beitchman. New York: Semiotext(e).
Bauman, R. 1987. 'The place of festival in the worldview of the seventeenth-century Quakers'. In A. Falassi (ed.), *Time Out of Time: Essays on the Festival*, pp. 93–8. Albuquerque: University of New Mexico Press.
BBC. 2010. 'BBC events spending should be better regulated', BBC News [online], 28 January. Available at: http://news.bbc.co.uk/1/hi/entertainment/8484852.stm (last accessed 11 June 2015).
BBC. 2013a. 'Man died after "paranoid drugs reaction" at Bestival', *BBC News Hampshire & Isle of Wight*, 2 July. Available at: www.bbc.co.uk/news/uk-england-hampshire-23144976 (last accessed 7 August 2015).
BBC. 2013b. 'Ecstasy warning for T in the Park', *BBC News Glasgow & West Scotland*, 10 July. Available at: www.bbc.co.uk/news/uk-scotland-glasgow-west-23263680 (last accessed 7 August 2015).
BBC Suffolk. 2014. 'Yoga added to "middle class" Latitude Festival', *BBC News Suffolk*, 10 June. Available at: www.bbc.co.uk/news/uk-england-suffolk-27780521 (last accessed 25 August 2016).
Beardsworth, L. 2015. 'V Festival 2015: the DiS review', *Drowned in Sound*, 20 August. Available at: http://drownedinsound.com/in_depth/4149326-v-festival-2015--the-dis-review (last accessed 22 July 2016).
Beaumont, M. 2015. 'V festival 2015 review – Sam Smith's cruise-ship soul leads chart-chasing bill', *The Guardian* [online], 24 August. Available at: www.theguardian.com/music/2015/aug/24/v-festival-2015-review-sam-smiths-cruise-ship-soul-leads-chart-chasing-bill (last accessed 22 July 2016).
Beckett, A. 2009. *When the Lights Went Out. What Really Happened to Britain in the Seventies*. London: Faber & Faber.
Bell, D. 2006. 'Variations on the rural idyll'. In P. Cloke, T. Marsden & P.H. Mooney (eds), *Handbook of Rural Studies*, pp. 149–60. London: Sage.
Bennett, A. 2004. '"Everybody's happy, everybody's free": representation and nostalgia in the Woodstock film'. In A. Bennett (ed.), *Remembering Woodstock*, pp. 43–54. Aldershot: Ashgate Publishing Ltd.

Bennett, A. 2013. *Music, Style, and Ageing: Growing Old Disgracefully?* Philadelphia: Temple University Press.

Bennett, A., Taylor, J. & Woodward, I. (eds) 2014. *The Festivalization of Culture*. Farnham: Ashgate.

Bey, H. 1991. *T.A.Z. The Temporary Autonomous Zone, Ontological Anarchy, Poetic Terrorism*. New York: Autonomedia.

Billboard. 1972. 'Bank holiday fest gets site after hassle', *Billboard*, 22 April, p. 20 & 22.

Bitner, M.J. 1992. 'Servicescapes: the impact of physical surroundings on customers and employees', *Journal of Marketing*, 56(2): 57–71.

Blake, A. 1997. *The Land Without Music: Music, Culture and Society in Twentieth-Century Britain*. Manchester & New York: Manchester University Press.

Bloustein, G. 2004. 'Still picking children from the trees? Reimagining Woodstock in twenty-first-century Australia'. In A. Bennett (ed.), *Remembering Woodstock*, pp. 127–45. Aldershot: Ashgate Publishing Ltd.

BluePeg. 2015. 'Diesel at Festival No. 6', *BluePeg* [website]. Available at: www.bluepeg.co.uk/case_studies/diesel_no6.html (last accessed 9 June 2015).

Boardman, D. 2016. *Safe Music: Making Gigs and Festivals Safer for Women. A report by the White Ribbon Campaign UK*. Available at: www.whiteribboncampaign.co.uk/sites/www.whiteribboncampaign.co.uk/files/Safe%20Music%20Guide%20Final%20PDFX.pdf.

Booker, M.K. & Juraga, D. 1995. *Bakhtin, Stalin, and Modern Russian Fiction. Carnival, Dialogism and History*. Westport, CT: Greenwood Press.

Bowen, H.E. & Daniels, M.J. 2005. 'Does the music matter? Motivations for attending a music festival', *Event Management*, 9: 155–64.

Boyd, J. 2006. *White Bicycles. Making Music in the 1960s*. London: Serpent's Tail.

Boyes, G. 1993. *The Imagined Village: Culture, Ideology and the English Folk Revival*. Manchester & New York: Manchester University Press.

Brady, T. & Cox, L. 2014. 'BBC sends 300 staff to cover Glastonbury Festival: that's 28 more than its Brazil World Cup crew', *The Daily Mail* [online], 6 June. Available at: www.dailymail.co.uk/news/article-2650797/ (last accessed 11 June 2015).

Brazier, C. 1979. 'Glastonbury Fayre: set the controls for the brown rice stall', *Melody Maker*, 30 June, p. 9.

Brennan, M. 2010. 'Constructing a rough account of British concert promotion history', *Journal of the International Association for the Study of Popular Music*, 1(1): 4–13.

Brennan, M. & Webster, E. 2010. 'The UK Festival Market Report 2010', *Festival Awards Programme 2010*, pp. 25–39.

Brocken, M. 2003. *The British Folk Revival, 1944–2002*. Aldershot: Ashgate Publishing Limited.

Brooks, S., O'Halloran, D. and Magnin, A. 2007. *The Sustainable Music Festival: A Strategic Guide*. Available at: www.artisterformiljon.se/afm_2/wp-content/uploads/2014/10/BTH-Master-20070604_MusicFestivalsGuidebook.pdf (last accessed 2 August 2015).

Brown, S. 2014. 'Emerging professionalism in the event industry: a practitioner's perspective', *Event Management*, 18: 15–24.

Bryman, A. 2004. *The Disneyization of Society*. London: Sage.

Bunce, M. 1994. *The Countryside Ideal: Anglo-American Images of Landscape*. London: Routledge.

Bunce, M. 2003. 'Reproducing rural idylls'. In P. Cloke (ed.), *Country Visions*, pp. 14–30. Harlow: Pearson.
Burke, P. 1994. *Popular Culture in Early Modern Europe*. Aldershot: Scholar Press.
Butler, J. 1990. *Gender Trouble*. London: Routledge.
Butler, J. 1993. *Bodies that Matter*. London: Routledge.
Caillois, R. 2001. *Man, Play and Games*, trans. M. Barash. Urbana & Chicago: University of Illinois Press.
Cambridge City Council Arts & Entertainments. (2004). Market research data for the Cambridge Folk Festival 2003. Provided via personal communication.
Cambridge News. 2004. 'Hall's well for future of festival', *Cambridge News*, 2 August. Available at: www.cambridge-news.co.uk/halls-future-festival/story-22464417-detail/story.html (last accessed 11 July 2016).
Campbell, C. 1987. *The Romantic Ethic and the Spirit of Modern Consumerism.* Oxford: Blackwell.
Carah, N. 2010. *Pop Brands: Branding, Popular Music, and Young People*. New York: Peter Lang.
Carroll, I. 2007. *The Reading Festival. Music, Mud and Mayhem: The Official History*. London: Reynolds & Hearn Ltd.
Carù, A. & Cova, B. 2007a. 'Consumer Immersion in an experiential context'. In A. Carù & B. Cova (eds), *Consuming Experience*, pp. 34–47. London & New York: Routledge.
Carù, A. & Cova, B. 2007b. 'Consuming experiences: an introduction'. In A. Carù & B. Cova (eds), *Consuming Experience*, pp. 3–16. London & New York: Routledge.
Cassidy, A. 2009. 'BMA calls for ban on alcohol advertising', *Campaign* [online], 8 September 2009. Available at: www.campaignlive.co.uk/article/936601/bma-calls-ban-alcohol-advertising (last accessed 3 August 2015).
Chalcraft, J. & Magaudda, P. 2013. '"Space is the place": the global localities of the Sònar and WOMAD music festivals'. In G. Delanty, L. Giorgi & M. Sassatelli (eds), *Festivals and the Cultural Public Sphere*, pp. 173–89. New York: Routledge.
Clarke, M. 1982. *The Politics of Pop Festivals*. London: Junction Books.
Cloonan, M. 1997. 'State of the nation: "Englishness," pop, and politics in the mid-1990s, *Popular Music & Society*, 21(2): 47–70.
Cloonan, M. 2012. 'Selling the experience: the worldviews of British concert promoters', *Creative Industries Journal*, 5(1–2): 151–70.
Cochrane, G. 2011. 'Music festivals struggling due to "overcrowded" market', *BBC Newsbeat*, 8 August. Available at: www.bbc.co.uk/newsbeat/article/14446562/music-festivals-struggling-due-to-overcrowded-market (last accessed 23 July 2015).
Collin, M. with Godfrey, J. 1997. *Altered State: The Story of Ecstasy Culture and Acid House*, 2nd edition. London: Serpent's Tail.
Connell, J. & Gibson, C. 2003. *Soundtracks: Popular Music, Identity and Place*. London: Routledge.
Cooper, Q. & Sullivan, P. 1994. *Maypoles, Martyrs and Mayhem. 366 Days of British Customs, Myths and Eccentricities*. London: Bloomsbury Publishing Ltd.
Corner, L. 2012. 'Music festivals: are our field days over?', *Independent (UK)*, 25 January. Available at: www.independent.co.uk/travel/news-and-advice/music-festivals-are-our-field-days-over-6293950.html (last accessed 16 June 2015).
Cosmopolitan. 2012. 'Festival sex', *Cosmopolitan* [online]. Available at: www.cosmopolitan.co.uk/love-sex/sex/tips/g832/festival-sex/?slide=1 (last accessed 6 August 2015).

Cox, H. 1969. *The Feast of Fools: A Theological Essay on Festivity and Fantasy*. Cambridge, MA: Harvard University Press.

Cresswell, T. 1996. *In Place/Out of Place: Geography, Ideology, and Transgression*. Minneapolis, MN: University of Minnesota Press.

Csikszentmihalyi, M. 1974. *Flow. Studies of Enjoyment*. University of Chicago, PHS Grant Report.

Csikszentmihalyi, M. 1975. *Beyond Boredom and Anxiety: The Experience of Play in Work and Games*. San Francisco: Jossey–Bass.

Cummings, J. 2008. 'Trade mark registered: sponsorship within the Australian Indie music festival scene', *Continuum: Journal of Media & Cultural Studies*, 22(5): 675–85.

Cummings, J. & Herborn, J. 2015. 'Festival bodies: the corporeality of the contemporary music festival scene in Australia'. In G. McKay (ed.), *The Pop Festival: History, Music, Media, Culture*, pp. 99–114. New York & London: Bloomsbury Academic.

Davies, D. 2005. 'Keeping the customer satisfied', *IQ*, 3: 24–9.

Deflem, M. 1991. 'Ritual, anti-structure, and religion: a discussion of Victor Turner's processual symbolic analysis', *Journal for the Scientific Study of Religion*, 30(1): 1–25.

Denham, J. 2014. 'Metallica hit back at "ridiculous" Glastonbury critics: "Huh? What? Who are you?"', *The Independent*, 9 June. Available at: www.independent.co.uk/arts-entertainment/music/news/metallica-hit-back-at-ridiculous-glastonbury-critics-huh-what-who-are-you-9513698.html (last accessed 4 June 2015).

De Pelsmacker, P., Geuens, M. & Van den Bergh, J. 2010. *Marketing Communications: A European Perspective*, 4th edition. Harlow: Financial Times Prentice Hall.

Derrett, R. 2003. 'Making sense of how festivals demonstrate a community's sense of place', *Event Management*, 8: 49–58.

Dewsbury, J.D. 2000. 'Performativity and the event: enacting a philosophy of difference', *Environment & Planning D: Society & Space* 18(4): 473–96.

Dimond, B. 2013. 'The Beat-Herder organiser Nick Chambers: exclusive interview with Festivals For All', *Festivals For All* [website], 10 April. Available at: www.festivalsforall.com/article/the-beat-herder-organiser-nick-chambers-exclusive-interview-with-festivals-for-all (last accessed 14 June 2015).

DoE [Department of the Environment]. 1973. *Pop Festivals: Advisory [Stevenson] Committee on Pop Festivals Report and Code of Practice*. London: HMSO.

DoE [Department of the Environment]. 1976. *Free Festivals: First Report of the [Melchett] Working Group on Pop Festivals*. London: HMSO.

DoE [Department of the Environment]. 1978. *Pop Festivals and their Problems: Second Report [Stedman] of the Working Group on Pop Festivals*. London: HMSO.

Dowd, T.J., Liddle, K. & Nelson, J. 2004. 'Music festivals as scenes: examples from Serious Music, Womyn's Music and SkatePunk'. In A. Bennett & R.A. Peterson (eds), *Music Scenes. Local, Translocal, and Virtual*, pp. 149–67. Nashville, TN: Vanderbilt University Press.

Drengner, J., Gaus, H. & Jahn, S. 2008. 'Does flow influence the brand image in marketing', *Journal of Advertising Research*, 48(1): 138–47.

Drengner, J., Jahn, S. & Zanger, C. 2011. 'Measuring event-brand congruence', *Event Management*, 15(1): 25–36.

Drury, J. 2013. *The Festival Awards Market Report 2013*. The UK Festival Awards/CGA Strategy.

Duffy, M. 2000. 'Lines of drift: festival participation and performing a sense of place', *Popular Music*, 19(1): 51–64.

Duncan, R. 1984. *The Noise: Notes from a Rock and Roll Era*. New York: Ticknor & Fields.

Ear to the Ground. 2012. 'Connect #444: A Very fashionable tent for V Festival', *Ear to the Ground* [website]. Available at: http://eartotheground.ahoycreative.co.uk/case-studies/a-very-fashionable-tent-for-v-festival/ (last accessed 9 June 2015).

Eavis, E. 2015. 'Emily Eavis on Kanye at Glastonbury: "Who are these people throwing out threats from behind their screens?"', *The Guardian* (online), 20 March. Available at: www.theguardian.com/music/2015/mar/20/emily-eavis-on-kanye-at-glastonbury-we-have-got-one-of-the-greatest-artists-of-his-generation-headlining (last accessed 4 June 2015).

Ehrenreich, B. 2006. *Dancing in the Streets. A History of Collective Joy*. New York: Henry Holt & Co LLC.

Ehrlich, C. 1985. *The Music Profession in Britain since the Eighteenth Century: A Social History*. Oxford: Clarendon Press.

EIF: Events Industry Forum. 2014. *The Purple Guide to Health, Safety and Welfare at Music and Other Events* [Website with subscription-based access model]. Available at: www.thepurpleguide.co.uk/ (last accessed 3 August 2015).

embok.org. 2015. *EMBOK. Event Management Body of Knowledge* [website]. Available at: www.embok.org/ (last accessed 1 August 2015).

Evans, M. 2017. 'Anti-drug campaigners slam plans to introduce drug testing tents at music festivals', The Telegraph [online], 22 May. Available at: www.telegraph.co.uk/news/2017/05/21/anti-drug-campaigners-slam-plans-introduce-drug-testing-tents/ (last accessed 21 June 2017).

Fahey, D. 2008. 'V Festival 2008: Rated!', *Virtualfestivals.com*, 18 August. Available at: www.virtualfestivals.com/latest/news/5184 (last accessed 4 June 2015).

Fairs Archive. 2015. *The Fairs Archive: The East Anglian Fairs, 1972 to 1986* [website]. Available at http://fairsarchive.org.uk/ (last accessed 2 July 2015).

Falassi, A. 1987. 'Festival: definition and morphology'. In A. Falassi (ed.), *Time Out of Time: Essays on the Festival*, pp.1–10. Albuquerque: University of New Mexico Press.

Farren, M. 2010. *Give the Anarchist a Cigarette*. Vintage Digital [ebook edition].

Faulkner, B., Fredline, E., Larson, M. & Tomljenovic, R. 1999. 'A marketing analysis of Sweden's Storsjoyran music festival', *Tourism Analysis*, 4: 157–71.

Fellowes, F. 2012. 'Oversaturated, maybe, but festivals are far from over: festivals large and small continue to close across the UK – is the 'cream rising' in the market?', *Music Week*, 18 May, p. 23.

Fenwick, H. 2007. *Civil Liberties and Human Rights*, 4th edition. Oxford & New York: Routledge-Cavendish.

Firat, A.F. & Venkatesh, A. 1995. 'Liberatory postmodernism and the reenchantment of consumption', *The Journal of Consumer Research*, 22(3): 239–67.

Fiske, R. 1990. 'Music and society'. In H.D. Johnstone & R. Fiske (eds), *The Blackwell History of Music in Britain, Volume 4: The Eighteenth Century*, pp. 3–27. Oxford: Basil Blackwell Ltd.

Flanigan, C.C. 1990. 'Liminality, carnival, and social structure. The case of late mediaeval biblical drama'. In K.M. Ashley (ed.), *Victor Turner and the Construction of Cultural Criticism. Between Literature and Anthropology*, pp. 42–63. Bloomington & Indianapolis: Indiana University Press.

Flinn, J. & Frew, M. 2013. 'Glastonbury: managing the mystification of festivity', *Leisure Studies*, 33(4): 418–33.

Florek, M. & Insch, A. 2013. 'When fit matters: leveraging destination and event image congruence'. In L. Dwyer & E. Wickens (eds), *Event Tourism and Cultural Tourism. Issues and Debates*, pp. 27–48. Abingdon & New York: Routledge.

Fonarow, W. 2006. *Empire of Dirt: The Aesthetics and Rituals of British Indie Music*. Middletown, CT: Wesleyan University Press.

Forde, E. 2015. 'The cost of staging a music festival: "We spent £30,000 on the waste"', *The Guardian* [online], 9 July. Available at: www.theguardian.com/music/2015/jul/09/cost-of-staging-music-festival (last accessed 8 August 2015).

Foucault, M. 1986. 'Of other spaces' (trans. J. Miskowiec), *Diacritics*, 16(1): 22–7.

Freeman, H. 2015. 'Wake up, rock dinosaurs – Kanye West belongs at Glastonbury', *The Guardian* (online), 25 March. Available at: www.theguardian.com/commentisfree/2015/mar/25/kanye-west-glastonbury-guitar-rock-england (accessed 4 June 2015).

Freidson, E. 1994. *Professionalism Reborn: Theory, Prophecy and Policy*. Oxford: Blackwell.

Frith, S. 1978. *The Sociology of Rock*. London: Constable.

Frith, S. 1984. 'Rock and the politics of memory', *Social Text*, 9(10): 59–69.

Frith, S., Brennan, M, Cloonan, M. & Webster, E. 2013. *The History of Live Music in Britain, Volume I: 1950–1967. From Dance Hall to the 100 Club*. Abingdon & New York: Routledge.

Frith, S., Brennan, M, Cloonan, M. & Webster, E. [forthcoming]. *The History of Live Music in Britain, Volume 2: 1968–1984. From Hyde Park to the Hacienda*. Abingdon & New York: Routledge.

Frith, S. & McRobbie, A. 2007. 'Rock and sexuality' [first published 1978]. In S. Frith (ed.), *Taking Popular Music Seriously*, pp. 41–57. Aldershot: Ashgate Publishing.

Frukt. 2013a. 'Get seen at Glastonbury. Hunter. Welly exchange', *Frukt* [website], 2013. Available at: www.wearefrukt.com/work/welly-exchange (last accessed 11 June 2015).

Frukt. 2013b. *Field Work. The Definitive Global Guide to Brand Activations at Music Festivals*. London: Frukt.

Gelder, G. & Robinson, P. 2009. 'A critical comparative study of visitor motivations for attending music festivals: a case study of Glastonbury and V Festival', *Event Management*, 13(3): 181–96.

Gebhardt, N. 2015. '"Let There Be Rock!" Myth and mythology in the rock festivals of the transatlantic counterculture'. In G. McKay (ed.), *The Pop Festival: History, Music, Media, Culture*, pp. 49–59. New York & London: Bloomsbury Academic.

Getz, D. 1991. *Festivals, Special Events, and Tourism*. New York: Van Nostrand Reinhold.

Getz, D. & Andersson, T.D. 2008. 'Sustainable festivals: on becoming an institution', *Event Management*, 12: 1–17.

Getz, D. & Page, S. 2016. *Event Studies. Theory, Research and Policy for Planned Events*, 3rd edition. Abingdon & New York: Routledge.

Getz, D. & Wicks, B. 1994. 'Professionalism and certification for festival and event practitioners: trends and issues', *Festival Management and Event Tourism*, 2(2): 103–9.

Gibson, C. 1999. 'Subversive sites: rave culture, spatial politics and the Internet in Sydney, Australia', *Area*, 3(1): 19–33.

Gillespie, A.K. 1987. 'Folk festivals and festival folk in twentieth-century America'. In A. Falassi (ed.), *Time Out of Time: Essays on the Festival*, pp. 152–61. Albuquerque: University of New Mexico Press.

Gimme Shelter. 1970. Directed by Albert Maysles, David Maysles & Charlotte Zwerin. US: Maysles Films & Penforta. [Available on DVD: Warner Home Video].

Glade Official. 2010. 'Glade Official Statement 11th May 2010', *Glade Festival* [official website]. Archived page available at: http://web.archive.org/web/20100516192908/www.gladefestival.com/news/?p=72 (last accessed 8 August 2015).

Gladwell, M. 2000. *The Tipping Point. How Little Things Can Make a Big Difference*. London: Little, Brown & Company.

Glastonbury. 2015. 'The Glastonbury broadcaster, filming and internet policy 2015', *Glastonbury Festival of Contemporary Performing Arts* [website], June 2015. Available at: www.glastonburyfestivals.co.uk/information/media/broadcaster-internet-and-filming-access-policy/ (last accessed 15 June 2015).

Glastonbury Fayre. 1972. Directed by Nicholas Roeg (uncredited) & Peter Neal. UK: Goodtimes Enterprises and Si Litvinoff Film Production. [Available on DVD: Odeon Entertainment].

Glastonbury Fayre [album]. 1972. *Various Artists – Glastonbury Fayre – The Electric Score*. Revelation Enterprises Ltd, catalogue no. REV1, REV2, REV3.

GLC. 1976. *Code of Practice for Pop Concerts: A Guide to Safety, Health and Welfare at One Day Events*. London: Greater London Council.

Goffman, E. 1956. *The Presentation of Self in Everyday Life*. New York: Doubleday.

Goffman, E. 1963. *Behaviour in Public Places*. New York: The Free Press of Glencoe.

Goffman, E. 1967. *Interaction Ritual: Essays on Face-to-Face Behaviour*. New York: Doubleday.

Goldblatt, J. 2011. *Special Events. A New Generation and the Next Frontier*, 6th edition. Hoboken, NJ: John Wiley & Sons Ltd.

Gomme, Sir L. & Lady A. 2012. *British Folk-lore, Folk Songs and Singing Games* [originally published in 1916]. London: Forgotten Books.

Goodall, M. 2013. *Gathering of the Tribe: Music and Heavy Conscious Creation*. London: Headpress.

Goodall, M. 2015. 'Out of sight: the mediation of the music festival'. In G. McKay (ed.), *The Pop Festival: History, Music, Media, Culture*, pp. 33–48. New York & London: Bloomsbury Academic.

Gration, D., Arcodia, C., Raciti, M. & Stokes, R. 2011. 'The blended festivalscape and its sustainability at nonurban festivals', *Event Management*, 15: 343–59.

Gregson, N. and Rose, G. 2000. 'Taking Butler elsewhere: performativities, spatialities and subjectivities', *Environment & Planning D: Society & Space*, 18(4): 433–52.

Grimes, R.L. 1990. 'Victor Turner's definition, theory, and sense of ritual'. In M.A. Kathleen (ed.), *Victor Turner and the Construction of Cultural Criticism. Between Literature and Anthropology*, pp. 141–46. Bloomington & Indianapolis: Indiana University Press.

Gunn, C.A. 1972. *Vacationscape: Designing Tourist Regions*, 2nd edition. New York: Van Nostrand.

Halfacree, K. 1996a. 'Out of place in the country: travellers and the "rural idyll"', *Antipode*, 28(1): 42–72.

Halfacree, K. 1996b. 'Trespassing against the rural idyll: the Criminal Justice and Public Order Act 1994 and access to the countryside'. In C. Watkins (ed.), *Rights of Way: Policy, Culture and Management*, pp. 179–93. London: Pinter.

Bibliography

Halfacree, K. 2006. 'From dropping out to leading on? British counter-cultural back-to-the-land in a changing rurality', *Progress in Human Geography*, 30: 309–36.

Halfacree, K. 2009. '"Glow worms show the path we have to tread": the counterurbanisation of Vashti Bunyan', *Social & Cultural Geography*, 10(7): 771–89.

Hannam, C. 2009. *Health and Safety Management in the Live Music and Events Industry*. Cambridge: Entertainment Technology Press Ltd.

Hardt, M. & Negri, A. 2000. *Empire*. Cambridge, MA & London: Harvard University Press.

Harker, D. 1985. *Fakesong. The Manufacture of British 'Folksong' 1700 to the Present Day*. Milton Keynes & Philadelphia: Open University Press.

Harris, V. 2004. 'Event management: a new profession?', *Event Management*, 9: 103–9.

Harrison, C. 1991. *Countryside Recreation in a Changing Society*. London: TMS Partnership.

Havas. 2012. *Digging the Dirt on European Music Festival Sponsorship*. Report by Havas Sports & Entertainment, Ignition, and Cake.

Hemment, D. 1998. 'Dangerous dancing and disco riots: the northern warehouse parties'. In G. McKay (ed.), *DiY Culture: Party and Protest in Nineties Britain*, pp. 208–27. London & New York: Verso.

Henderson, S. & Wood, E. 2009. 'Dance to the music: fans and socialities in the festival audience'. *Live Music Exchange Resources*. Available at: http://livemusicexchange.org/wp-content/uploads/Dance-To-The-Music-Fans-and-Socialites-in-the-festival-audience.pdf (last accessed 30 October 2016).

Hesmondhalgh, D. 1999. 'Indie: the institutional politics and aesthetics of a popular music genre', *Cultural Studies*, 13(1): 34–61.

Hetherington, K. 1992. 'Stonehenge and its festival: spaces of consumption'. In R. Shields (ed.), *Lifestyle Shopping: The Subject of Consumption*, pp. 83–98. London: Routledge.

Hetherington, K. 1994. 'The contemporary significance of Schmalenbach's concept of the Bund', *The Sociological Review*, 42(1): 1–25.

Hetherington, K. 1998a. 'Vanloads of uproarious humanity: New Age Travellers and the utopics of the countryside'. In T. Skelton & G. Valentine (eds), *Cool Places: Geographies of Youth Cultures*, pp. 328–42. London & New York: Routledge.

Hetherington, K. 1998b. *Expressions of Identity: Space, Performance, Politics*. London: SAGE Publications Ltd.

Hetherington, K. 2001. *New Age Travellers: Vanloads of Uproarious Humanity*. London: Cassell.

Hewison, R. 1986. *Too Much. Art and Society in the Sixties, 1960–75*. London: Methuen.

Hinton, B. 1995. *Message to Love: The Isle of Wight Festivals, 1968–70*. Chessington: Castle Communications.

Hirschman, E.C. & Holbrook, M.B. 1982. 'Hedonic consumption: emerging concepts, methods, and propositions', *Journal of Marketing*, 46: 92–101.

Holden, P. 2001. 'A festival for "people like us"', *Audience.uk*, July 2001, pp. 8–12.

Hop Farm. 2012. 'Info: General', *Hop Farm Music Festival* [official website]. Available at: http://hopfarmfestival.com/info/general (last accessed 15 June 2015).

Howe, N. & Strauss, W. 2000. *Millennials Rising: The Next Great Generation*. New York: Vintage.

HSE [Health & Safety Executive]. 1993. *A Guide to Health, Safety and Welfare at Pop Concerts and Similar Events*. Norwich: HSE Books.

Hudson, S. & Hudson, R. 2013. 'Engaging with consumers using social media: a case study of music festivals', *International Journal of Event and Festival Management*, 4(3): 206–23.

Hudson, S., Roth, M.S., Madden, T.J. & Hudson, R. 2015. 'The effects of social media on emotions, brand relationship quality, and word of mouth: an empirical study of music festival attendees', *Tourism Management*, 47: 68–76.

Hughes, M. & Stradling, R. 2001. *The English Musical Renaissance 1840–1940: Constructing a National Music*, 2nd edition. Manchester: Manchester University Press.

Humphreys, C. 2001. *The Politics of Carnival: Festive Misrule in Medieval England*. Manchester: Manchester University Press.

Humphries, P. 1982. 'After the deluge', *Melody Maker*, 26 June, p. 8.

Huntley Film Archives. 2014. 'Woburn Festival, 1960s – Film 17360'. *Huntley Film Archives*. Available on YouTube at: www.youtube.com/watch?v=rJvSEaniH3c (last accessed 9 July 2015).

ICC. 2003. *ICC International Code on Sponsorship*. Paris: International Chamber of Commerce. Available at: www.sponsorship.org/freePapers/fp01.pdf (last accessed 4 June 2015).

IEG. 2000. 'Year One of IRL Title Builds Traffic, Awareness for Northern Light', *IEG Sponsorship Report*, 19(23): 1, 3.

Ilbery, B. & Bowler, I. 1998. 'From agricultural productivism to post-productivism'. In B. Ilbery (ed.), *The Geography of Rural Change*, pp. 57–84. Harlow: Longman.

Ingham, J., Purvis, M. & Clarke, D.B. 1999. 'Hearing places, making spaces: sonorous geographies, ephemeral rhythms, and the Blackburn warehouse parties', *Environment & Planning D: Society & Space*, 17(3): 283–305.

Iso-Ahola, S. 1980. *The Social Psychology of Leisure and Recreation*. Dubuque, IA: Brown.

Iso-Ahola, S. 1983. 'Towards a social psychology of recreational travel', *Leisure Studies*, 2(1): 45–57.

Jago, L. & Shaw, R. 1998. 'Special events: a conceptual and differential framework', *Festival Management and Event Tourism*, 5(1/2): 21–32.

Jago, L. & Shaw, R. 1999. 'Consumer perceptions of special events: a multi-stimulus validation', *Journal of Travel and Tourism Marketing*, 8(4): 1–24.

Jaimangal-Jones, D., Pritchard, A. & Morgan, N. 2010. 'Going the distance: locating journey, liminality and rites of passage in dance music experiences', *Leisure Studies*, 29(3): 253–68.

Jaimangal-Jones, D., Pritchard, A. & Morgan, N. 2015. 'Exploring dress, identity and performance in contemporary dance music culture', *Leisure Studies*, 34(5): 603–20.

Jazz on a Summer's Day. 1960. Directed by Bert Stern & Aram Avakian. USA: Galaxy Productions. [Available on DVD: Snapper Music].

Jennings, M. 2010. 'Realms of re-enchantment: socio-cultural investigations of festival music space', *Perfect Beat*, 11(1): 67–83.

Jensen, J. 1992. 'Fandom as pathology: the consequences of characterisation'. In L.A. Lewis (ed.), *The Adoring Audience: Fan Culture and Popular Media*, pp. 9–29. London: Routledge.

Karsten, K. 2009. 'Experiential marketing and brand experiences: a conceptual framework'. In A. Lindgreen, J. Vanhamme & M.B. Beverland (eds), *Memorable Customer Experiences: A Research Anthology*, pp. 25–44. Farnham: Gower Publishing.

Kemp, C., Hull, I., Upton, M. & Hamilton, M. 2007. *Case Studies in Crowd Management*. Cambridge: Entertainment Technology Press Ltd.

Kerr, A. & May, D. 2011. 'An exploratory study looking at the relationship marketing techniques used in the music festival industry', *Journal of Retail & Leisure Property*, 9(5): 451–64.

Kinser, S. 1999. 'Why is carnival so wild?' In K. Eisenbichter & W. Hüsken (eds), *Carnival and the Carnivalesque. The Fool, the Reformer, the Wildman, and Others in Early Modern Theatre*, pp. 43–87. Atlanta, GA: Editions Rodopi B.V.

Klein, N. 2000. *No Logo*. London: Flamingo.

Knight, R., Miller, V., O'Connell, D., Siegle, L., Tucker, I. & Vernon, P. 2003. 'A to Z of summer (part one)', *The Observer* [online], 8 June. Available at: www.theguardian.com/lifeandstyle/2003/jun/08/ethicalliving1 (last accessed 27 July 2015).

Kotler, P. 1973. 'Atmospherics as a marketing tool', *Journal of Retailing*, 4: 48–64.

Kotler, P., Haider, D.H. & Rein, I. 1993. *Marketing Places – Attracting Investment, Industry, and Tourism to Cities, States, and Nations*. New York: The Free Press.

Kozinets, R.V. 1999. 'E-tribalized marketing? The strategic implications of virtual communities of consumption', *European Management Journal*, 17(3): 252–64.

Kubernik, H. & Kubernik, K. 2011. *A Perfect Haze. The Illustrated History of the Monterey International Pop Festival*. Solana Beach, CA: Santa Monica Press LLC.

Laing, D. 2004. 'The three Woodstocks and the live music scene'. In A. Bennett (ed.), *Remembering Woodstock*, pp. 1–17. Aldershot: Ashgate Publishing Limited.

Laing, D. & Newman, R. (eds) 1994. *Thirty Years of the Cambridge Folk Festival. The Definitive History of the World's Premier Acoustic Music Event*. Ely: Music Maker Books Ltd.

Lambert, S. 2000. 'Relationships in music', *Audience*, September, pp. 20–4.

Lammiman, J. & Syrett, M. 2004. *Cool Search*. Chichester: Capstone Publishing Ltd.

Lanier, C.D. & Hampton, R.D. 2009. 'Experiential marketing: understanding the logic of memorable customer experiences'. In A. Lindgreen, J. Vanhamme & M.B. Beverland (eds), *Memorable Customer Experiences: A Research Anthology*, pp. 9–23. Farnham: Gower Publishing.

Larsen, G. & O'Reilly, D. 2009. 'Festival tales: utopian tales'. *Academy of Marketing Annual Conference*, Aberdeen, Scotland.

Lazzarato, M. 1996. 'Immaterial labour' (trans. P. Colilli & E. Emory). In P. Virno & M. Hardt (eds) *Radical Thought in Italy*, pp. 132–46. Minneapolis: University of Minnesota Press.

Lefebvre, H. 1991. *The Production of Space*, trans. D. Nicholson-Smith. Oxford: Basil Blackwell Ltd.

Leyshon, A., Matless, D. & Revill, G. 1995. 'The place of music', *Transactions of the Institute of British Geographers*, 20: 423–33.

Li, X. & Petrick, J.F. 2006. 'A review of festival and event motivation studies', *Event Management*, 9: 239–45.

Life. 1969. 'Woodstock Music Festival: the great Woodstock rock trip', *Life* magazine, special edition, 1969.

Lindley, A. 1996. *Hyperion and the Hobbyhorse. Studies of Carnivalesque Subversion*. London: Associated University Presses.

Lingerieblog. 2007. 'Sloggi at V Festival', *Lingerieblog.co.uk*, 24 August. Available at: www.lingerieblog.co.uk/news/sloggi-at-v-festival/ (last accessed 4 June 2015).

Little, J. & Austin, P. 1996. 'Women and the rural idyll', *Journal of Rural Studies*, 12: 101–11.

Lloyds. 2013. 'Game, set, cancelled?', *Lloyds.com* [website], 25 June. Available at: www.lloyds.com/news-and-insight/news-and-features/market-news/industry-news-2013/game-set-cancelled (last accessed 2 August 2015).

Logan, G.M. & Adams, R.M. 2002. *Thomas More: Utopia*. Cambridge: Cambridge University Press.

Lowe, R. & Shaw, R. 1993. *Travellers: Voices of the New Age Nomads*. London: Fourth Estate.

Lull, J. 2000. *Media, Communication, Culture. A Global Approach*. 2nd edition. Cambridge, UK & Malden, MA: Polity Press.

Maffesoli, M. 1996. *The Time of the Tribes: The Decline of Individualism in Mass Society*, trans. D. Smith. London: SAGE Publications Ltd.

Mair, J. & Jago, L. 2010. 'The development of a conceptual model of greening in the business events tourism sector', *Journal of Sustainable Tourism*, 18(1): 77–94.

Malbon, B. 1998. 'The club. Clubbing: consumption, identity and the spatial politics of every-night life'. In T. Skelton & G. Valentine (eds), *Cool Places: Geographies of Youth Cultures*, pp. 266–86. London: Routledge.

Malbon, B. 1999. *Clubbing: Dancing, Ecstasy and Vitality*. London: Routledge.

Mandler, P. 1997. 'Against "Englishness": English culture and the limits to rural nostalgia, 1850–1940', *Transactions of the Royal Historical Society*, Sixth Series, Vol. 7: 155–75.

Martin, G. 1998. 'Generational differences amongst New Age travellers', *The Sociological Review*, 46(4): 735–56.

Martin, G. 2002. 'New Age travellers: uproarious or uprooted?', *Sociology*, 36(3): 723–35.

Martin, G. 2014. 'The politics, pleasure and performance of New Age travellers, ravers and anti-road protestors: connecting festivals, carnival and new social movements'. In A. Bennett, J. Taylor & I. Woodward (eds), *The Festivalization of Culture*, pp. 87–106. Farnham: Ashgate.

Maslow, A.H. 1999. *Toward a Psychology of Being*, 3rd edition. New York: John Wiley & Sons.

Massey, D. 1994. *Space, Place and Gender*. Minneapolis: University of Minnesota Press.

Massey, D. 2005. *For Space*. London: Sage.

Masson, G. 2004. 'Vitality vindicates V visionaries', *Audience*, July, pp. 18–25.

Masson, G. 2008. 'Power presses on despite opposition', *Music Week*, 29 November, p.11.

Masson, G. 2011. 'Crimewave fear for boutique festivals', *Music Week*, 5 February, p.10.

Matless, D. 1993. 'Appropriate geography: Patrick Abercrombie and the energy of the world', *Journal of Design History*, 6: 167–78.

Matless, D. 1998. *Landscape and Englishness*. London: Reaktion Books.

McAllister, M.P. 1996. *The Commercialization of American Culture: New Advertising, Control and Democracy*. Thousand Oaks, CA: Sage Publications.

McBride, T. & Muhle, B. 2008. *Meet the Millennials. Fans, Brands and Cultural Communities*. London: MusicTank.

McCabe, M. 2013. 'ISBA dismisses calls to ban alcohol ads at festivals and sports events', *Campaign* [online], 12 June. Available at: www.campaignlive.co.uk/news/1185978/ (last accessed 3 August 2015).

McGuinness, R. & Johnstone, H.D. 1990. 'Concert life in England'. In H.D. Johnstone & R. Fiske (eds), *The Blackwell History of Music in Britain, Volume 4: The Eighteenth Century*, pp. 31–95. Oxford: Basil Blackwell Ltd.

McKay, G. 1996. *Senseless Acts of Beauty: Cultures of Resistance since the Sixties*. London: Verso.

McKay, G. 2000. *Glastonbury: A Very English Fair*. London: Victor Gollancz.

McKay, G. 2004. '"Unsafe things like youth and jazz": Beaulieu Jazz Festivals (1956–61), and the origins of pop festival culture in Britain'. In A. Bennett (ed.), *Remembering Woodstock*, pp. 90–110. Aldershot: Ashgate.

McKay, G. (ed.). 2015. *The Pop Festival: History, Music, Media, Culture*. New York & London: Bloomsbury Academic.

McKelvey, S. 1994. 'Sans legal restraint, no stopping brash, creative ambush marketers', *Brandweek*, 35(16): 20.

McVeigh, S. 1993. *Concert Life in London from Mozart to Haydn*. Cambridge: Cambridge University Press.

McVeigh, S. 1999. 'The benefit concert in nineteenth-century London: from "tax on the nobility" to "monstrous nuisance"'. In B. Zon (ed.), *Nineteenth-Century British Music Studies, I*, pp. 242–66. Aldershot: Ashgate.

McWilliams, A. & Siegel, D.S. 2000. 'Corporate social responsibility and finance performance: correlation or misspecification?', *Strategic Management Journal*, 21(5): 603–09.

McWilliams, D. 2006. 'The boutique generation that refuses to grow up', *Sunday Business Post* [Ireland], 3 September. Also available at: www.davidmcwilliams.ie/2006/09/03/the-boutique-generation-that-refuses-to-grow-up (last accessed 27 July 2015).

Measham, F. 2016. 'Time to test: the festival drug report – Part II', Volteface Magazine [online]. Available at: http://volteface.me/features/the-festival-drug-report-part-ii/ (last accessed 21 June 2017).

Meenaghan, T. 1998. 'Ambush marketing: corporate strategy and consumer reaction', *Psychology & Marketing*, 15(4): 305–22.

Meenaghan, T. 2001. 'Understanding sponsorship effects', *Psychology & Marketing*, 18(2): 95–122.

Melody Maker. 1992a. 'Pressgang: the great festival debate', *Melody Maker*, 27 June, pp. 41–4.

Melody Maker. 1992b. 'Levellers blast festivals', *Melody Maker*, 13 June, p. 4.

Melody Maker. 1993. 'The empire strikes back. The Maker hit squad's definitive guide to the best of '93', *Melody Maker*, 25 September, pp. 40–2.

Met Police. 2015. *Unlicensed Music Events (Raves) Policy Statement*, v.1.1. Metropolitan Police, April 2015. Available at: www.met.police.uk/foi/pdfs/policies/unlicensed_music_policy.pdf (last accessed 9 August 2015).

Michaels, L. 2002. 'Has Glastonbury sold out?', *Corporate Watch*, 5 June. Available at: http://web.archive.org/web/20061014042358/http://archive.corporatewatch.org/news/glastonbury.htm (last accessed 13 July 2015).

Middleton, R. 1988. 'Popular music in the lower classes'. In N. Temperley (ed.), *The Blackwell History of Music in Britain. The Romantic Age 1800–1914*, pp. 63–91. Oxford: Basil Blackwell Ltd.

Miles, S. 1998. *Consumerism: As a Way of Life*. London: Sage.

Mintel. 2010. *Music Concerts and Festivals – UK – August 2010*. London: Mintel.

Mintel. 2013. *Music Concerts and Festivals – UK – August 2013*. London: Mintel.

Mintel. 2014. *Music Concerts and Festivals – UK – October 2014*. London: Mintel.
Mirza, M. (ed.). 2006. *Culture Vultures: Is UK Arts Policy Damaging the Arts?* London: Policy Exchange.
Mixmag. 2015. '43 People arrested at bank holiday rave in Lincolnshire', *Mixmag* [online], 27 May. Available at: www.mixmag.net/read/43-people-arrested-at-bank-holiday-rave-in-lincolnshire-news (last accessed 9 August 2015).
Monterey Pop (1967). Directed by D.A. Pennebaker. USA: The Foundation. [Available on DVD: The Criterion Collection].
Moore, T. 2013. *Audience Attitudes on the Environmental Impact of Events*. Report produced on behalf of A Greener Festival. Summary and findings available at: www.agreenerfestival.com/summary-of-research/ (last accessed 2 August 2015).
Morey, Y., Bengry-Howell, A., Griffin, C. Szmigin, I. & Riley, S. 2014. 'Festivals 2.0: consuming, producing and participating in the extended festival experience'. In A. Bennett, J. Taylor & I. Woodward (eds), *The Festivalization of Culture*, pp. 251–68. Farnham: Ashgate.
Music Week. 1998. 'Goldsmith: be sensible about live music', *Music Week*, 20 June, p.1.
Nakamura, J. & Csikszentmihalyi, M. 2003. 'The construction of meaning through vital involvement'. In L.M. Corey & J. Haidt (eds), *Flourishing: Positive Psychology and the Life Well-Lived*, pp. 83–104. Washington: American Psychological Association.
Nazerali, S. 1998. 'What sponsors can learn from music festival flops', *Marketing Week*, 27 August, p. 14.
NCCL: National Council for Civil Liberties. 1986. *Stonehenge*. London: NCCL.
Nelson, K.B. 2009. 'Enhancing the attendee's experience through creative design of the environment: applying Goffman's dramaturgical perspective', *Journal of Convention and Event Tourism*, 10: 120–33.
Neslen, A. 1994. 'Fest full of dealers', *NME*, 17 September, pp. 6–7.
Nettl, B. (ed.). 1978. *Eight Urban Musical Cultures: Tradition and Change*. Urbana, IL: University of Illinois Press.
Nicholson, R. & Pearce, D.G. 2011. 'Why do people attend events? A comparative analysis of visitor motivations at four South Island events', *Journal of Travel Research*, 39: 449–60.
NME. 1993. 'Thrill special. The bluffer's guide to crusty', *NME*, 9 January, p. 47.
NME. 1994. 'CJB: people can make a stand', *NME*, 10 September, p. 6.
Norwood, G. 2007. 'Beds and rugs and … rock'n'roll', *The Guardian* [online], 20 May. Available at: www.theguardian.com/money/2007/may/20/property.business (last accessed 8 August 2015).
O'Grady, K.A. & Kill, R. 2013. 'Exploring festival performance as a state of encounter', *Arts and Humanities in Higher Education*, 12(2–3): 268–83.
One iota. 2014. 'Very @ V Festival', *One iota* [website]. Available at: www.itsoneiota.com/portfolio/very-v-festival/ (last accessed 9 June 2015).
Operation Solstice. 1991. *Operation Solstice: The Battle of the Beanfield*. Directed by Gareth Morris, Russell Morris & Neil Goodwin. Channel 4 Television.
Orme, J. 1977. 'Festivals galore, but who's going to play?', *Melody Maker*, 18 June, pp. 30–1.
Osler, F. 2005. 'Know your enemy: the end of Glastonbury?', *Red Pepper*, July 2005. Available at: http://web.archive.org/web/20070702182827/www.redpepper.org.uk/KYE/x-kye-July2005.htm (last accessed 13 July 2015).

OutCider. 2015. 'OutCider Festival, July 31st – August 2nd 2015', *OutCider Festival* [website]. Available at: www.outciderfestival.co.uk/ (last accessed 27 July 2015).

Page, W. & Carey, C. 2009. 'Adding up the UK music industry for 2009', *Economic Insight*, Issue 20. Available at: www.prsformusic.com/creators/news/research/Documents/Economic%20Insight%2020%20web.pdf (last accessed 27 July 2015).

Palmer, H. & Thelwall, S. 2013. 'Smaller arts festivals: what is the most sustainable business model?', *The Guardian* [online], 13 February. Available at: www.theguardian.com/culture-professionals-network/culture-professionals-blog/2013/feb/13/arts-festivals-funding-local-authorities (last accessed 31 July 2015).

Palmley, G. 2002. 'Running the Metropolis', *Audience.uk*, September, pp. 8–13.

Partridge, C. 2006. 'The spiritual and the revolutionary: alternative spirituality, British free festivals, and the emergence of rave culture', *Culture & Religion*, 7(1): 41–60.

Partridge, R. 1973. 'Caught in the act: Glastonbury Fayre', *Melody Maker*, 9 June, p.53.

Paterson, C. 2008. 'Hip-hop "wrong" for Glastonbury', *BBC News*, 14 April. Available at: http://news.bbc.co.uk/1/hi/entertainment/7345780.stm (last accessed 4 June 2015).

Pearsall, R. 1973. *Victorian Popular Music*. Newton Abbot, Devon: David & Charles (Publishers) Limited.

Pegg, S. & Patterson, I. 2010. 'Rethinking music festivals as a staged event: gaining insights from understanding visitor motivations and the experiences they seek', *Journal of Convention and Event Tourism*, 11(2): 85–99.

Perez Falconi, J. 2011. 'Space and festivalscapes', *Platform: Postgraduate Journal of Theatre Arts*, 5(2): 5–18.

Peterson, R.A. 1973. 'The unnatural history of rock festivals: an instance of media facilitation', *Popular Music & Society*, 2(2): 97–123.

Peterson, R.A. & Bennett, A. 2004. 'Introducing music scenes'. In A. Bennett & R.A. Peterson (eds), *Music Scenes. Local, Translocal and Virtual*, pp. 1–16. Nashville: Vanderbilt University Press.

Petridis, A. 2003. 'Travel: boutique festivals of Britain', *The Guardian*, 21 June, p.13.

Pine, B.J, & Gilmore, J.H. 1999. *The Experience Economy: Work is Theatre and Every Business a Stage*. Boston, MA: Harvard Business School Press.

Porter, M.E. & Kramer, M.R. 2006. 'Strategy and society: the link between competitive advantage and corporate social responsibility', *Harvard Business Review*, 84 (12): 78–93.

Portman Group. 2014. *Code of Practice on Alcohol Sponsorship, First Edition*. London: Portman Group. Available at: www.portmangroup.org.uk/docs/default-source/recruitment-jds/alcohol-sponsorship-code.pdf?sfvrsn=0 (last accessed 3 August 2015).

Pratt, A.C. 2008. 'Locating the cultural economy'. In H. Anheier & Y.R. Isar (eds), *Cultures and Globalization: The Cultural Economy*, pp. 42–51. London: Sage.

Press, J. 1994. 'The killing of Crusty', *Spin*, 1 October, pp. 68–76.

Proud, A. 2015. 'Today's festivals are elitist, corporate and a million miles from their alternative roots', *The Telegraph* [online], 25 June. Available at: www.telegraph.co.uk/men/thinking-man/11697087/Todays-festivals-are-elitist-corporate-and-a-million-miles-from-their-alternative-roots.html (last accessed 5 August 2015).

PRS for Music/Frukt. 2013. *UK Brand Spend in Music*. Report by PRS for Music/Frukt.

PSA. 2016. *Psychoactive Substances Act 2016*. London: TSO.

PSI Act. 2001. *The Private Security Industry Act 2001*. London: HMSO.
Quinn, B. & Burn-Murdoch, J. 2012. 'Revealed: types and quantities of drugs seized by police at UK music festivals', *The Guardian* [online], 21 May. Available at: www.theguardian.com/uk/2012/may/21/music-festivals-drugs (last accessed 7 August 2015).
Quinn, B. & Wilks, L. 2013. 'Festival connections: people, place and social capital'. In G. Richards, M.P. de Brito & L. Wilks (eds), *Exploring the Social Impacts of Events*, pp. 15–30. Oxford: Routledge.
Rao, A.R. 1997. 'Strategic brand alliances', *Journal of Brand Management*, 5: 111–19.
Ravenscroft, N. & Gilchrist, P. 2009. 'Spaces of transgression: governance, discipline and reworking the carnivalesque', *Leisure Studies*, 28(1): 35–49.
Relph, E. 1976. *Place and Placelessness*. London: Pion.
Renov, M. 2004. *The Subject of Documentary*. Minneapolis: University of Minnesota Press.
Revill, G. 2000. 'Music and the politics of sound: nationalism, citizenship and auditory space', *Environment & Planning D: Society & Space*, 18(5): 597–613.
Reynolds, S. 2013. *Energy Flash: A Journey Through Rave Music and Dance Culture*, revised edition. London: Picador.
Rietveld, H. 1993. 'Living the dream'. In S. Redhead (ed.), *Rave Off: Politics and Deviance in Contemporary Youth Culture*, pp. 41–78. Aldershot: Avebury.
Rietveld, H. 1998. 'Repetitive beats: free parties and the politics of contemporary DiY dance culture in Britain'. In G. McKay (ed.), *DiY Culture: Party and Protest in Nineties Britain*, pp. 243–67. London & New York: Verso.
Ritzer, G. 1993. *The McDonaldization of Society*. London: Sage.
Ritzer, G. 1999. *Enchanting a Disenchanted World: Revolutionizing the Means of Consumption*. Thousand Oaks, CA: Pine Forge Press.
Ritzer, G. & Jurgenson, N. 2010. 'Production, consumption, prosumption. The nature of capitalism in the age of the digital "prosumer"', *Journal of Consumer Culture*, 10(1): 13–36.
Robinson, R. 2015a. *Music Festivals and the Politics of Participation*. Farnham: Ashgate.
Robinson, R. 2015b. 'No spectators! The art of participation, from Burning Man to boutique festivals in Britain'. In G. McKay (ed.), *The Pop Festival: History, Music, Media, Culture*, pp. 165–81. New York & London: Bloomsbury Academic.
Rojek, C. 2000. *Leisure and Culture*. Basingstoke: Macmillan Press Ltd.
Rojek, C. 2013. *Event Power: How Global Events Manage and Manipulate*. London: Sage.
Roland, M. 1998. 'Festival guide '98: Druid's Dream is so passé', *Melody Maker*, 27 June, p. 34.
Rolfe, H. 1992. *Arts Festivals in the UK*. London: Policy Studies Institute.
RT Worldwide. 2015. 'Festival insurance', *Robertson Taylor W&P Longreach* [website]. Available at: http://rtworldwide.com/music-event-insurance/festival-insurance/ (last accessed 2 August 2015).
Russell, D. 1987. *Popular Music in England, 1840–1914. A Social History*, 2nd edition. Manchester: Manchester University Press.
Rycroft, S. 1998. 'Global undergrounds: the cultural politics of sound and light in Los Angeles, 1965–1975'. In A. Leyshon, D. Matless & G. Revill (eds), *The Place Of Music*, pp. 222–48. New York: The Guildford Press.
St John, G. 2001. 'Alternative cultural heterotopia and the liminoid body: beyond Turner at ConFest', *The Australian Journal of Anthropology*, 12(1): 47–66.

St John, G. 2008. *Victor Turner and Contemporary Cultural Performance*. New York & Oxford: Berghahn Books.
St John, G. 2009. *Technomad. Global Raving Countercultures*. London & Oakville, CT: Equinox.
St John, G. 2010. 'Liminal culture and global movement: the transitional world of psytrance'. In G. St John (ed.) *The Local Scenes and Global Culture of Psytrance*, pp. 220–46. London: Routledge.
St John, G. 2017. *Weekend Societies: Electronic Dance Music Festivals and Event-Cultures*. New York: Bloomsbury Academic.
Salmon, C. 2011. 'UK festivals: has the bubble burst?', *The Guardian* [online], 15 September. Available at: www.guardian.co.uk/music/2011/sep/15/uk-festivals-bubble-burst (last accessed 23 July 2015).
Sandford, J. & Reid, R. 1974. *Tomorrow's People*. London: Jerome Publishing Company.
Sanghani, R. 2015. 'The dark truth about rape at UK music festivals', *The Telegraph* [online], 25 August. Available at: www.telegraph.co.uk/women/womens-life/11822420/Bestival-UK-music-festivals-have-a-rape-problem-that-needs-action-now.html (last accessed 20 August 2016).
Santoro, C. & Troilo, G. 2007. 'The drivers of hedonic consumption experience. A semiotic analysis of rock concerts'. In A. Carù & B. Cova (eds), *Consuming Experience*, pp. 109–25. London & New York: Routledge.
Schmalenbach, J. 1977. 'Communion – a sociological category'. In G. Lüschen & G.P. Stone (eds), *Herman Schmalenbach: On Society and Experience*, pp. 64–125. Chicago, University of Chicago Press.
Schmid, C. 2008. 'Henri Lefebvre's theory of the production of space. Towards a three-dimensional dialectic' (trans. B. Goonewardena). In K. Goonewardena, S. Kipfer, R. Milgram & C. Schmid (eds), *Space, Difference, Everyday Life. Reading Henri Lefebvre*, pp. 27–45. New York & London: Routledge.
Schofield, N. 2002. *Fairport unConventionAL*. Belper, Derbyshire: Free Reed Music.
Schowalter, D.F. 2000. 'Remembering the dangers of rock and roll: toward a historical narrative of the rock festival', *Critical Studies in Media Communication*, 17(1): 86–102.
Shambala Festival. 2015. 'Our guiding principles', *Shambala Festival* [website]. Available at: www.shambalafestival.org/essential-info/our-guiding-principles/ (last accessed 15 June 2015.
Sherwin, A. 2006. '2006: the year festivals killed the golden goose', *The Times* [London], 11 August, p. 14.
Shields, R. 1989. 'Social spatialization and the built environment: the West Edmonton Mall', *Environment & Planning D: Society & Space*, 7: 147–64.
Shields, R. 1991. *Places on the Margin: Alternative Geographies of Modernity*. London: Routledge.
Short, B. 2006. 'Idyllic ruralities'. In P. Cloke, T. Marsden & P.H. Mooney (eds), *Handbook of Rural Studies*, pp. 133–48. London: Sage.
SIA [Security Industry Authority]. 2008. *Security at Events. Guidance on the Private Security Industry Act 2001* (updated edition, February 2008). Liverpool: Security Industry Authority.
Sibley, D. 1994. 'The sin of transgression', *Area*, 26: 300–3.
Skinner, B.E. & Rukavina, V. 2003. *Event Sponsorship*. Hoboken, NJ: John Wiley & Sons Inc.

Slocombe, M. 1998. 'The festival experience™', *The Big Issue*, May 1998. Also available at: www.urban75.com/Rave/bigissue.html (last accessed 13 July 2015).

Smith, A. 1995. 'The Criminal Justice and Public Order Act: the public order elements', *Criminal Law Review*, January 1995: 19–27.

Smith, A. 2011. 'The transition town network: a review of current evolutions and renaissance', *Social Movement Studies: Journal of Social, Cultural & Political Protest*, 10(1): 99–105.

Smyth, D. 2004. 'V. good music festival', *Evening Standard*, 23 August. Available at: www.thisislondon.co.uk/showbiz/article-12739308-v-good-music-festival.do (last accessed 16 June 2015).

Sonisphere. 2015. 'No Sonisphere Knebworth in 2015', *Sonisphere.co.uk*, 16 January. Available at: http://sonisphere.co.uk/news/no-sonisphere-knewborth-in-2015/ (last accessed 4 June 2015).

Spence, A. 2014. 'BBC sends more people to Glasto than Brazil', *The Times* [online], 7 June. Available at: www.thetimes.co.uk/tto/news/medianews/article4111743.ece (last accessed 11 June 2015).

Stadler, R., Fullagar, S.P. & Reid, S. 2014. 'The professionalization of festival organizations: a relational approach to knowledge management'. *Event Management*, 18(1): 39–52.

Stallybrass, P. & White, A. 1986. *The Politics and Poetics of Transgression*. Ithaca, New York: Cornell University Press.

Stoeltje, B.J. 1989. 'Festival'. In E. Barnouw, G. Gerbner, W. Schramm, T.L. Worth & L. Gross (eds), *International Encyclopedia of Communications, Volume 2*, pp. 161–6. New York & Oxford: Oxford University Press.

Stoodley, T. & Grainger, E. 2001. 'Cambridge Folk Club. A history', *Cambridge Folk Club History* [web resource]. Available at: https://web.archive.org/web/20060108235252/www.shpltd.co.uk/cfc/history.html (last accessed 9 July 2016).

Stout, A. 2003. 'The world turned upside down: Stonehenge summer solstice before the hippies', *3rd Stone*, 46: 38–41.

Street, J. 2004. '"This is your Woodstock": popular memories and political myths'. In A. Bennett (ed.), *Remembering Woodstock*, pp. 29–42. Aldershot: Ashgate Publishing Limited.

Street, J. 2005. 'Wellies, check. Bolly, check', *Times Higher Education Supplement*, 8 July. Available at: www.timeshighereducation.com/features/wellies-check-bolly-check/197199.article (last accessed 30 October 2016).

Street, J. 2012. *Music and Politics*. Cambridge & Malden, MA: Polity.

Sturdy, M. 2003. *Truth and Beauty: The Story of Pulp*. London: Omnibus Press.

Sunrise Celebration. 2015. 'About us'. *Sunrise Celebration* [website]. Available at: www.sunrisecelebration.com/about/about-us (last accessed 212 June 2015).

Swash, R. 2008a. 'Gallagher brands Jay-Z "wrong for Glasto"', *The Guardian* (online), 14 April. Available at: www.theguardian.com/music/2008/apr/14/jayz.urban (last accessed 4 June 2015).

Swash, R. 2008b. 'Reading and Leeds festival cans Carling sponsorship', *The Guardian* (online), 21 January. Available at: www.theguardian.com/music/2008/jan/21/festivals.news (last accessed 7 June 2015).

Tapscott, D. 2009. *Grown Up Digital. How the Net Generation is Changing Your World*. New York: McGraw-Hill.

Tayler, F. 2013. 'Something Else in the Dean 2013 review', *efestivals.co.uk*. 3 October. Available at: www.efestivals.co.uk/festivals/somethingelse/2013/review-overview.shtml (last accessed 27 July 2015).

Bibliography

TerraChoice. 2010. 'The "seven sins of greenwashing": home and family edition'. Available at: http://sinsofgreenwashing.org/findings/the-seven-sins/ (last accessed 2 August 2015).

Thames Valley Police. 2014. 'TVP@RDG 2014', *Thames Valley Police* [online], August 2014. Available at: www.thamesvalley.police.uk/newsevents/newsevents-events/newsevents-events-rdgfestival.htm (last accessed 8 August 2015).

The Manufacturer. 2010. 'Coca-Cola awarded for festival recycling', *The Manufacturer*, 25 November. Available at: www.themanufacturer.com/articles/coca-cola-awarded-for-festival-recycling/ (last accessed 8 June 2015).

Thomas, R. & Thomas, H. 2013. 'What are the prospects for professionalizing events management in the UK?', *Tourism Management Perspectives*, 6: 8–14.

Thornton, S. 1995. *Club Cultures: Music, Media and Subcultural Capital*. Cambridge: Polity Press.

Thrift, N. 1989. 'Images of social change'. In C. Hammet, L. McDowell & P. Sarre (eds), *The Changing Social Structure*, pp. 12–42. London: Sage.

Time. 1967. 'People: Sep. 8 1967', *Time* [magazine], 8 September, p. 32.

Tinkler, J. 2012. 'Reality television hits new low with Channel 4's latest show, Summerdaze', *Sick Chirpse* [website], summer 2012. Available at: www.sickchirpse.com/reality-television-hits-new-low-with-channel-4s-latest-show-summerdaze/ (last accessed 20 December 2015).

Tjora, A. 2016. 'The social rhythm of the rock music festival', *Popular Music*, 35(1): 64–83.

Tobin, B. 2014. 'Music festivals becoming too expensive and repetitive', *YouGovUK* [website], 14 May. Available at: https://yougov.co.uk/news/2014/05/14/music-festivals-becoming-too-expensive-and-repetit/ (last accessed 3 August 2015).

Tönnies, F. 2001. *Community and Civil Society*, ed. & trans. J. Harris, trans. M. Hollis. Cambridge: Cambridge University Press.

Tuan, Y-F. 1977. *Space and Place: The Perspective of Experience*. Minneapolis: University of Minnesota Press.

Turner, V. 1969. *The Ritual Process: Structure and Anti-Structure*. London: Routledge & Kegan Paul.

Turner, V. 1982. *From Ritual to Theatre. The Human Seriousness of Play*. New York: PAJ Publications.

Turner, V. 1987. 'Carnival, ritual, and play in Rio de Janiero'. In A. Falassi (ed.), *Time Out of Time: Essays on the Festival*, pp. 76–90. Albuquerque: University of New Mexico Press.

UK Folk Festivals. 2015. 'Folk music festivals in the UK', *UK Folk Festivals* [website]. Available at: www.ukfolkfestivals.co.uk/viewall.php (last accessed 9 July 2015).

UK Music. 2011. *Destination Music: The Contribution of Music Festivals and Major Concerts to Tourism in the UK*. London: UK Music.

UK Music. 2013. *Wish You Were Here. Music Tourism's Contribution to the UK Economy*. London: UK Music.

UK Music. 2016. *Wish You Were Here 2016. The Contribution of Live Music to the UK Economy*. London: UK Music.

Urban75. 1998. 'Rave: the hard sell. Rave is big business', *Urban75.com*, January 1998. Available at: www.urban75.com/Rave/raverant.html (last accessed 13 July 2015).

Urry, J. & Larsen, J. 2011. *The Tourist Gaze 3.0*. London: Sage.

van Gennep, A. 1960. *The Rites of Passage*, trans. M.B. Vizedom & G.L. Caffee. London: Routledge & Kegan Paul Ltd.

V Festival. 2014. 'V Festal Info Guide'. Supplied with the *Official V Festival Programme 2004*. London: Blue Grape Ltd.

V Festival. 2015. 'Festival safety – getting intimate', *V Festival* [website]. Available at: www.vfestival.com/festival-safety/ (last accessed 6 August 2015).

Vincent, A. 2014. 'Where are all the women headlining music festivals?', *The Telegraph* [online], 8 August. Available at: www.telegraph.co.uk/culture/music/music-festivals/11016441/Where-are-all-the-women-headlining-music-festivals.html (last accessed 10 August 2015).

Wakefield, K.L. 2012. 'How sponsorships work: the sponsorship engagement model', *Event Management*, 16(2): 143–55.

Waller, J. 2013. 'V-Festival: a chav paradise', *Sabotage Times*, 16 August. Available at: http://sabotagetimes.com/music/v-festival-a-chav-paradise (last accessed 4 June 2015).

Waterman, S. 1998. 'Carnivals for elites? The cultural politics of arts festivals', *Progress in Human Geography*, 22(1): 54–74.

Watson, I. 1983. *Song and Democratic Culture in Britain. An Approach to Popular Culture in Social Movements*. Beckenham, Kent: Croom Helm Ltd.

Watts, G. 1986. *Parks Service Information*. Leaflet produced by Cambridge City Council Amenities and Recreation Department.

Watts, M. 1974. 'Knebworth. Great music but a non-event', *Melody Maker*, 27 July, pp.8,9,56.

Weber, D. 1995. 'From limen to border: a meditation on the legacy of Victor Turner for American Cultural Studies', *American Quarterly*, 47(3): 525–36.

Weber, M. 1992. *The Protestant Ethic and the Spirit of Capitalism*, trans. T. Parsons. London & New York: Routledge.

Weber, W. 2000. 'Miscellany vs. homogeneity: concert programmes at the Royal Academy of Music and the Royal College of Music in the 1880s'. In C. Bashford & L. Langley (eds), *Music and British Culture, 1785–1914: Essays in Honour of Cyril Ehrlich*, pp. 299–320. Oxford: Oxford University Press.

Webster, E. 2014. *Association of Independent Festivals Six-Year Report 2014*. Available at: http://aiforg.com/wp-content/uploads/AIF-Six-Year-Report-2014.pdf (last accessed 3 August 2015).

Webster, E. & McKay, G. 2016. *From Glyndebourne to Glastonbury: The Impact of British Music Festivals*. Norwich: Arts & Humanities Research Council/University of East Anglia.

Weston Park. 2016. 'About Weston Park – The Weston Park Foundation'. *Weston Park* [official website]. Available at: www.weston-park.com/about/the-foundation/ (last accessed 26 July 2016).

Whistler, L. 1947. *The English Festivals*. London: William Heinemann Ltd.

whynotfindout.org. 2015. *Homepage* [website]. Available at: www.whynotfindout.org/ (last accessed 3 August 2015).

Wikström, P. 2009. *The Music Industry: Music in the Cloud*. Cambridge, UK & Malden, MA: Polity Press.

Wilks, L. 2011. 'Bridging and bonding: social capital at music festivals', *Journal of Policy Research in Tourism, Leisure and Events*, 3(3): 281–97.

Wilks, L. & Quinn, B. 2016. 'Linking social capital, cultural capital and heterotopia at the folk festival', *Journal of Comparative Research in Anthropology and Sociology*, 7(1): 23–39.

Wiseman-Trowse, N. 2008. *Performing Class in British Popular Music*. London: Palgrave Macmillan.

Woods, M. 2006. 'Redefining the "rural question": the new "politics of the rural" and social policy', *Social Policy and Administration*, 40(6): 579–95.

Woods, M. 2011. *Rural*. London: Routledge.

Woodstock – Three Days of Peace and Music. 1970. Directed by Michael Wadleigh. USA: Wadleigh-Maurice/Warner Bros. [Available as an extended Director's Cut from Warner Home video, 2002].

Worthington, A. 2004. *Stonehenge: Celebration and Subversion*. Loughborough: Alternative Albion.

Worthington, A. 2005. *The Battle of the Beanfield*. Teignmouth, Devon: Enabler Publications.

WSTA [Wine and Spirit Trade Association]. 2015. *Challenge 25*. Available at: www.wsta.co.uk/challenge-25 (last accessed 9 August 2015).

Young, R. 2010. *Electric Eden: Unearthing Britain's Visionary Music*. London: Faber & Faber.

Index

AC/DC 141
acid house 16–17, 33, 108; *see also* raves
AEG Live / AEG Presents 35, 48, 50
affordability of festivals 43, 62, 110
A Greener Festival 57–8
AIF (Association of Independent Festivals) 57–8, 64, 66, 69
Albion Fairs 13, 14, 15, 25
alcohol: consumption 65, 138; sponsorship 70–1, 82; pouring rights 86
Also Festival 45
Altamont 10, 23
Alt-fest 48
anti-social behaviour 36, 119, 152
Anti-structure 104, 105; *see also* liminality; communitas
Arcadia 155
Arctic Monkeys 79–80
Arts Council 49, 52, 82
atmosphere 32, 134, 135, 153–62: atmospherics 154; belonging 143; domestication of a site 43, 118; fandom 145; role of audiences 44, 118–19, 140, 151–2; role of brand sponsors 98; role of organisers 139, 151, 153–6; experience economy 154; servicescapes 155; temporal rhythms 156; zoning of sites 156, 157–9
audiences/festivalgoers: affective labour 97–8; demographics/psychographics 40, 67, 76–7, 153; immaterial labour 97–8, 100; loyalty 72, 78, 104, 133, 135–6; 'middle youth' 44, 62; millennials 99–100; motivations 44, 135–48, 152, 162; transcendence 22, 136, 139, 146–8, 161; use of space 103, 109, 157–9; *see also* authenticity; belonging; experience; participation; sociality; spectacular consumption
authenticity: audiences 25, 29, 138–43; festivals 139–40, 142, 143; utopia/utopianism 138–9, 141

Bakhtin, M. 19–22, 103, 107–8, 159; *see also* carnival/carnivalesque
Bannister, F. 83
Barsham Faire 14
Barthes, R 147–8, 161–2
Bath Festival of Blues and Progressive Music 31, 83
Battle of the Beanfield 16, 18; *see also* Stonehenge Free Festival
BBC: 30, 78, 90, 91, 94, 130
Beacon Festival 52
Bearded Theory 29
Beat-Herder Festival 95
Beaulieu Jazz Festival 29–30
Beautiful Days 148
Bell, D. 132
belonging 135, 143–5, 149–50, 162
Ben & Jerry's Sundae on the Common 85–6
Benn, M. 67, 69, 85, 153, 159
Bennett, A. 2, 63
Bestival 44, 62, 65–6, 147, 156
Bey, H. 107–8, 110, 112
Big Chill 33, 39, 43
Bitner, M.J. 154, 155
Bjork 41–2
Blake, A. 19
Blissfields 52, 144
Block 9 155
Bloodstock Open Air 75, 148
Bolan, M. 131
Boomtown Fair 75, 92, 105, 138, 155

boutique festivals 14, 43–5, 94: characteristics 43–4, 68, 142; design 44–5, 76, 155; family orientation 44; programming 14, 44, 46, 156
Boyes, G. 25, 130
branding 84, 95–7, 99, 124: brand experience 96–8, 112–14; brand fit/ congruence 76–80, 100; brand matrix 74–5; growth of 74, 85; *see also* sponsorship
British Summer Time Festival 50–1, 85, 107
Britpop 34, 119, 120
broadcasting of festivals 41, 56, 78: broadcast rights 90–1; mainstreaming 127; *see also* mediation of festivals
Brocken, M. 24, 28–9
Bryman, A. 97
Butler, J. 134, 151

Caillois, R. 136–7
Cambridge Folk Festival 29, 32, 52: audiences 138, 140–1, 144, 151, 155, 160; case study 114–19; sponsorship 84
Campbell, C. 136, 142
Camp Bestival 138, 144–5
CND (Campaign for Nuclear Disarmament) 32
camping; 41, 43–4, 156–7: boutique camping/glamping 44, 67–8, 153
Carah, N. 98, 100, 143
Carling Weekend *see* Reading Festival and Leeds Festival
Carlsberg UK 82, 86
carnival/carnivalesque 19–20, 22, 36, 41, 124, 139: as safety valve 23–4; behaviours associated with 19–22, 103, 147, 160; critique of 21, 23; feast of fools 22; flattening of hierarchy 19, 159–60; 'second world' 20, 22, 71; *see also* countercultural carnivalesque
Castlemorton Common mega-rave 17–18, 69
celebrity culture 89–90, 92
Channel 4 84, 91–2, 121
Clarke, M. 9, 14, 15, 22, 62, 64
class 149, 153, 159–61; boutique festivals 94, 159; carnivalesque 22, 23–4; folk culture and 24, 25, 27, 29; middle class counterculture 14; New Age Travellers 12, 18; *see also* 'weekend hippies'

Cloonan, M. 49–50, 54, 129
club culture 16, 18, 34
Coca-Cola 83, 87–8
co-creation 135, 142, 164
Collin, M. 12, 15, 16, 17
commercialisation of festivals 33–6, 143, 147; *see also* raves
communitas 104, 146–7, 158, 161
ConFest 109
Cornbury Music Festival 29, 159
Corona SunSets 50
corporate hospitality 55–6
corporate social responsibility 54–5, 56, 62, 81
costume/fancy dress 46, 112, 138, 147
countercultural carnivalesque 3–4, 22–3, 45, 105; commercialisation of 62–71, 122; disorder 16, 69–71, 71–2; drugs 15–17, 64–7; historical narratives of 7–19, 32–34; marketing 80, 95; mediation 135, 138–9, 155–6; sex/nudity 63–4; space/place 130–2; sponsorship 95–8, 120–1; squalor 67–68; *see also* commercialisation of festivals; mainstreaming
Creamfields 33–4, 39, 50, 72
crime 17, 64, 69–71
Criminal Justice and Public Order Act 1994 33–4, 59, 69, 72; protests and criticisms 17–19, 61, 120–1
Cropredy Festival 32, 44, 148; audiences 141–2; 144–5; 159–60; *see also* Fairport Convention
crowd-funding 48
Csikszentmihalyi, M. 146, 147
cultural economy 3
cyclic place 111, 125–28; annual reconstruction 111, 125, 126; continuity vs. ephemerality 112, 125, 127; 'insideness' 114, 133; mediation 111, 126–7; narrativisation 112, 113–14, 126; relationship with host location 111, 114, 125–6, 128; representations 112–13; *see also* place; sense of place

dance-orientated festivals 16, 33–4, 95, 103, 137; *see also* acid house; free parties
Deeply Vale Festival 13, 106
Deutsche Entertainment AG 51
DF Concerts 34, 51, 120
DHP Family Ltd 48, 51

digital technology 66, 91, 101, 110
disorder 4, 15–16, 69–71, 131
Download Festival 50, 65, 75, 107, 141, 148, 155
drugs 64–7, 131: drug-testing and other actions 66–7, 69–70, 122, 152; representations 8–10, 15; *see also* legal highs
Dylan, B. 28, 96

Eavis, E. 78
Eavis, M. 10, 116
economic recession 43
Ecstasy 16, 65–6
Ehrenreich, B. 137, 143, 159
Electric Picnic (Ireland) 44, 45
electronic dance music (EDM) 2, 103; *see also* acid house; raves
Events Management Body of Knowledge (EMBOK) 53
Englishness 129–30
environmental sustainability 18, 56–8, 94–5: Love Your Tent campaign 57–8; mainstreaming of 56–7, 131; sponsorship and 87–8, 93; 'triple bottom line' 57, 62
escapism 14, 25, 95, 135, 136–8
European festivals 43, 97
exclusivity deals 42, 44, 62, 72, 78
experience 15, 32, 62–71, 75–76, 110–11: authenticity 138–43; co-creation 87; commercialisation 122–4, 143; experience generation 99; hedonic pleasure 16, 139, 142–3, 162; heterogeneity 109; 112–114, 135, 147; immersion 85, 88, 146; jouissance 147–8, 161; peak experience 146–7; plaisir 147–8, 161; standardisation 61, 86, 95; tourist gaze 45; *see also* atmosphere; belonging; branding; communitas; flow; liminality; 'specialness'

Facebook 82, 89, 113, 126
Fairport Convention 12, 28, 131, 145, 148; *see also* Cropredy Festival
Falassi, A. 6, 159
family-friendly festivals 116–19, 141–5; *see also* boutique festivals
fashion 30, 87, 89, 92, 160–1
festivals: charitable events 26, 49, 50, 87; codes of practice 59–60, 70–71; competitive events 23–4, 46; cultural stereotypes 10–19, 29, 127, 135; customer service orientation 37, 41, 72, 124; diversification 45–6; failure 39, 47, 48–9, 51, 60, 77; festival season 26, 40–1; growth 29–30, 33, 35, 38–40, 140; municipal events 25–7, 52; volatility 47–9, 72–3; *see also* atmosphere; commercialisation of festivals; countercultural carnivalesque; mainstreaming; marketing; mediation
Festival No. 6 51, 89, 102
Festival of the Flower Children 8, 30–1
Festival Republic (formerly Mean Fiddler) 39, 45, 50, 93
Festival Welfare Services 15
flow 142, 146–8, 158
folk music 13, 115–16, 129–30, 151: First Folk Revival 23–5; Second Folk Revival 27–9
folk-rock 28, 32, 44, 131
Fonarow, W. 158
Foucault, M. 5, 103, 112, 126; *see also* heterotopia
Found Series 48, 51
free festivals 1–2, 11–13, 14–16, 22, 131: People's Free Festivals 12; regulation 59; *see also* New Age Travellers; free parties; Stonehenge Free Festival
free parties 17–19, 49, 59, 61, 72: Advance Party 18; licensing 16–18; Spiral Tribe 17–18; street protests 18, 120–1; UK Tek 71–2; Unlicensed Music Events (UMEs) 71–2; *see also* acid house; raves
Frith, S. 2, 7, 9, 33
Frukt Agency 80, 88, 92, 100

Gallagher, N. 78
Getz, D. 39, 52, 54, 115, 134, 161
Gimme Shelter (1970) 9–10
Glade Festival 70
glamping *see* camping
Glastonbury Fayre (1972) 10–11, 164
Glastonbury Festival 32, 70, 102, 140, 149–50: BBC 78, 91; drugs 64–5; environmentalism 10–11, 32; mediation 80, 90–1, 119; mythology 11, 46, 61, 131, 155; New Age Travellers 138–9; politics 32; programming 32, 46, 78–80, 156; sponsorship 74, 92, 95; *see also Glastonbury Fayre*

194 *Index*

Global 51, 72
Goffman, E. 150–1
Goldblatt, J. 53–4
Great Western Festivals 58
Green Man Festival 43, 82, 94, 106

Halfacree, K. 59, 131
Hawkwind 10, 12, 18
headline acts 33–4, 39, 42, 77–80; *see also* exclusivity deals
heavy metal 33, 75, 79–80, 151
Hendrix, J. 8, 30
Here & Now 12
heterotopia 108–11, 112, 117: alternative cultural heterotopia 103, 109; cyclic place 126
heritage artists 42–3
Hetherington, K. 3, 9, 13, 106–7, 149–50, 152
High Voltage Festival 39
Hillage, S. 32
hippies 8–9, 11, 18; *see also* 'weekend hippies'
Hop Farm Festival 48, 74, 96
house music *see* acid house
hybrid festivals 45–6, 49, 72, 148, 165
Hyde Park concerts 8, 50–1, 85, 107
hyperreality 97

independence 95, 141
Innocent Village Fete 86
Instagram 80, 87, 113, 123, 126, 154
insurance 56, 57
Isle of Wight Festival: 1968–70 8, 18, 31, 58; 2002 to date 65, 68, 70, 85
Iso-Ahola, S.E. 135

Jay-Z 78, 79
jazz festivals 8, 29–30, 115
Jazz on a Summer's Day 115
Jefferson Airplane 8, 10
Julie's Bicycle 58

Kilimanjaro Live 51
Knebworth 31–2, 33
Kotler, P. 135, 154–5
Kozinets, R. 154

Laing, D. 31, 52, 140
Larmer Tree Festival 29, 144
Latitude Festival 45, 92, 94, 153
Lefebvre, H. 112–14, 126, 127, 150

Leeds Festival 36, 67, 70, 85, 94
legal highs 65–7, 122
Let's Rock festivals 42, 48, 51
Levellers, The 18, 61, 148
licensing 58–61, 70, 71, 132–3, 139
liminality 103–7
Lindley, A. 20, 21
live music sector 2–3, 38–9: festival touring 42, 62, 141; revenue streams 41–2
Live Nation Entertainment 34, 35, 42, 51: sponsorship 86, 93, 94
Lloyd, A.L. 27–8
Longstock Summer Solstice Festival 17
Loop, The 66–7

MacColl, E. 27–8
McKay, G. 2, 15, 19, 22, 125
Maffesoli, M. 14–50
Mainstreaming of festivals 37, 41, 61–2, 126–7
Malbon, B. 16, 137, 158
MAMA & Co / MAMA Group 39, 43, 48, 50
Mamas and the Papas, The 8
markets 28, 116, 122, 157
marketing of festivals 49–50, 61, 76–7, 135–6: added value 84, 86–7, 93, 122, 124; ambush marketing 91–2; engagement 82, 88, 98; event marketing 88–9, 143; experiential marketing 41, 68, 74, 86–90, 100–1; post-event marketing 113, 143, 154; use of social media 80, 82, 83–4. 87. 89, 98; *see also* branding; sponsorship
Maslow, A. 146, 147
Massey, D. 112, 126, 127
Matless, D. 128–9
MCD Productions 34, 50, 90, 96, 119
Mean Fiddler 85, 90, 96, 119: and commercial raves 33–4; *see also* Festival Republic
Measham, F. 66–7
mediation of festivals 8, 46, 161: countercultural carnivalesque 135; cyclic place 126–7; Glastonbury 78–80; media rights 90–1; meta-sociality 150, 152; social media 46, 98, 113; traditional media 46; *see also* BBC
merchandising 42, 83, 88, 145, 150
Metallica 34, 79–80

meta-sociality 134, 150–3: behavioural and social norms 150–1; organiser control 151–2; performativity 151; spatiality 150, 152–3
Metropolis Music 34, 51, 120
Mintel 38, 44, 68, 72
Monsters of Rock Festival 32, 60, 85
Monterey International Pop Festival 8, 9, 23, 30
mosh pit 151, 158

national identity 35, 130; *see also* Englishness
National Jazz Federation *see* Reading Festival
neo-tribes 149–50, 160
New Age Travellers (NATs) 12–19, 25, 59, 69: media representations 2, 14–15; liminality and space 106, 109; 'Peace Convoy' 15; *see also* Stonehenge Festival
Night Assemblies Bill 58
North Wales Blues and Soul Festival 52
'no spectators' philosophy 105
nudity 10, 19, 63

O2 51, 82
OutCider Festival 45
OutKast 42
Ozric Tentacles 2, 18

pagan and neo-pagan beliefs 13, 17, 19, 61, 106
participation 12, 75, 105, 110, 136, 143
payment schemes 62
programming 14, 77–80, 115, 121, 124, 155, 159; *see also* boutique festivals
Partridge, C. 11, 17
Pendleton, H. 30
Pennebaker, D.A 8
place 45, 102–3, 109–10, 127: destination image 135–6; place and space 111–12, 126, 150; place identity/image 112, 124, 127; placelessness 124; *see also* cyclic place; rurality; sense of place
play 14, 22, 88, 97, 100, 104–5
policing 15–6, 17, 59, 69–70, 71–2; *see also* drugs
politics 37, 58, 136, 169; folk revivals 24, 27–8; free festivals 12, 15, 17, 69, 106; rurality 128

Port Eliot Lit Fest 14, 46
post-productivist countryside *see* rurality
pouring rights 86
Power, V. 48, 96
Private Security Industry Act 2001 60–1
professionalism 49–50, 52–6, 57, 166
promoters: rave promoters 16–17, 33–4; typologies 49–52
PRS for Music 41, 52, 80, 82
Psychoactive Substances Act 2016 66
Public Order Act 1986 16
Pulp 77, 80, 119, 120
'Purple Guide' 60, 166
Pyramid Stage 11, 78–9; *see also* Glastonbury Festival

Quinn, B. & Wilks, L. 157

raves 16–19: commercialisation 18, 34, 37, 61; liminality 103, 105; rural 128, 131; TAZ 107–8; unlicensed events 33, 59, 71–2; *see also* free parties
Reading Festival 4, 18: final night riots 33, 36, 70; image 140, 141; National Jazz Federation 30–31; ownership 45, 50; programming 30, 33–4; sponsorship 85, 90, 94; *see also* Festival Republic
religion 8, 11, 19–21, 105
Relph, E. 114, 124, 152–3; *see also* sense of place
Revill, G. 128, 129
revivalist fairs 13–14, 25, 119, 131
Rewind Festival 42, 48, 51
RFID (Radio Frequency Identification) 110, 143
risk management 4, 39, 52: licensing 60–1, 70; sponsorship and branding 56, 80, 94, 101, 120
Ritzer, G. 87, 97, 142
Robinson, R. 2, 44, 105
Rojek, C. 1, 27, 97, 105, 161
Rolfe, H. 26–7
Rolling Stones 10, 30, 79
rurality 13, 16, 106–7, 128–33: back-to-the-land movement 131; Britishness 128–32; conflict 15, 17, 131; countercultural understandings 130–2; folk revivals 25, 117; noise 56, 128, 131–3, 155; patriotism 130; planner-preservationists 128–30; post-

rurality (*cont.*)
    productivist countryside 132–3; rural idyll 128, 131, 132; *see also* revivalist fairs
Russell, D. 21, 24

St John, G. 2, 61, 109, 149
Sandford, J. 9, 11, 12, 31, 169
'Second Summer of Love' 16–17
Secret Garden Party 63, 67, 75, 105, 138
security 69–70, 158, 159: Hells Angels 10; visibility 64; *see also* policing
Security Industry Authority (SIA) 60–1, 71
Security Task Force 69
sense of place 111, 114, 125–6, 144, 152–3
sex 14–15, 131: campaigns 63–64; free love 10, 19; sexual harassment/assault 64
Shambala 43, 56–7, 95, 141
Shields, R. 21, 106–7, 113
SJM Concerts 34, 48, 51, 120, 122–3
social media: audience interaction 87, 89, 97–8, 100; data mining 84; *see also* Facebook; Instagram; marketing of festivals; mediation of festivals; Twitter
sociality 145, 148–9: and neo-tribes 149–50; and TAZ 107; *see also* meta-sociality
Somerset House concerts 43–4, 51
Something Else in the Dean 45
Sonisphere Festival 51, 65, 77
Southern Comfort 88
space, construction of 112–14, 126; *see also* cyclic place; sense of place; place
'specialness' 134, 161–2, 169
spectacular consumption 14, 22–3, 25–6, 106, 142–3, 147, 153
Spiral Tribe 17–18
sponsorship 80–93: badging 83–85, 86; critiques/opposition 96–100; leveraging 84–85, 86; media rights 90–91; pouring rights 86; pseudo-sponsorship 91–3; reciprocity 83; strategies 93–96; title sponsorship 84–6, 91, 120; *see also* branding; mediation of festivals
stadium concerts 31, 32
staycation 43

Stonehenge 10, 13, 106, 112, 129
Stonehenge Free Festival 9, 12, 13, 15–16, 69
Street, J. 78
Summer Daze (TV series) 92–3
'Summer of Love' 8–9, 31
sun worship 13
Sunrise Celebration 56–7, 94

T in the Park 50, 66, 75, 84, 85
TAZ (Temporary Autonomous Zone) 107–8
television *see* mediation of festivals
Thatcher, M. 15
Themed festivals 45, 76, 102, 115, 154–5
ticketing 30, 42–3, 62, 96: discounts 60, 116; early bird 75; exclusives 89; poor sales and sponsors 83–84; VIP 44, 55, 67, 81, 89, 159
Tjora, A. 144, 147, 156–7
toilets 67–8, 116, 122
Torpedo Town Festival 16, 106
tourism 26–7, 97, 107, 132: attendee motivations 135; fast and slow leisure 161; tourist gaze 45
transcendence 22, 136–7, 146–8, 161–2
translocal scenes 148
travellers *see* New Age Travellers
Tribal Gathering 18, 33, 34, 138
Turner, V. 103–7, 138; *see also* communitas; liminality
Twitter 80, 82, 89, 92

UK Events and Production 48
UK Festival Awards 55, 87, 97
Urry, J. 44–5
utopia/utopianism 13, 19, 71: carnival 21–3; class 159; liminality 105; rurality 25; sponsorship 93, 96; TAZ 108; *see also* authenticity; heterotopia
Uxbridge Blues (and Folk) Festivals 30–1

V Festival 114, 119–24: audiences 63, 65, 122, 137, 139–40, 146, 157–8; branding 77, 85, 97, 120; mediation 76–7, 89, 99, 123–4, 138; ownership 34, 120; space/place 107, 122–3; sponsorship 68, 76–7, 84–5, 89, 121
VIP areas 67, 159: sponsors 55–6, 81, 89–90; *see also* ticketing

Virtual Communities Marketing (VCM) 154
Virtual Festivals (website) 77

waste 56–8, 88
Waterman, S. 114
weather 9, 31, 39, 40, 56
Webster, E. 57, 69, 141
'weekend hippies' 13, 14, 105
West, K. 78–9

Wireless Festival 42, 48, 50, 85
WOMAD 32
Woodstock - Three Days of Peace and Music (1970) 9–10, 11
Woodstock Festival 11, 23
Woollard, K. 115–17
world music 29, 32, 115
Worthington, A. 3, 17

Young, R. 130–1